The
RAYNORS
of
Ketchaponack

A GENEALOGY OF THE DESCENDANTS OF JONATHAN RAYNOR, GRANDSON OF THURSTON RAYNOR OF SOUTHAMPTON, LONG ISLAND, NEW YORK

*Dedicated to the memory of
Carrie Marguerite (Raynor) Howell
—my mother and a proud Raynor—*

COMPILED BY
Stuart Payne Howell, Jr., Ed.D.

HERITAGE BOOKS
2012

HERITAGE BOOKS

AN IMPRINT OF HERITAGE BOOKS, INC.

Books, CDs, and more—Worldwide

For our listing of thousands of titles see our website
at
www.HeritageBooks.com

Published 2012 by
HERITAGE BOOKS, INC.
Publishing Division
100 Railroad Ave. #104
Westminster, Maryland 21157

International Standard Book Numbers
Paperbound: 978-0-7884-0065-0
Clothbound: 978-0-7884-9332-4

TABLE OF CONTENTS

	Page
INTRODUCTION, by Art Raynor	v
PREFACE	xiii
RAYNORS OF KETCHAPONACK	1
Third Generation	3
Fourth Generation	5
Fifth Generation	7
Sixth Generation	15
Seventh Generation	24
Eighth Generation	43
Ninth Generation	67
Tenth Generation	93
Eleventh Generation	120
Twelfth Generation	153
Thirteenth Generation	160
INDEX	161
REFERENCES	184
APPENDIX	188
(Art Raynor's 30's Map & Guide)	

I-N-T-R-O-D-U-C-T-I-O-N

Welcome!

If you are the least bit interested in the RAYNOR family of eastern Long Island, you have come to the right place.

If you are new to genealogy, or an old, practiced hand, you are in the right place - meaning that the information gathered here can verify what you already know and/or take you all the way back to the *ELIZABETH* and that voyage in the spring of 1634.

Understand, this does not attempt in any way to be a directory to the world's supply of RAYNORs. We are not, by any stretch of the imagination, an endangered species. (A recent publisher offered a list of 2298 Raynor families with telephones under the title, "The National Registry of Living Raynors").

This work, rather, concentrates on a listing of people with a direct connection to ONE GRANDSON of the original immigrant Thurston whose name is Jonathan. He was born at Southampton, Long Island in 1681 - no TV - quiet nights - time to start a dynasty.

The FIRST ROUNDUP

Rounding up RAYNORs is not an easy task. To quote Lorraine, the late wife of the late George Lafayette Raynor, "The trouble of it is none of you damnraynors give your right name". She should know. She had married 2 at different times - "Bud" (Chester S., Jr.) and "Let" (George Lafayette). To top it off, Chester S. III is known as "Syd", his son, Chester S. IV, is "Corkey", and finally, Chester S. V is currently called "Chet". Of course, at this writing, "Chet" is very young and could be renamed at the drop of a Chet.

In Westhampton and Westhampton Beach, L.I., NY, during the 1930s, it was no novelty being a

v

mere Raynor. This was especially true at some public function like High School Graduation when Principal E.J. Brong would do his best to suppress a giggle as he read off RAYNOR after RAYNOR after RAYNOR, 'ad hysterium' in the audience.

It took Mrs. Henry Howell (mother of Hampton) to make me know for certain that RAYNOR was an honorable name, and had been in America since a few years after those very same Pilgrims and the Mayflower that we heard about in grade school. She was a very upright and positive person. I caddied for her and her husband and son many times at their special request. Indicentally, she was a darn good golfer in a day and time when there weren't that many lady golfers. (Tuesdays, please). You can only imagine what a boost it was for the lowly servant type to be elevated to a place of some importance by the employer. Quantity no longer diminished quality.

Here and now I find myself indebted to another Howell - Stuart Payne Howell, who is no less RAYNOR than any of us with 2 parents, for his mother was Carrie Raynor Howell. My first meeting with him was somewhat strained, since he was busy learning to walk and talk, and I was a sophisticated eight and a half year old. My sister and I were told to call Stuart's mother "Aunt Carrie". Innocent enough - but -

Talk about confusion! Stuart's mother was Kenneth Raynor's sister. Stuart's father was Alice (Mrs. Frank) Bishop's brother. Frank Bishop was my father's first cousin via his mother, Helen Fournier Raynor, and Frank's mother, Edith Fournier Bishop. The key to this nightmare is this: as children, we all called each other's mother "aunt". So, Alice Howell Bishop with 3 girls and 2 boys, Catherine Jessup (Mrs. Kenneth) Raynor with her 5 girls, Carrie Raynor Howell with her son and daughter, and Irene Cody (Mrs. Daniel T.) Raynor with my sister and me, managed to warp the genealogical

minds of their 14 children, some of whom were
actual nieces and nephews, others of whom were
not related within five gnerations. "You can
choose your friends - ".

SELECT YOUR FRIENDS

A good many Ketchaponack area people wind
up in Florida, and among these, originally from
Massena, NY, was one of the teachers who got
stuck with me as a "student" in Westhampton
Beach, Leslie Danforth, "The Senator". "Let"
Raynor recognized Les in a grocery store in
Jensen Beach, Florida, and I finally got over to
see him.

He remembered me all right from my
connection with that less than famous music
appreciation group, "The Long Island
Mountaineers," but more to the point, thought I
was connected with the "Raynor with the outboard
motors".

It was easy to understand how that could
have happened. In the 1930s, my grandfather,
Arthur Halsey Raynor, attributed some of the
mixups to what he thought were "5 separate and
distinct families" of Raynors in the area.

In Grandpa's mind, Jess Raynor, Quiogue
outboard motor king, was an entity unto himself.
That's one.

Then there was the Incorporated Village
types with such famous people as Gus, Madison,
Emerson, and the father of the latter 2, "Uncle
Mitch", Ken, Bill, Doc, Lydia, Elijah, and some
more. That's two.

The 3rd contingent was literally "up the
creek" - Beaver Dam Creek: Fletcher, Archie,
Chester, Big John, Little John, Ralph, Thurston,
Dan, and his father, Arthur H.

Slightly further west, near Fordham's Mill,

Ansel had started a tribe of his own...group
4...and the 5th element was better known than
all the rest with his wheelbarrow type
transportation, rear view mirror and all, and
the sign, "Russ Raynor - Organs Repaired -
Pianos Tuned", wheeling down the middle of Main
Street, Westhampton Beach, more interested in
where he had been than where he was going.

Now, you have to understand that I'm simply
naming the older folks of the day, all of whom
had kids or grandkids in the WHB public school
system. This says absolutely nothing about
other towns in every direction but south, each
with their own supply of Raynors. Elsewhere in
this document you will find a map indicating the
homes of 27 families of Raynors, in about a 3/4
mile radius from Culvertown, containing over 90
Raynors.

But Grandpa was right about the 5 groups,
except they were not all that 'separate and
distinct'.

It's a little more than you can expect of
even a brilliant school teacher to have
separated all these Raynors at the time, no less
50 years later!

RAYNORS vs RABBITS

While my 1937 or 8 cap is on, let me tell
you a true story of a thing a young fellow by
the name of Ralph Gay put on with me. It was at
one of those variety shows Mike Parlato's wife,
Rica, used to direct at Mechanic's Hall as a
fund raiser for the Beach Methodist Church.

Apparently, they were scraping the bottom
of the local talent barrel, since we were
invited to perform almost as an afterthought.
The fact that we had not really rehearsed
anything didn't slow us down a whole lot - I was
ad libbing the names of all the Raynors in the
chorus on stage and in the audience when Ralph
arrived late (as per plan A) with the excuse

that he'd been hunting rabbits and the time had gotten away. I went on introducing more Raynors when he broke in with: "Why are there so many Raynors in Westhampton Beach?" After a thoughtful Jack Benny type pause, I came up with what I believe is my all time best one liner: "I don't know - why are there so many rabbits?"

HOW MANY RAYNORS DOES IT TAKE TO PAINT A PORCH?

Consider this - following World War II, I came home to work in the office of E. Raynor's Sons on Library Avenue in the village, the then leading home builder in the area. A man came in one day to pay his bill for some painting he'd had done. While he was writing the check, he said casually: "You know, this has been quite an experience."
"Really? In what way?"
"Well, I came in here from the city to get the porch painted on a house I just bought, stopped by this place and talked to an old fellow who said he would send the painter."
"That was J. Mitchell Raynor, one of the original sons."
"I know - a couple of days later a guy drives up in the yard with this black Chevvy coupe with ladders hanging all over it. Said he was Ken Raynor. He gave me an estimate I approved, and in a few days he came back with his brother Bill."
"Was the job all right?"
"Just fine - so good, in fact, I dropped by the office to make arrangements to have more work done, but the guy in the office said he just handled insurance and real estate - I'd have to talk to his brother, Madison."
"That was Emerson."
"Right - Emerson - but the point is, I had to talk to FIVE Raynors just to get this little porch painted!"
"Yessir - 5 Raynors! Here is your receipt, sir. Thank you."
It might have been better if I hadn't signed my name so big on the receipt...he was really talking to himself as he went out the

front door..."SIX...six...SIX Raynors!"

MY KIND OF HELP

Five years ago, to help straighten some of
this out, some data entitled, "The Raynor
Ancestral Line of Stuart Payne Howell, Jr."
graced my mailbox. Attached was a note
including the words, "There are still many
missing pieces, but I have decided to call it
quits, after 19 years. Perhaps, someone in the
next generation may want to carry on the
research at some point in time."

Since his recent retirement, the spark has
been rekindled. What follows represents a
quarter of a century's interest and effort in
the research of this one line of RAYNORs. He
could have gone fishing - he could have done any
number of things with his time - but even his
vacations were genealogy oriented and speaking
for myself, I appreciate it, for getting
accurate information at this distance from the
scene (Florida) is most difficult.

Stuart Payne Howell, Jr. has been active in
the Howell Family Association, his doctorate in
Education, his conscientious research and yen
for accuracy, both in this country and in
England, and his long hours pulling it all
together are gifts that future generations will
be free to relish.

Roger Tory Peterson said: "If it isn't
written down, it didn't happen". Consider
direct lines responsible for the birth of a
child: 2 parents, 4 grandparents, 8 great-
grandparents, etc. - doubling each generation
for 13 generations in America, like my
grandchildren - 4096 getting together for the
birth of that one child. These are the people
we are attempting to identify.

Welcome to the world of RAYNORS as seen
through the eyes of Stuart Payne Howell, Jr.,
10th generation descendant of Thurston Raynor

x

(Carrie M.[9], Frederick W.[8], Elijah P.[7], William[6], William[5], William[4], Jonathan[3], Jonathan[2], Thurston[1])!

July 1992   s/ Arthur Daniel Raynor
                              # 830

PREFACE

Jonathan Raynor, the common ancestor of all Raynor descendants in this genealogy, was the first white resident of Ketchaponack, the area encompassed by the villages of Westhampton and Westhampton Beach on eastern Long Island. From that one seed, many little Raynors have sprouted to abundantly populate the hamlets of Westhampton and Westhampton Beach, as well as the larger world beyond.

Jonathan Raynor was the grandson of Thurston Raynor, our first ancestor in America, who immigrated to New England from England in 1634 with his wife and children and an orphaned nephew, Edward Raynor, and in the 1640's, settled in Southampton, Long Island. Since the genealogy of Jonathan Raynor includes nearly 1400 known direct descendants (there are actually many more), and as Thurston Raynor had seven children who lived to adulthood, and probably 30 - 40 grandchildren, it is not hard to imagine the number of Thurston's descendants in the hundreds of thousands.

Originally, the village of what is now Westhampton Beach was laid out in three distinct divisions; eventually, all three divisions of the new settlement became known as Ketchaponack (or Catchaponack, or any of eight other spellings) - an Indian term meaning a place where large roots grow.

This current genealogy defines the relationship of each early Westhampton/Westhampton Beach Raynor family to all the others. Some local area Raynor families are not, however, descended from Jonathan Raynor; specifically, Ansel Raynor, the son of Napoleon Raynor, came from Greenport, and Jesse L. Raynor of Quiogue, came from either Eastport or Bay Shore.

THE RAYNORS OF KETCHAPONACK was originally compiled and published in 1992 in conjunction with the first RAYNOR ROUNDUP, which was held on October 3, 1992 at the Westhampton Beach Methodist Church and attended by more than

150 Raynor relatives. Since that time, information about a substantial number of additional descendants of Jonathan Raynor has been made available, thus warranting this current revision of the original genealogy.

The format of this genealogy facilitates following a family line from one generation to the next. All descendants are numbered consecutively starting with Jonathan[3] Raynor (#1); each generation is identified by a superscript number, i.e., fourth generation (from our common ancestor, Thurston) descendants have a [4] behind their first, or middle, names, those of generation five have a [5], and so on. A descendant's children are listed as "issue", and each descendant with children has an asterisk ("*") before his/her name, indicating that same individual appears in the next generation as a parent, with the same identifying number.

An index of names is included to facilitate location of a particular individual. Also included is a list of references. Specific sources for all data in the genealogy may be ascertained by contacting the author. In those few instances where different sources present contradictory information (usually dates), the author has taken the liberty of listing the best documented date(s), or has presented the alternative date thusly: 15 Jan (or 16 Feb). The sign, "ca" refers to "about" when an exact date is not known.

Identification of adoptions and divorces has been intentionally omitted from this genealogy. Since adopted children are reared as Raynor descendants as much as are biological children, differentiating adopted from biological children would serve no useful purpose in this type of family history. Likewise, each marriage is important and has been noted, but identification of divorces would not enhance the utility of this document.

Art Raynor, of Bartow, Florida (formerly of Westhampton), has literally been the inspiration for this project. Without his encouragement and assistance, this genealogy would never have seen the light of day. Art not only provided considerable Raynor information and assisted in editing drafts of this document, but he also created the cover design and prepared the Introduction as well as the 30's map and guide of the Westhampton and Westhampton Beach Raynors. Art, too, was my savior during the innumerable times I encountered computer problems in preparing the manuscript.

The author wishes to acknowledge his gratitude to the many other individuals and organizations whose contributions of time, information and suggestions have helped to make this genealogy as complete and accurate as possible. Without their tremendous help, *THE RAYNORS OF KETCHAPONACK* would be very incomplete and lacking in other ways. Contacts with these Raynor descendant contributors have been the most gratifying aspect of this project for the author. (Individual and organizational contributors are identified under **REFERENCES**).

This genealogy represents only a beginning, a first attempt to identify and link the Westhampton/Westhampton Beach Raynor families - descendants of but one of Thurston Raynor's grandchildren. Perhaps, this research effort may stimulate one or more Raynor descendants of a younger generation to undertake a comprehensive Raynor genealogy, to include all of Thurston Raynor's known descendants. In the meantime, it is hoped this present, limited work may be of interest to members of the Raynor "clan".

Stuart P. Howell, Jr.

THE RAYNORS OF KETCHAPONACK

Raynor (Rayner) is a distinguished name of Teutonic origin. The Anglo-Saxon Regenhere d. 617 A.D. He was the son of Raedwald, King of East Anglia, an ancient division of England which is the modern day Norfolk and Suffolk Counties.

Among the first instances of the surname in England were those of Rayner in Blake in County Norfolk during the year 1273; Reyner, son of Reyner Fleming, a Yorkshireman in the 13th year of Edward II's reign; and Thomas Rayner, also of Yorkshire (1379).

The Raynor Coat of Arms was granted in 1588: Ermine above two etoiles on a blue background; crest: golden leopard walking on green mount.

The first of our Raynor line about whom there is recorded information was Robert Raynere, who was born ca 1525 at Wickham Market, Suffolk, England and died between 4 Oct 1571 and 5 Dec 1571, when his will was proved. Robert Raynere's children were Edward, John, Dorothie and Rose. Edward Reyner, Robert Raynere's son, b. 1540, married sometime after 4 Oct 1571, Margery _____, and they were the parents of nine children: Thurston, John, Samuel, Anna, Richard, Edward, Robert, Joseph, and Margery. Edward Reyner undoubtedly died in 1621 for his will was dated 22 Mar 1620/21, and proved 7 July 1621 at Elmsett, County of Suffolk, England.

Thurston[1] Raynor, Edward Reyner's son, was baptized 21 Sept 1593 in Elmsett, England. By 13 Apr 1620, he had married Elizabeth _____, who was born in 1598. Thurston and Elizabeth, and their children, Thurston, 13, Joseph, 11, Elizabeth, 9, Sarah, 7, and Lydia, 1, immigrated to America, departing from Ipswich, England in April 1634 aboard the ship, *Elizabeth*, and landing in Boston in July 1634. Thurston Raynor was one of the early settlers of Southampton, L.I., NY, arriving there about 1646 by way of Watertown, Massachusetts, and Wethersfield and

Stamford, Connecticut. While in Wethersfield, Thurston was a delegate to the First Connecticut General Assembly, under Governor Haynes.

Thurston[1] Raynor left Wethersfield, CT with a group to found a village at Stamford (Rippowams), CT; they are credited with being the founding fathers of that town. In 1644, they established a colony at Hempstead, L.I. Later, Thurston and others went on to Southampton. For the past 350 years, Thurston Raynor's descendants have distinguished themselves on Eastern Long Island as farmers and tradesmen. Thurston Raynor himself was a prominent man; he was a Judge and member of the Legislature in Connecticut, and a Judge, Magistrate, and Freeman in Southampton, L.I. His direct descendants are numerous throughout Eastern Suffolk County, New York as well as elsewhere in the United States.

Edward Raynor, Thurston[1] Raynor's orphaned nephew, accompanied Thurston to America in 1634 aboard the ship, *Elizabeth*, and settled in Hempstead, L.I. in the 1640's. One of Edward's descendants, John Raynor, moved to East Moriches, L.I. about 1800 and had a large family there. Many of the East Moriches Raynors are thus descended from Edward Raynor.

Thurston Raynor's first wife, Elizabeth, was mother of the children they brought with them to America. Elizabeth probably did not survive very long, and apparently, most of her children did not survive to adult years. Thurston Raynor married second, probably by 1638, Martha Wood, daughter of Edmund and Martha (Lum) Wood. The Wood family was at Wethersfield and Stamford while the Raynors were in those places, and also removed to Long Island. Thurston[1] Raynor died in Oct 1667. It is likely that he had six children by his first wife, Elizabeth: Thurston[2], bapt. 19 Sept 1620; Joseph[2], b. 1623, d. 1682; Elizabeth[2], b. 1625; Sarah[2], b. 1627; Lydia[2], b. 1633; Hannah[2], m. Arthur Howell. Thurston[1] Raynor had five children by his second wife, Martha: Mary[2],

Abigail[2], Deborah[2], Jonathan[2], and probably
another daughter, whose name is not known.
Probably only seven of his eleven children were
still living when he made his will, 6 July 1667
(proved 4 Nov 1667), since he mentioned only
seven children and his wife, Martha ("wife,
Martha, sons Joseph and Jonathan, and 'my other
five children'").

Thurston[1] Raynor's oldest son, Joseph[2], b.
ca 1623, d. 1682, m. Mary _____, and had the
following children: Thurston[3], Isaac[3], John[3],
and Josiah[3] Raynor. Joseph[2]'s son, Josiah[3], b.
before 1668, left Southampton, lived in
Southold, and later, in Lyme, CT, where his
children were born; eventually (after 1717),
Josiah[3] Raynor returned to Long Island and
settled in St. George's Manor (Manorville).
Most Raynors from Manorville and nearby
communities are from the Josiah[3] line.

Jonathan[2] Raynor, son of Thurston[1] and
Martha (Wood) Raynor, was born sometime between
1646 and 1661. On 2 June 1680, Jonathan[2] Raynor
married in Southampton Town, Sarah Pierson, born
20 Jan 1660/61, daughter of Henry and Mary
(Cooper) Pierson. Jonathan[2] and Sarah Raynor
were the parents of: (1) Jonathan[3], born
1681/82; (2) Deborah[3]; and (3) Hannah[3] (1698
Census). The family lived on the road to the
beach in Southampton. Jonathan[2] Raynor died
sometime after 1714.

Third Generation

1. JONATHAN[3] RAYNOR (Jonathan[2], Thurston[1]), b. 4
Mar 1681 at Southampton, L.I., NY, d. 31 Jan
1741; m. 27 July 1704, Irene Herrick, d/o
William and Mehitable (Howell) Herrick.
Jonathan[3] was probably the first white resident
in Ketchaponack (Westhampton/Westhampton Beach),
having bought land there as early as 1707 and
resided there as early as 1738. Ketchaponack

(or Catchaponack or Ketchabonack) was an Indian
word meaning "a place where large roots grow".
Jonathan[3] and Irene Raynor had nine or ten
children, at least three of whom (Nathan,
William and Hugh) resided in the Westhampton-
Westhampton Beach area. The others may have
died early and/or remained in Southampton. It
is likely some of Jonathan[3] Raynor's children
(and their descendants) remained in Southampton.
In a will dated 31 Jan 1740/41, proved 7 Apr
1741, Jonathan[3] Raynor names no wife, but
disposes of his large holdings of land in
Southampton Town, and other possessions to his
family (Liber XIV, p. 46, N.Y. Wills). The
original Raynor homestead was located midway
between the Main Street and the beach on Beach
Lane, Westhampton Beach. The homestead remained
in the Raynor family until 1861, when it was
sold to Silas Tuttle. The house burned in 1884
and was rebuilt on the old foundation in 1886 by
Mr. Tuttle.

Jonathan[3] Raynor is the common ancestor of
all those Raynor descendants included in this
genealogy.
Issue:

  2. Jonathan[4] Raynor (twin), b. 18 Jan 1705/6
 *3. David[4] Raynor (twin), b. 18 Jan 1705/6
  4. Martha[4] Raynor
 *5. Adonijah[4] Raynor, b. 24 Aug 1708
  6. Elihu[4] Raynor, b. 18 Nov 1710
  7. Sarah[4] Raynor, b. 18 Mar (or 17 Aug) 1713
 *8. Nathan[4] Raynor, b. 14 Feb 1716/17
        (Southampton Town Records) or 1715
        (gravestone), d. 20 Nov 1772
 *9. William[4] Raynor, b. 1 Oct (or 10 Feb) 1719
        (or 1718), d. 3 (or 20 or 30) Jan 1784
        (or 1781)
?10. Henry[4] Raynor, b. 9 June 1722
*11. Hugh[4] Raynor, b. 1725 (or 1724 or 9 June
        1722), d. 1802, will proved 22 Dec 1802

4

Fourth Generation

3. DAVID[4] RAYNOR (Jonathan[3], Jonathan[2], Thurston[1]), twin, b. 18 Jan 1705/6; listed in the 1776 Census as a Head of Family in Southampton Town.
Issue:

*12. David[5] Raynor, b. 9 Aug 1740, Coram, L.I., d. 27 July 1823, Coram

*13. Jonathan[5] Raynor, b. ca 1743, Morristown, NJ, d. 20 Mar 1822, Greene Co., PA, bur. Washington Co., PA

14. Matthew[5] Raynor, of Morristown, NJ, m. 16 May 1777, Lottie Marschalk

5. ADONIJAH[4] RAYNOR (Jonathan[3], Jonathan[2], Thurston[1]), b. 24 Aug 1708.
Issue:

*15. Adonijah[5] Raynor, Jr., b. ca 1750

8. NATHAN[4] RAYNOR (Jonathan[3], Jonathan[2], Thurston[1]), b. 14 Feb 1716/17 (Southampton Town Records) or 1715 (gravestone), d. 20 Nov 1772, bur. Westhampton Cemetery; m. Jerusha Bowers, b. 21 Dec 1717, d. 1809. Nathan resided in Westhampton. Jerusha was living at Beaverdams (Westhampton), according to the 1790 Census. By his father's will, Nathan[4] was to inherit "all his lands and meadows in Apocock Neck West and half a lot in Cedar Swamp, Riverhead". Nathan and Jerusha are said to have been buried, without tombstones, on Apaucuck Neck, Westhampton. Apaucuck Neck is west of Beaverdam Stream, which was called Pocock River in old deeds. Nathan apparently left no will, but the testament of his widow, Jerusha, May 24 1801, proved August 26, 1809, names her daughters, Phoebe, Mehetable, Martha and her heirs (Lib. C, Suffolk County Wills).
Issue:

16. Nathan[5] Raynor, b. 11 Mar 1740; m. 26 Mar 1778 at Aquebogue, Juliana _____.

17. Jerusha[5] Raynor, b. 1 Nov 1742
18. Elizabeth[5] Raynor, b. 11 Oct 1747
19. Sarah[5] Raynor, b. 18 Mar 1749
*20. Phebe[5] Raynor, b. 15 Apr 1750, d. 17 Nov 1807, bur. Quogue
*21. Elihu[5] Raynor, b. 15 May 1752, d. 16 Jan 1826
22. Ichabod[5] Raynor, b. 2 Apr 1755; a soldier in the Revolutionary War; signed the Association from East Hampton Town, 5 May 1775; had a land grant near Albany.
23. Mehitable (Hetty)[5] Raynor, d. ca 1828, unmarried
24. Martha (Patty)[5] Raynor, b. ca 1768, d. 12 July 1835, ae 77yrs.; m. Edward Stephens of Quogue.

9. WILLIAM[4] RAYNOR (Jonathan[3], Jonathan[2], Thurston[1]), b. 1 Oct (or 10 Feb) 1719 (or 1718), d. 3 (or 20 or 30) Jan 1784 (or 1781), in the 66th year of his age; m. Esther Woodhull, b. 1728, d. 5 Aug 1817, in the 89th year of her age. Esther was d/o John (or Josiah) and Clementine (Holman or Homan) Woodhull of Wading River. Both William and Esther are bur. in the Westhampton Cemetery. William was listed in the 1776 Census as Head of a Family in Southampton Town.
Issue:
*25. Josiah Woodhull[5] Raynor, b. ca 1757 (or 1756), d. 24 Jan (or June) 1839, in his 83rd year, bur. Remsenburg Cemetery
*26. William[5] Raynor, b. ca 1760 (or 1745), d. Jan 1808, Westhampton
27. Nathaniel[5] Raynor, b. 1762, d. 29 Dec 1802, aged 40 years, bur. Westhampton Cemetery; m. Millicent Brewster, d. 19 Dec 1802, aged 34 years, bur. Westhampton Cemetery, d/o John Sills Brewster of Quiogue.
28. Rena[5] Raynor
? Henry[5] Raynor

6

11. HUGH[4] RAYNOR (Jonathan[3], Jonathan[2], Thurston[1]), b. 1725 (or 1724 or 9 June 1722), d. 1802, Southampton,; m. Sarah Halsey (or Horton), b. 1725, d. 26 Mar 1806, at the age of 81 yrs., bur. Quogue. Hugh was an early settler of Tanners Neck, Westhampton; he owned property west of Beaverdam River. Sarah was bur. in the plot of her son-in-law, Henry Jessup of Quogue (*HISTORY OF SUFFOLK COUNTY*, H. W. Munsell). His father (Jonathan[3]), by his will, gave to Hugh[4] and his male heirs a lot in Little "Onuck", and his home lot and buildings in Southampton. Hugh's will, dated 12 Mar 1799 and proved 22 Dec 1802, names wife, Sarah, sons, Stephen and Henry, the latter to have lands and a mill at Setuck River, daughters, Jane Jessup, Phoebe Foster and Abigail Tuthill, children of daughter, Prudence Pierson, and son, James, who is to have the residue of the estate. James sold his grandfather's homestead in Southampton to Elie Pelletreau in 1812 (Lib. B, 218, Suffolk County Wills, N.Y. Hist. Soc. Coll., 1894, p. 325). Hugh was listed in the 1776 Census as Head of a Family in Southampton Town.
Issue:

*29. Jane[5] Raynor, b. 14 Apr 1750, d. 6 May 1816, ae 66 yrs., 22 days, bur. Quogue

*30. James[5] Raynor, b. before 1760, Southampton

*31. Henry[5] Raynor, b. 8 Aug 1763, d. 2 Oct 1836 ae 73 yrs.

32. Stephen[5] Raynor, b. before 1765; listed in the 1776 Census as Head of a Family in Southampton Town.

*33. Phoebe[5] Raynor

*34. Abigail[5] Raynor, b. 12 July 1768, Southampton, d. ca 1802

*35. Prudence[5] Raynor

Fifth Generation

12. DAVID[5] RAYNOR, JR. (David[4], Jonathan[3], Jonathan[2], Thurston[1]), b. 9 Aug 1740, Coram,

L.I., d. 27 July 1823, Coram; m. 6 Dec 1769 in
Morristown, NJ, Elizabeth Lindsley of
Morristown, NJ, b. 22 Mar 1746, d. 17 Apr 1829,
Coram, L.I., d/o Daniel and Grace (Kitchell)
Lindsley. Children b. in Coram, L.I.
Issue:

?   Daniel Lindsley[6] Raynor, b. 1771
36. Irene[6] Raynor, b. 8 Feb 1771, d. 16 Jan
    1829; m. 15 Feb 1802 at Basking Ridge,
    NJ, I. R. Kinnan.
37. Azur (Asa)[6] Raynor, b. 13 Nov 1773, d. Nov
    1848; m. Ann Laws and removed to Cayuga
    County, NY.
38. Martha[6] Raynor, b. 4 Nov 1776, d. 7 Aug
    1825; m. M. R. McKensey.
39. Shuah[6] Raynor, b. 29 Jan 1779, d. 26 Mar
    1820; m. S. R. Riggs.
*40. Elizabeth Lindsley[6] Raynor, b. 3 Apr 1781,
    d. 18 Aug 1820, Basking Ridge, NJ
41. Naomi[6] Raynor, b. 3 Feb 1783 (or 1784),
    bapt. 18 Apr 1784 at Morristown, NJ, d.
    15 Nov 1825
42. Hannah[6] Raynor, b. 24 Mar 1786, d. 1853,
    Newark, NJ
43. Phebe[6] Raynor, b. 3 May 1789, d. 1853 (or
    24 Apr 1833); m. at Basking Ridge, NJ, P.
    R. Riggs.
44. Clarissa[6] Raynor, b. 23 (or 28) Nov 1791,
    d. 1818; m. C. R. Graham.

13. JONATHAN[5] RAYNOR (David[4], Jonathan[3],
Jonathan[2], Thurston[1]), b. ca 1743, Morristown,
NJ, d. 20 Mar 1822, Greene Co., PA, bur. Upper
Ten Mile Presbyterian Church Cemetery,
Washington Co., PA; m. 17 Oct 1771 in the
Whippany, NJ Presbyterian Church, Tryphenia
Fordham, d. 1828, Mt. Vernon, OH. Jonathan was
a private in the Continental Army during the
Revolutionary War. Jonathan and his family
moved from Morristown, NJ to Greene Co., PA.
Issue:

45. Pamella[6] Raynor, b. 1 Aug 1773; m. Bethuel

8

Day.

46. Cyrenus[6] Raynor, b. 12 May 1774, d. 1845

47. Eunice[6] Raynor, b. 16 Aug 1778; m. Benjamin Burnett.

*48. Prudence[6] Raynor, b. 3 Feb 1782, Morristown, NJ, d. 6 Sept 1851, Morristown, NJ

49. Hannah[6] Raynor, b. 12 Apr 1784; m. Benjamin Leach.

50. Jonathan[6] Raynor, b. 11 Apr 1787; m. Dianah Corcoran.

51. Triphena[6] Raynor, b. 29 Jan 1790; m. John Secor.

52. Stephen[6] Raynor, b. 19 Sept 1794

15. ADONIJAH[5] RAYNOR, JR. (Adonijah[4], Jonathan[3], Jonathan[2], Thurston[1]), b. ca 1750; m. Submit Fowler, b. 27 Apr 1762, d/o John and Abigail ( ) Fowler. Adonijah was listed in the 1776 Census as Head of a Family in Southampton Town. Issue:

53. Oliver[6] Raynor

*54. Catherine[6] Raynor, b. 1786, d. 19 June 1868

55. George[6] Raynor, bapt. 19 Oct 1788

56. Sylvanus[6] Raynor, d. 24 Feb 1841, ae 54 yrs.; m. Jerusha White, d. 25 Jan 1856, ae 61 yrs., bur. Old North End Cemetery, Southampton, d/o Ephraim and Hannah White; no children mentioned in Sylvanus's or Jerusha's wills.

*57. Abigail[6] Raynor, b. ca 1794, d. between 23 Nov 1855 (will date) and 1 Mar 1856 (will proved), ae 61 yrs.

58. Rebecca[6] Raynor

59. William[6] Raynor

60. Charles[6] Raynor

20. PHEBE[5] RAYNOR (Nathan[4], Jonathan[3], Jonathan[2], Thurston[1]), b. 15 Apr 1750, d. 17 Nov 1807, bur. Quogue; m. 3 Jan 1790, Dr. George Howell of Quogue, b. 10 Jan 1751, d. Missouri,

s/o Zebulon and Joanna (Howell) Howell.
Issue:
61. Hiram[6] Howell, b. 5 Dec 1790
62. Warren[6] Howell, b. 15 Nov 1793, d. 30 Apr
    1797, bur. Quogue

21. ELIHU[5] RAYNOR (Nathan[4], Jonathan[3],
Jonathan[2], Thurston[1]), b. 15 May 1752,
Southampton, d. 16 Jan 1826, ae 75 yrs., bur.
Westhampton Cemetery; m. 11 Dec 1780 at
Aquebogue, Elizabeth Albertson, b. 1758, d. 13
Jan 1801, ae 42 yrs., bur. Westhampton Cemetery.
Elihu lived at Beaverdams (Westhampton) in 1790.
In 1797, he built a house 100' south of South
Road and 350' west of Apaucuck Point Road.
Elihu was listed in the 1776 Census as Head of a
Family in Southampton Town.
Issue:
*63. Jonathan (or Jotham)[6] Raynor, b. 27 Apr
     1781, d. 19 Oct 1850, ae 69 yrs.
 64. Elizabeth[6] Raynor, b. 1783; m. _____
     Robertson.
 65. Ruth[6] Raynor, b, 1785; m. _____ Emmons.
*66. Nathan[6] Raynor, b. 1787, d. 1824
*67. John Cook[6] Raynor, b. 12 July 1789,
     Westhampton Beach, d. 12 Sept 1871,
     Westhampton, ae 82 yrs., 2 mos.
 68. Charity[6] Raynor, b. 1791, d. 13 Jan 1832,
     ae 41 yrs., bur. Westhampton Cemetery
 69. Nancy[6] Raynor, b. 1793, d. 30 Jan 1866, ae
     72 yrs., bur. Westhampton Cemetery
 70. Abigail[6] Raynor, b. 1796; unmarried in
     1821, at the time of her father's will
*71. Herrick[6] Raynor, b. 28 Aug 1798, d. 30 Mar
     1837
 72. William[6] Raynor, b. 1801, d. 1803

25. JOSIAH WOODHULL[5] RAYNOR (William[4],
Jonathan[3], Jonathan[2], Thurston[1]), b. ca 1757 (or
1756), d. 24 Jan (or June) 1839, in his 83rd
year, bur. Remsenburg Cemetery; m. 28 Dec 1783,
Mercy W. Aldridge, b. ca 1760, d. 19 Oct 1833,

10

in her 74th year. Josiah, a shoemaker, resided in Speonk.
Issue:
73. Jacob A.[6] Raynor, b. ca 1786, d. 7 Feb 1856 - 69 yrs., 6 mos., 5 days, bur. Remsenburg Cemetery; he was a carpenter.
74. Josiah Woodhull[6] Raynor, b. 1791, d. 1874, bur. Remsenburg Cemetery
*75. Caleb S.[6] Raynor, b. 26 Dec 1798 (or 1795), Speonk, d. 27 Nov 1864 - 68 yrs., 11 mos., bur. Remsenburg Cemetery

26. WILLIAM[5] RAYNOR (William[4], Jonathan[3], Jonathan[2], Thurston[1]), b. ca 1760 (or 1745), d. Jan 1808, Westhampton (will written 26 Jan 1808 and proved 19 Feb 1808); m. 27 June 1781 at Southampton, Mary Pierson of Southampton, d/o Timothy and Mary (Culver) Pierson. William and Mary may be bur. at Westhampton without tombstones. William's will names wife, Mary, sons, William, Woodhull, Elijah, daughter, Mary Jessup, three unmarried daughters, Sophia, Harriet, and Susannah, and sons-in-law, Henry W. Corwin and Lester G. Rogers (Lib. B, 488, Suffolk County Wills). Harriet afterwards married John Sills Brewster of Quiogue, and Susannah married Silas Jessup of Quogue.
Issue:
76. Mary[6] Raynor, b. 7 Mar 1782, d. 1846 (smallpox), Jamesport, bur. Jamesport; m. 1 Feb 1803, Richard Jessup, b. 1779, d. 6 Feb 1816 (smallpox), Jamesport, bur. Westhampton, s/o Stephen and Abigail (Albertson) Jessup.
*77. William R.[6] Raynor, b. 14 Mar 1784 (or 1783), d. 14 Apr 1849
*78. Nathaniel Woodhull[6] Raynor, b. 26 Jan 1786 (or 1787), d. 16 Mar (or 18 Mar) 1849, ae 63 (or 62) yrs.
79. Timothy[6] Raynor, b. 24 Sept 1787, d. 3 Nov 1806, ae 19 yrs.
80. Elihu[6] Raynor, b. 3 June 1789, d. 3 Apr 1790

11

*81. Susannah[6] Raynor, b. ca 1791, d. 21 Jan 1846, ae 55 yrs.

*82. Elijah[6] Raynor, b. 19 Dec 1792, d. 17 May 1853, ae 60 yrs., 4 mos., 28 days

83. Joffy[6] Raynor, b. 13 Nov 1796, probably d. young

84. Sophia[6] Raynor, b. 1797, d. 6 Apr 1849 (measles), ae 52 yrs., unmarried; resided in Westhampton.

*85. Harriet[6] Raynor, b. 11 Mar 1799, bapt. 11 Aug 1799 in the Westhampton Presbyterian Church, d. 18 Aug 1876, ae 77 yrs., 5 mos., 18 days, bur. Quogue

29. JANE[5] RAYNOR, (Hugh[4], Jonathan[3], Jonathan[2], Thurston[1]), b. 14 Apr 1750, d. 6 May 1816, ae 66 yrs., 22 days, bur. Quogue; m. ca 1769, Henry Jessup of Quogue, b. 25 June 1743, d. 30 June 1824, bur. Quogue, s/o Deacon Thomas and Mehetabel Jessup.
Issue:

86. Mehetabel[6] Jessup, b. 23 July 1770; m. _____ Foster.

87. Sarah[6] Jessup, b. 22 Dec 1772

88. Lewis[6] Jessup, b. 22 Nov 1774, resided at Palmyra, Wayne County, NY

89. Henry[6] Jessup, b. 11 Aug 1776, resided at Palmyra, NY

*90. Silas[6] Jessup, b. 10 (or 16) Mar 1779, d. 24 Sept 1841

91. Apollos[6] Jessup, b. 13 Sept 1782, d. 13 Sept 1824

92. Ruth[6] Jessup, b. 30 July 1786

93. Ebenezer[6] Jessup, b. 16 Sept 1789

30. JAMES[5] RAYNOR (Hugh[4], Jonathan[3], Jonathan[2], Thurston[1]), b. before 1760, Southampton, L.I.; removed to Cazenovia, NY.
Issue:

*94. James Hewitt[6] Raynor, b. 1786

*95. Lewis[6] Raynor, b. 6 June 1796, Southampton,

L.I., d. 7 Oct 1887, Cazenovia, NY

31. HENRY[5] RAYNOR (Hugh[4], Jonathan[3], Jonathan[2], Thurston[1]), b. 8 Aug 1763, d. 2 Oct 1836, ae 73 yrs.; m. (1) Jerusha Foster, b. 6 Apr 1766 (or 1767), d. 24 Feb (or 21 Feb) 1811, in the 45th year of her age, d/o Daniel and Temperance (Halsey) Foster of Quiogue; m. (2) 7 Aug 1811 by Rev. Zachariah Greene, Olivia Shaler, widow, b. 1774, d. 19 Mar 1826, ae 52 yrs.; m. (3) Nancy Saxon. Henry, Jerusha, and Olivia are bur. in the Westhampton Cemetery. Henry's will, written 7 Mar 1833, proved 2 Nov 1836, names his wife, Nancy.

Issue Wife (1):

*96. Elizabeth (Betsey)[6] Raynor, b. 12 July 1789, d. 6 Sept 1865

97. Miriam[6] Raynor, b. 17 May 1791, d. 1855; m. Seth Tuthill; may have m. (2) William Tuttle.

*98. Selah[6] Raynor, b. 28 Feb 1793, d. 2 May 1878, ae 85 yrs., 2 mos., 4 days, bur. Remsenburg

99. Jerusha[6] Raynor, b. 28 Apr 1795; m. John Penny

100. Nancy[6] Raynor, b. 4 Sept 1797, d. 21 Feb 1808, ae 11 yrs.

101. Joanna[6] Raynor, b. 11 Oct 1799, d. 26 Mar 1870, Tuthill's Mills (Riverhead), ae 71 yrs., 8 mos., 9 days, bur. Westhampton Cemetery; m. Oliver Tuthill, b. 1795, d. 1866, s/o Joshua and Hannah (Aldrich) Tuthill.

*102. Hannah[6] Raynor, b. 5 Dec 1801, d. 7 June 1879, ae 77 yrs., 6 mos., 2 days, bur. Speonk

103. Luther[6] Raynor, b. 21 May 1804, d. Mar 1805, bur. Westhampton Cemetery

104. Merritt (or Herrick)[6] Raynor, b. 19 Aug 1806

105. Phoebe[6] Raynor, b. 5 Dec 1809, Setauket, L.I., d. 14 Jan 1876, Sayville, L.I.; m. 1834, Charles Tuthill, b. 1807, d. 1890,

13

s/o Joshua and Hannah (Aldrich) Tuthill.
Issue Wife (2):
106. Harriet[6] Raynor, b. 7 Aug 1812; m. James
    Stanborough, b. 1807, d. 1844 (lost at
    sea). Residence: Bellport.

33. PHOEBE[5] RAYNOR (Hugh[4], Jonathan[3], Jonathan[2],
Thurston[1]), m. Daniel Foster, s/o Jonas and
Eunice (Culver) Foster.
Issue:
107. Sarah[6] Foster, bapt. 22 July 1798 in
    Southampton Presbyterian Church

34. ABIGAIL[5] RAYNOR (Hugh[4], Jonathan[3],
Jonathan[2], Thurston[1]), b. 12 July 1768,
Southampton, d. ca 1802, Brookhaven, L.I.; m. ca
1792 at Southampton, as his 2nd wife, Josiah
Tuthill, b. ca 1759, d. 18 June 1819,
Brookhaven, s/o Benjamin Tuthill.
Issue:
108. Josiah[6] Tuthill, b. 24 Jan 1793, d. 28 Apr
    1854, Greenport, bur. Greenport; m. 19
    Feb 1817 at Moriches, Harriet ("Hattie")
    Bishop, b. 4 June 1850, d/o Solomon and
    Mehetable (Reeves) Bishop. Residence:
    Moriches until 1841, then Greenport.
109. Richard[6] Tuthill, b. 9 Dec 1794, Middle
    Island, L.I., d. 27 Aug 1865, bur. Mt.
    Sinai, L.I.; m. 9 July 1798, Joanna
    Davis, d/o Daniel and Joanna (Robbins)
    Davis.
110. Isaac[6] Tuthill, b. 29 Nov 1796, Brookhaven
111. Zophar[6] Tuthill, b. 4 May 1799, Brookhaven
112. Daniel[6] Tuthill, b. 11 June 1801
Note: Josiah Tuthill had four other children by
    his first wife and two children by his
    third wife.

35. PRUDENCE[5] RAYNOR (Hugh[4], Jonathan[3],
Jonathan[2], Thurston[1]), m. _____ Pierson.
Issue:
113. Ruth[6] Pierson

14

40. ELIZABETH LINDSLEY[6] RAYNOR (David[5], David[4], Jonathan[3], Jonathan[2], Thurston[1]), b. 3 Apr 1781 at Coram, L.I., d. 18 Aug 1820, Basking Ridge, NJ; m. 26 Jan 1803 at Basking Ridge, Col. John R. Breese, b. 20 Sept 1778, Basking Ridge, NJ, d. 17 Jan 1861, s/o Azariah and Susanna (Gildersleeve) Breese. John m. (2) Mrs. Maria (Mandaville) Winney, widow, b. 17 June 1795, d. 15 Jan 1836, and they were the parents of four children: John, Caroline, Henry Mandaville, and Maria Mandaville Breese. Maria also had at least seven children by her first husband. Issue:

114. Eliza Lindsley[7] Breese, b. 23 Jan 1804

*115. Silas Gildersleeve[7] Breese, b. 4 June 1805 on L.I., d. 23 Oct 1863, Serena, IL

*116. Robert Finley[7] Breese, twin, b. 22 June 1807

*117. David Raynor[7] Breese, twin, b. 22 June 1807

118. Susan Day[7] Breese, b. 6 May 1809, d. 7 Jan 1905, ae 95 yrs., 8 mos.

*119. Mary Ann[7] Breese, b. 2 Mar 1811

*120. Augustus[7] Breese, b. 25 Oct 1812

*121. Hannah[7] Breese, b. 8 Oct 1815

122. Phebe[7] Breese, b. 20 May 1817; m. Thomas Willet

*123. Sarah Naomi[7] Breese, b. 30 Aug 1819

48. PRUDENCE[6] RAYNOR (Jonathan[5], David[4], Jonathan[3], Jonathan[2], Thurston[1]), b. 3 Feb 1782, Morristown, NJ, d. 6 Sept 1851, Morristown, NJ; m. John Mattox, Jr., b. ca 1779, NJ, d. 1 July 1858, Washington Co., PA, s/o John A. and Rebeckah (   ) Mattox, Sr. Issue:

*124. Rebecca[7] Mattax, b. 29 May 1816, Lindley's Mills, PA, d. 7 Oct 1904, Rock Falls, IL

54. CATHERINE[6] RAYNOR (Adonijah, Jr.[5],

Adonijah[4], Jonathan[3], Jonathan[2], Thurston[1]), b.
1786, d. 19 June 1868; m. 17 Nov 1806, Jared
(Jeremiah) Wade, Sr., b. 1776, d. 6 May 1849;
both bur. Oakland Cemetery, Sag Harbor. Jared
was a whaling ship Captain. Residence: Sag
Harbor, L.I.
Issue:

125. Jared[7] Wade, Jr., a famous ship captain,
who sailed to China and to San Francisco
at the opening of the California gold
rush.

*126. Oliver R.[7] Wade, a ship outfitter; resided
in Sag Harbor and bur. Oakland Cemetery,
Sag Harbor.

*127. Benjamin[7] Wade, b. 1809, d. 1867

57. **ABIGAIL[6] RAYNOR** (Adonijah, Jr.[5], Adonijah[4],
Jonathan[3], Jonathan[2], Thurston[1]), b. ca 1794, d.
between 23 Nov 1855 (will written) and 1 Mar
1856 (will proved), ae 61 yrs.; m. 1819, Harvey
Penny, b. June 1797, d. 22 Feb 1865, s/o Joseph
and Deborah (Squires) Penny.
Issue:

128. Frances Matilda[7] Penny

129. Harriet Amanda[7] Penny, m. A. Frank Trask

130. George Sylvanus[7] Penny

*131. Mary Jane[7] Penny, b. 9 Oct 1836, d. 21 Aug
1879

132. Catherine R.[7] Penny, m. Thomas P. Ripley

133. Abigail[7] Penny, may have m. Joseph A.
Williams; resided in Pennsylvania in
1841.

134. Phebe R.[7] Penny, m. Norton F. Robinson

135. William[7] Penny, probably d. before 1856 as
he was not named in his mother's will.

63. **JONATHAN ("JOTHAM")[6] RAYNOR** (Elihu[5],
Nathan[4], Jonathan[3], Jonathan[2], Thurston[1]), b. 27
Apr 1781, d. 19 Oct 1850, Westhampton, ae 69
yrs., bur. Westhampton Cemetery; m. Sarah A.
("Sally") Tuttle (Tuthill) of Speonk (or
Eastport), b. 20 Sept 1784, d. 5 Feb 1859, ae 75

yrs., bur. Westhampton Cemetery, d/o Daniel and Sarah (Parshall) Tuthill of Eastport. Jonathan was a farmer.
Issue:

*136. William[7] Raynor, b. 18 Feb 1805, d. 12 Nov 1857, ae 52 yrs., 8 mos., 24 days

137. Sarah R. ("Sally")[7] Raynor, b. 25 Jan 1807, d. 10 Aug 1879 (or 1877), ae 72 yrs.

*138. Hannah[7] Raynor, b. 25 Oct 1808 (or 24 or 29 Oct 1809), d. 10 Feb (or 11 Feb) 1848, ae 39 yrs.

*139. Millicent[7] Raynor, b. 25 Jan 1811, d. 6 Dec 1895, aged 84 yrs., 10 mos., 19 days

*140. Nathan[7] Raynor, b. 25 Mar 1813, d. 16 (or 15) May 1890

*141. Daniel[7] Raynor, b. 25 Jan 1815

142. Phoebe[7] Raynor, b. 23 Jan 1817, d. 10 July 1885

143. Mary T.[7] Raynor, bapt. 11 Feb 1819, d. 13 July 1888

*144. Uriah[7] Raynor, bapt. 28 Apr 1822, d. 9 May 1897 (or 1898), Good Ground

*145. Elizabeth ("Eliza")[7] Raynor, b. 1 Nov 1824, bapt. 7 Nov 1824

*146. Elihu[7] Raynor, b. 20 Jan 1827, d. 2 Dec 1894

66. NATHAN[6] RAYNOR (Elihu[5], Nathan[4], Jonathan[3], Jonathan[2], Thurston[1]), b. 1787, d. 1824; m. Mary Hoffman, b. 1787, d. 1828. They removed to Philadelphia.
Issue:

147. Maria[7] Raynor, b. 1815, d. 1879

*148. Charles[7] Raynor, b. 1816

149. Elizabeth[7] Raynor, b. 1818, d. 1826

150. Catherine[7] Raynor, b. 1821, d. 1846

151. George[7] Raynor, b. 1823, d. 1824

67. JOHN COOK[6] RAYNOR (Elihu[5], Nathan[4], Jonathan[3], Jonathan[2], Thurston[1]), b. 12 July

1789, Westhampton Beach, d. 12 Sept 1871,
Westhampton, ae 82 yrs., 2 mos.; m. 5 Mar 1833,
Mehitable Jagger, b. 13 Feb 1808, d. 15 July
1880, d/o Enoch and Abigail (Post) Jagger; both
bur. Westhampton Cemetery.
Issue:

*152. John Morrison[7] Raynor, b. 19 Dec 1834,
    Greenport, d. 1 Mar 1906, bur.
    Westhampton
*153. Herrick Jagger[7] Raynor, b. 8 Dec 1838,
    Westhampton, d. 16 May 1909

71. HERRICK[6] RAYNOR (Elihu[5], Nathan[4], Jonathan[3],
Jonathan[2], Thurston[1]), b. 28 Aug 1798, d. 30 Mar
1837; m. (1) Harriet Halsey, b. 12 Feb 1795, d.
25 Dec 1833, in her 38th year; m. (2) Almine
Benjamin. Herrick, a farmer, was born in the
Raynor homestead. Herrick and Harriet are bur.
in the Westhampton Cemetery. In his will,
Herrick leaves his daughter, Harriet, a chest of
"my first wife with initial HH and my first
wife's things"; she also received a gold ring of
her mother's. The balance of Herrick's estate
was left to his son, Oscar Bingley, and $200 "to
my present wife". Will proved 15 May 1837.
After their mother's (Harriet Halsey Raynor)
death in childbirth, 25 Dec 1833, the children,
Oscar Bingley and Harriet, went to live with
their Uncle and Aunt, John Cook and Mehitable
(Jagger) Raynor.
Issue Wife (1):

*154. Oscar Bingley[7] Raynor, b. 9 Oct 1828, d.
    18 Feb 1900
*155. Harriet[7] Raynor, twin, b. 23 Dec 1833, d.
    31 Jan 1912, ae 78 yrs., 1 mo., 8 days,
    bur. Northville Cemetery, Riverhead
  156. _____[7] Raynor, twin, b. & d. 23 Dec 1833

75. CALEB S.[6] RAYNOR (Josiah Woodhull[5],
William[4], Jonathan[3], Jonathan[2], Thurston[1]), b.
26 Dec 1798 (or 1795), Speonk, d. 27 Nov 1864,
ae 68 yrs., 11 mos., bur. Remsenburg Cemetery;
m. (1) Hulda A. Corwin, d. ae 33 yrs., 1 mo., 15

days; may have m. (2) Martha _____, d. at 72 yrs., 1 mo., 19 days.
Issue:
*157. Jacob A.[7] Raynor, b. 1 July 1834, d. 17 Jan 1914
*158. Joseph[7] Raynor

77. WILLIAM R.[6] RAYNOR (William[5], William[4], Jonathan[3], Jonathan[2], Thurston[1]), b. 14 Mar 1784 (or 1783), Westhampton, d. 14 Apr 1849 (general debility), ae 66 yrs., Westhampton, bur. Westhampton Cemetery; m. 1813, in the Westhampton Presbyterian Church, Harriett Jagger, b. 3 Feb 1789, d. 14 Feb (or 13 Feb) 1882, ae 93 yrs., 11 days, at Ketchabonack, d/o Enoch and Mehitable (Fanning) Jagger. William was a farmer in Westhampton Beach. The 1820 U.S. Census listed William Raynor as Head of a Family in Southampton Town. The 1850 U.S. Census listed Harriett Raynor as a resident of Southampton Town along with her daus., Nancy, 23, and Polly, 21. The family was also listed in the 1865 Southampton Town Census: widow, Harriett; son, William, his wife and dau.; son, Elijah, his wife and four sons. Harriett Raynor's will, dated 14 Oct 1871, proved 16 Feb 1882, names dau., Betsey Rogers; grandson, Harrison H. Corwin of Riverhead; dau., Susan Tyler's children: John, Fanny and Roscoe Tyler of Eastport; dau., Nancy Bishop's children: Ida May Raynor and Stanton R. Bishop, both of Westhampton; son, William Raynor's widow, Mary Jane Raynor, and children: Antoinette, Louise and William Raynor, all of Westhampton; and son, Elijah Raynor.
Issue:
*159. Miriam Wickes[7] Raynor, b. 15 Jan 1815, Westhampton, d. Aquebogue, 5 Oct 1861, bur. Riverhead Cemetery
*160. William Jagger[7] Raynor, b. 20 (or 19) Dec 1816, d. 11 Jan 1882, ae 65 yrs., 22 days
*161. Elizabeth[7] Raynor, b. 4 Mar 1820, d. 17 Dec 1893, ae 73 yrs., 9 mos., 13 days

*162. Susan[7] Raynor, b. 1824, d. 6 Mar 1873

*163. Nancy P.[7] Raynor, b. 5 Mar 1827, d. 21 Feb 1869

164. Mary J. ("Polly")[7] Raynor, b. 1829, d. 30 Mar 1856, ae 27 yrs., unmarried, bur. Westhampton Cemetery

*165. Elijah Pierson[7] Raynor, b. 21 Oct 1833, d. 30 May 1911

78. NATHANIEL WOODHULL[6] RAYNOR (William[5], William[4], Jonathan[3], Jonathan[2], Thurston[1]), b. 26 Jan 1786 (or 1787), d. 16 Mar (or 18 Mar) 1849, Westhampton, (measles), ae 63 yrs. (or 62 yrs.); m. Harmony Howell, b. 1793, d. 5 Dec 1857, ae 64 yrs., d/o Usher Howell; both Woodhull and Harmony are bur. Westhampton Cemetery. Nathaniel was a carpenter.
Issue:

166. Charles L.[7] Raynor, b. 1830; m. Sarah LeVelley

167. Marriette[7] Raynor, m. Daniel Aldridge

168. Elizabeth[7] Raynor, m. Norstrand Bennett

*169. Mulford T.[7] Raynor

170. Fannie[7] Raynor

171. Milicent[7] Raynor

172. John[7] Raynor

81. SUSANNAH[6] RAYNOR (William[5], William[4], Jonathan[3], Jonathan[2], Thurston[1]), b. ca 1791, d. 21 Jan 1846, ae 55 yrs.; m. after 1808, # **90. SILAS[6] JESSUP** of Quogue, b. 10 Mar 1779, d. 24 Sept 1841, s/o Henry and Jane (Raynor) Jessup; both bur. Quogue Cemetery.
Issue:

*173. Egbert[7] Jessup, b. 16 (or 30) June 1818, Quogue, d. 22 Mar 1876, ae 57 yrs., 9 mos., 6 days

*174. William Henry[7] Jessup, b. 21 Nov 1819, d. 30 Apr 1852, ae 32 yrs., 5 mos., 22 days

175. Mary Jane[7] Jessup, b. 2 Feb 1821, d. 4 July 1900; m. after 1841 as his 2nd

wife, Capt. Henry Gardiner, b. ca 1789, d. 24 Apr 1867; both bur. Quogue.

82. ELIJAH^6 RAYNOR (William^5, William^4, Jonathan^3, Jonathan^2, Thurston^1), Captain, b. 19 Dec 1792, d. 17 May 1853, ae 60 yrs., 4 mos., 28 days; m. 1815, Hannah Terry, b. 23 Oct 1814, d. 13 June 1882, ae 67 yrs., 7 mos., 21 days. Hannah m. (2) Herman D. Bishop, b. 1797, d. 20 July 1885, ae 87 yrs., 9 mos., 2 days. Capt. Elijah, wife, Hannah, and Hannah's 2nd husband, Herman D. Bishop, are all bur. in the Westhampton Cemetery. Elijah was listed in the 1850 U.S. Census as a farmer in Southampton Town along with his wife, Hannah, son, Henry, and dau., Mary.
Issue:

176. Henry T.^{7} Raynor, b. 31 Dec 1843, d. 9 June 1851, ae 7 yrs., 5 mos., 9 days, bur. Westhampton Cemetery

*177. Mary Frances^7 Raynor, b. 17 Oct 1846, d. 24 Feb 1930

85. HARRIET^6 RAYNOR (William^5, William^4, Jonathan^3, Jonathan^2, Thurston^1), b. 11 Mar 1799, bapt. 11 Aug 1799 in the Westhampton Presbyterian Church, d. 18 Aug 1876, ae 77 yrs., 5 mos., 18 days; m. John Sills Brewster of Quiogue, d. 4 Aug 1872, ae 83 yrs., 9 mos., 28 days, s/o William and Hannah (Foster) Brewster. Harriet was bur. in Quogue.
Issue:

178. Milicent^7 Brewster, b. 17 Aug 1799, d. 12 July 1819, bur. Westhampton

179. William^7 Brewster

180. Eliza^7 Brewster, m. Jeremiah Hedges of Brookhaven

90. SILAS^6 JESSUP (Jane^5, Hugh^4, Jonathan^3, Jonathan^2, Thurston^1), b. 10 Mar 1779, d. 24 Sept 1841; m. after 1808, # 81. SUSANNAH^6 RAYNOR, b. ca 1791, d. 21 Jan 1846, ae 55 yrs.,

d/o William[5] and Mary (Pierson) Raynor; both Silas and Susannah are bur. at Quogue. Issue: See **81.** SUSANNAH[6] RAYNOR.

94. JAMES HEWITT[6] RAYNOR (James[5], Hugh[4], Jonathan[3], Jonathan[2], Thurston[1]), b. 1786; m. Elizabeth Shay of Jamaica, NY; removed to Brooklyn.
Issue:
181. Melvinna[7] Raynor, b. 1828; m. Henry Meyer
182. James[7] Raynor, b. 1835, d. 1838
183. Jane Alice[7] Raynor, b. 1836; m. Robert Whittemore
*184. Cyrus Timothy[7] Raynor, b. 1842
185. Nicholas[7] Raynor
186. James Huit[7] Raynor
187. John Lawrence[7] Raynor
188. Cornelius[7] Raynor, twin
189. Mary[7] Raynor, twin

95. LEWIS[6] RAYNOR (James[5], Hugh[4], Jonathan[3], Jonathan[2], Thurston[1]), b. 6 June 1796, Southampton, L.I., d. 7 Oct 1887, Cazenovia, NY; m. 1 Jan 1819, Anna Tillotson, b. 6 Dec 1798, Cazenovia, d. 4 Aug 1845, Cazenovia, d/o Abraham and Abigail (Backus) Tillotson.
Issue:
190. Charles A.[7] Raynor; resided in Syracuse, NY
191. Phebe Ann[7] Raynor, b. 1819; m. 1836 in Cazenovia, William Brown Slocum, b. 6 Aug 1809, Groton, CT, s/o Caleb and Sarah (Batty) Slocum.
192. James A.[7] Raynor, d. NYC, aged 56 yrs.

96. ELIZABETH ("BETSEY")[6] RAYNOR (Henry[5], Hugh[4], Jonathan[3], Jonathan[2], Thurston[1]), b. 12 July 1789, d. 6 Sept 1865; m. 5 Mar 1809 at East Moriches, Joel Hawkins, b. 28 Feb 1785, Moriches, d. 14 Feb 1867, s/o Joseph and Ruth (Hulse) Hawkins. Residence: Brookhaven, L.I.

22

Issue:

*193. Nancy[7] Hawkins, b. 26 Apr 1811, d. 25 Mar
       1890, bur. South Haven, L.I.
*194. Elmira[7] Hawkins, b. 15 Aug 1815, d. 20 Feb
       1912, bur. Woodland Cemetery, Bellport,
       L.I.
*195. Sylvester[7] Hawkins, b. 1818, Brookhaven,
       d. 1882, bur. Southold
*196. William Henry[7] Hawkins, b. 24 Apr 1829,
       Brookhaven, d. 1 Aug 1907, bur.
       Greenfield Cemetery, Hempstead, L.I.

98. SELAH[6] RAYNOR (Henry[5], Hugh[4], Jonathan[3],
Jonathan[2], Thurston[1]), b. 28 Feb 1793, d. 2 May
1878, ae 85 yrs., 2 mos., 4 days, bur.
Remsenburg; m. Sophia Foster, b. 1797, d. 25
June 1867, ae 69 yrs., 10 mos., 11 days.
Issue:

197. William Foster[7] Raynor, bapt. 6 Apr 1834
     in the Westhampton Presbyterian Church

102. HANNAH[6] RAYNOR (Henry[5], Hugh[4], Jonathan[3],
Jonathan[2], Thurston[1]), b. 5 Dec 1801, d. 7 June
1879, ae 77 yrs., 6 mos., 2 days, bur. Speonk;
m. 1820, Jeremiah Rogers, b. 1796, d. 15 Nov
1859, Speonk, s/o Jesse and Amelia (Jagger)
Rogers.
Issue:

*198. Angeline Cecelia[7] Rogers, b. 24 Sept 1825,
       d. 27 Jan 1897, bur. Cedar Grove
       Cemetery, Patchogue, L.I.
199. Henry Merritt[7] Rogers, b. 24 Mar 1827, d.
     22 Feb 1903; m. 23 Dec 1858/9,
     Georgianna Saxton, b. 1840, d. 1908.

Seventh Generation

115. SILAS GILDERSLEEVE[7] BREESE (Elizabeth
Lindsley[6], David[5], David[4], Jonathan[3], Jonathan[2],
Thurston[1]), b. 4 June 1805 on L.I., d. 23 Oct
1863 at Serena, IL, bur. in a small country

cemetery just west of Serena on Hwy 52; m. (1) 21 Feb 1826, Anna Heath, b. 1808, d. 11 June 1837; m. (2) 19 Nov 1837, Henrietta Rosina Larwill, b. England, d. 9 July 1886, Serena, IL, bur. Serena country Cemetery.
Issue Wife (1):
*200. Mary Elizabeth[8] Breese, b. 15 Apr 1827, NJ
*201. John Heath[8] Breese, b. 20 Oct 1830, NJ
Issue Wife (2):
*202. Lucilla Larwill[8] Breese, b. 28 Jan 1839, Newark, NJ
*203. Henrietta Rosina[8] Breese, b. 31 Jan 1841, d. 12 June 1911
*204. Silas Howard[8] Breese, b. 10 Mar 1843
 205. Edwin Augustus[8] Breese, b. 23 Mar 1848, d. 23 Feb 1850
*206. Harriet Maria[8] Breese, b. 22 Mar 1851
*207. Ella Florence[8] Breese, b. 11 Oct 1854
*208. Eugenia Artilisa[8] Breese, b. 9 Apr 1857, d. 8 Dec 1910
*209. Thurlow Ellsworth[8] Breese, b. 29 June 1861, d. 12 Apr 1933

116. ROBERT FINLEY[7] BREESE (Elizabeth Lindsley[6], David[5], David[4], Jonathan[3], Jonathan[2], Thurston[1]), twin, b. 22 June 1807, bur. Princeville, IL; m. Hannah _____. Residence: Princeville, IL.
Issue:
 210. Ambrose[8] Breese
 211. Finley[8] Breese
 212. David[8] Breese, d. in the Civil War

117. DAVID RAYNOR[7] BREESE (Elizabeth Lindsley[6], David[5], David[4], Jonathan[3], Jonathan[2], Thurston[1]), twin, b. 22 June 1807; m. Hannah Vail.
Issue:
 213. Robert[8] Breese
 214. Cecil[8] Breese

*215. Augustin[8] Breese
216. Susan[8] Breese
*217. Agnes[8] Breese

119. MARY ANN[7] BREESE (Elizabeth Lindsley[6], David[5], David[4], Jonathan[3], Jonathan[2], Thurston[1]), b. 2 Mar 1811; m. as his 3rd wife, Thomas Teeple.
Issue:
218. Libbie[8] Teeple
219. Susan[8] Teeple

120. AUGUSTUS[7] BREESE (Elizabeth Lindsley[6], David[5], David[4], Jonathan[3], Jonathan[2], Thurston[1]), b. 25 Oct 1812; m. Susan _____.
Issue:
*220. Lizzie[8] Breese
221. Laura[8] Breese, m. Will Van Fleet
*222. Emma[8] Breese
223. Frances[8] Breese, m. Victor Van Fleet
224. Amelia[8] Breese, m. Eddie Lord

121. HANNAH[7] BREESE (Elizabeth Lindsley[6], David[5], David[4], Jonathan[3], Jonathan[2], Thurston[1]), b. 8 Oct 1815; m. (1) _____ Winne; m. (2) _____ Corbet; m. (3) William Stevens.
Issue Husband (1):
225. Rachel[8] Winne

123. SARAH NAOMI[7] BREESE (Elizabeth Lindsley[6], David[5], David[4], Jonathan[3], Jonathan[2], Thurston[1]), b. 30 Aug 1819; m. Thomas Clark.
Issue:
*226. Anna[8] Clark
227. Lizzie[8] Clark, m. George Lawrence
228. Emily[8] Clark
229. Frank[8] Clark

124. REBECCA[7] MATTAX (Prudence[6], Jonathan[5], David[4], Jonathan[3], Jonathan[2], Thurston[1]), b. 29 May 1816, Lindley's Mills, PA, d. 7 Oct 1904, Rock Falls, IL; m. 8 Sept 1832, Jeptha N. Nightser, Jr., b. 27 July 1808, Morris Co., NJ, d. 23 May 1867, Morrison, IL, s/o Jeptha and Abigail (Guest) Nightser.
Issue:
  230. William Morgan[8] Nightser, b. 20 Feb 1848, Mt. Vernon, OH, d. 16 May 1930, Sedgwick, KS.

126. OLIVER R.[7] WADE (Catherine[6], Adonijah, Jr.[5], Adonijah[4], Jonathan[3], Jonathan[2], Thurston[1]), a ship outfitter; residence: Sag Harbor; bur. Oakland Cemetery, Sag Harbor.
Issue:
  231. Edgar[8] Wade
  232. Oliver[8] Wade

127. BENJAMIN[7] WADE (Catherine[6], Adonijah, Jr.[5], Adonijah[4], Jonathan[3], Jonathan[2], Thurston[1]), b. 1809, d. 1867; m. Nov 1834, Sarah Pierson, b. 1814, d. 1902. Benjamin was a ship builder. Residence: Sag Harbor. Both Benjamin & Sarah bur. Oakland Cemetery, Sag Harbor.
Issue:
*233. Lillie[8] Wade, b. 11 Feb 1850, d. 12 Feb 1917

131. MARY JANE[7] PENNY (Abigail[6], Adonijah, Jr.[5], Adonijah[4], Jonathan[3], Jonathan[2], Thurston[1]), b. 9 Oct 1836, d. 21 Aug 1879; m. William Bishop, b. 7 Mar 1829, d. 29 Mar 1908. William Bishop m. (2) Susan E. Raynor, b. 27 Nov 1834, d. 15 July 1909.
Issue:
  234. George P.[8] Bishop, b. 1 Feb 1859, d. 2 Nov 1882; m. Harriet M. _____, b. 22 Dec 1856, d. 20 Feb 1927.
*235. Florence[8] Bishop, b. 1860, d. 1941

136. WILLIAM[7] RAYNOR (Jonathan[6], Elihu[5], Nathan[4], Jonathan[3], Jonathan[2], Thurston[1]), b. 18 Feb 1805, d. 12 Nov 1857, ae 52 yrs., 8 mos., 24 days; m. Sarah Ann ("Sally") Robinson of Patchogue, d. 16 July 1866, d/o Joseph and Elizabeth J. (Clark) Robinson of Manor. Sarah Ann was b. Sept 1811, d. 15 July 1886, Westhampton, ae 74 yrs., 10 mos. Both William and Sarah Ann are bur. in the Westhampton Cemetery. Sarah and her three sons resided in Speonk on 25 July 1860, at the time of the 1860 Federal Census.
Issue:

236. Joseph Clark[8] Raynor, b. 1842, d. 2 Apr 1879, San Francisco (dropsy), unmarried. He left Westhampton for California via Cape Horn in 1863. At the time of his death, only his mother was living; his father died (drowned) 20 years previously and his two brothers were also dead. Joseph Clark Raynor was a boatman in 1860.

237. Joshua[8] Raynor, b. 1844

*238. George W.[8] Raynor, b. 16 Dec 1847, d. 30 Oct 1873, ae 25 yrs., 10 mos., 14 days, bur. Westhampton Cemetery

239. Angelina[8] Raynor, b. 17 Jan (or Feb) 1849

240. Charles Russell[8] Raynor, b. 30 Mar 1850, d. 13 Aug (or July) 1873, NYC (Bright's disease), ae 23 yrs., 4 mos., 14 days, bur. Westhampton Cemetery; m. 27 Nov 1869 at Center Moriches by Rev. Robert Scott, Eliza E. Terry, d/o Samuel Terry. Charles was a member of the Metropolitan Police of New York City.

138. HANNAH[7] RAYNOR (Jonathan[6], Elihu[5], Nathan[4], Jonathan[3], Jonathan[2], Thurston[1]), b. 25 Oct 1808 (or 24 or 29 Oct 1809), d. 10 (or 11) Feb 1848, ae 39 yrs.; m. Abraham ("Abram") Stevens, b. 7 May 1805, d. 1 July 1882 (or 1883), s/o Charles and Nancy (Howell) Stevens; Abraham m. (2) **139. MILLICENT[7] RAYNOR.** Both Hannah and Abraham are

bur. Westhampton Cemetery.
Issue:
241. Nancy[8] Stevens, b. 23 May 1828, d. 1907;
     m. Jesse W. Pelletreau.
242. Sarah[8] Stevens, b. 25 Jan 1830, d. 21 July
     1889
243. Lina[8] Stevens, b. 26 Jan 1833, d. 20 (or
     30) Dec 1863
*244. John Mitchell[8] Stevens, b. 25 June 1840,
     d. 1 Feb 1922
245. Hubert F.[8] Stevens, b. 25 Feb 1845, d. 21
     Dec 1901; m. 5 Oct 1867, Susan Margaret
     Tuthill, b. 28 Mar 1847, d. 20 May 1937,
     d/o Silas Tuthill.
246. Charles B.[8] Stevens, b. 8 May 1847, d. 11
     Feb 1883, ae 35 yrs., 9 mos., 2 days,
     bur. Westhampton Cemetery

139. **MILLICENT**[7] **RAYNOR** (Jonathan[6], Elihu[5],
Nathan[4], Jonathan[3], Jonathan[2], Thurston[1]), b. 25
Jan 1811, d. 6 Dec 1895, aged 84 yrs., 10 mos.,
19 days, bur. Westhampton Cemetery; m. (1)
William Jessup, b. 17 Aug 1807, d. 28 Sept 1840,
ae 33 yrs., 1 mo., 11 days; m. (2) Abraham
("Abram") Stevens, b. 7 May 1805, d. 1 July 1882
(or 1883), s/o Charles and Nancy (Howell)
Stevens and widower of **138.** **HANNAH**[7] **RAYNOR**,
Millicent's sister.
Issue Husband (1):
247. Richard[8] Jessup, b. 2 Dec 1831, d. 28 Feb
     1857, ae 25 yrs. 2 mos., 20 days
248. Stephen[8] Jessup, b. 8 May 1833, d. 1879
249. Daniel R.[8] Jessup, b. 13 Jan 1835, d. 9
     Dec 1866, ae 31 yrs., 11 mos., 23 days
250. Laura P.[8] Jessup, b. 15 Aug 1837, d. 30
     May 1852, ae 15 yrs., 9 mos., 15 days
251. William C.[8] Jessup, b. 25 Nov 1839, d. 9
     Jan 1867, ae 27 yrs., 2 mos., 14 days
Issue Husband (2):
252. Hannah ("Annie") R.[8] Stevens, b. 17 Feb
     1849, d. 1936; m. (1) 24 Dec 1869, **238.**
     GEORGE W.[8] **RAYNOR**, b. 16 Dec 1847, d. 30

Oct 1873, ae 25 yrs., 10 mos., 14 days, bur. Westhampton Cemetery, s/o William^7 and Sarah Ann (Robinson) Raynor; m. (2) Israel Monroe Rose. Issue: See 238. GEORGE W.^{8} RAYNOR.

253. Abraham Howell^8 Stevens, b. 25 Apr 1852, d. 15 Apr 1853, ae 11 mos., 20 days, bur. Westhampton Cemetery

140. NATHAN^7 RAYNOR (Jonathan^6, Elihu^5, Nathan^4, Jonathan^3, Jonathan^2, Thurston^1), b. 25 Mar 1813, d. 16 (or 15) May 1890 at Westhampton; m. Sarah Jane ("Sally") Carter, b. 21 July 1823 (or 1822), d. 3 Jan 1890, ae 67 yrs., d/o David J. and Huldah (Raynor) Carter of Manor. Both Nathan and Sarah Jane are bur. Westhampton Cemetery.
Issue:

*254. William Clark^8 Raynor, b. 10 Sept 1839, d. 1921

*255. John Gilbert^8 Raynor, b. 12 Oct 1841, d. 17 May 1916, bur. Westhampton Cemetery

*256. George Clinton^8 Raynor, b. 30 Aug 1843 (or 1842), d. 17 May 1901, bur. Westhampton Cemetery

*257. Millicent^8 Raynor, b. ca 1846

*258. Nathan Sidney^8 Raynor, b. 15 Oct 1848, d. 13 Nov 1904

*259. Charlotte Elizabeth^8 Raynor, b. 3 June 1852, Westhampton

*260. Charles Wesley^8 Raynor, b. 28 Nov 1856, Westhampton, d. 18 May 1943, White Haven, MD, bur. Dolbey Cemetery, White Haven, MD

*261. Hettie Jane^8 Raynor, b. 29 Jan 1858, d. 24 July 1941

*262. Sarah Rupell^8 Raynor, b. ca 1859

*263. Walter Scott^8 Raynor, b. 20 Aug 1860 (or 1862 or 1864), d. 8 Feb 1921, ae 59 yrs.

264. Rose Belle^8 Raynor, b. 29 July 1862, d. 23 Mar 1886, Bluepoint, L.I.; m. 3 July 1880 in Westhampton, William T. Arthur,

d. 1886.

265. Grace Alice[8] Raynor, b. 13 (or 1) Feb 1865, d. 14 May 1946; m. 15 Dec 1885, Merten Jarvis Hawkins, b. 17 May 1860, d. 10 Apr 1923, s/o William Sidney and Ann Jemima (Wines) Hawkins; no issue. Both bur. Mt. Pleasant Cemetery, East Moriches.

?   Fred[8] Raynor

?   Arthur[8] Raynor

141. DANIEL[7] RAYNOR (Jonathan[6], Elihu[5], Nathan[4], Jonathan[3], Jonathan[2], Thurston[1]), b. 25 Jan 1815; m. Laura P. _____. Daniel, a farmer, resided in Brookhaven Town.
Issue:

*266. William[8] Raynor, b. 1840

 267. Nancy[8] Raynor, b. 1843

 268. Martha[8] Raynor, b. 1845

 269. Grace[8] Raynor, b. 1855

144. URIAH[7] RAYNOR (Jonathan[6], Elihu[5], Nathan[4], Jonathan[3], Jonathan[2], Thurston[1]), bapt 28 Apr 1822, d. 9 May 1897 (or 1898), Good Ground, ae 75 yrs., 11 days, bur. Methodist Cemetery, Hampton Bays; m. (1) Mary Foster, d. Jan 1866 (or 1861), d/o Maltby Foster; m. (2) Julia (Foster) Wells, b. ca 1830, widow of Ransford Wells and sister of Mary Foster; m. (3) 26 Apr 1875, Maria H. Payne of Greenport. Uriah came to Good Ground from Westhampton and bought land in 1863 of Joshua Squires, the homesite Joshua bought long before, probably from John Bellows.
Issue Wife (1):

 270. Mary Alice[8] Raynor, b. 18 Oct 1849

*271. Sarah Tuthill[8] Raynor, b. ca 1852

*272. John Fletcher[8] Raynor, b. 26 Nov 1855, d. 8 May 1913

*273. William Anderson[8] Raynor, b. ca 1861, d. 20 Jan 1934, Hampton Bays

145. ELIZABETH ("ELIZA")[7] RAYNOR (Jonathan[6],

30

Elihu[5], Nathan[4], Jonathan[3], Jonathan[2], Thurston[1]), b. 1 Nov 1824, bapt. 7 Nov 1824; m. 16 Aug 1846 at the Westhampton Presbyterian Church, by Rev. Nathan Price, Erastus Hubbard, b. ca 1822.
Issue:
*274. Elijah (or Elihu)[8] Hubbard, b. ca 1847
*275. William[8] Hubbard

146. ELIHU[7] RAYNOR (Jonathan[6], Elihu[5], Nathan[4], Jonathan[3], Jonathan[2], Thurston[1]), b. 20 Jan 1827, d. 2 Dec 1894, ae 67 yrs., 10 mos., 12 days; m. Hannah Maria Tuttle, b. 10 Dec 1831, d. 18 Mar 1888, ae 56 yrs., 3 mos., 8 days, d/o Wells and Penelope ("Nellie") (Hallock) Tuttle. According to the 1865 Southampton Town Census, Elihu, a farmer, and his family resided in Westhampton. Elihu, his wife, Hannah, and their children, Ella G., Erastus W., and Elihu J., were listed in the 1865 Southampton Town Census as residents of Westhampton.
Issue:
276. Ella Grace[8] Raynor, b. 29 Aug 1851, Westhampton; m. 7 Sept 1871 at Westhampton, Gideon Henry Raynor, b. 23 Dec 1850, d. 29 Jan 1910, ae 59 yrs., 1 mo., 16 days, s/o Laban and Elizabeth (Robinson) Raynor, Sr.
*277. Erastus W.[8] Raynor, b. 9 Mar 1853, Westhampton, d. 10 Mar 1923, bur. Westhampton Cemetery
*278. Elihu Jotham[8] Raynor, b. 19 Jan 1855, d. 19 Feb 1938

148. CHARLES[7] RAYNOR (Nathan[6], Elihu[5], Nathan[4], Jonathan[3], Jonathan[2], Thurston[1]), b. 1816; m. Anna M. Dungan; removed to Philadelphia.
Issue:
*279. Kate[8] Raynor
280. Charles[8] Raynor, b. 1853, d. 1854
281. Charles[8] Raynor, b. 1855; m. Annie Potter
282. Nathan H.[8] Raynor, b. 1857; a physician in

31

Philadelphia
283. Mary[8] Raynor, b. & d. 1865
284. William[8] Raynor, b. 1866
285. George[8] Raynor, b. 1867
286. John[8] Raynor, b. & d. 1869
287. Anna[8] Raynor, b. 1870
288. Hetty[8] Raynor, b. 1873
289. Herrick[8] Raynor, b. 1875

152. JOHN MORRISON[7] RAYNOR (John Cook[6], Elihu[5], Nathan[4], Jonathan[3], Jonathan[2], Thurston[1]), b. 19 Dec 1834, Greenport, d. 1 Mar 1906, Greenport, bur. Westhampton; m. Frances J. Robinson, b. 17 Sept 1843, d. 6 Feb 1927, ae 83 yrs., bur. Westhampton. John's will, dated 16 Apr 1898, was proved 5 Apr 1906 (Liber 47, p. 188, Suffolk County Surrogate's Court).
Issue:
*290. Mary Jagger[8] Raynor, b. 10 Sept 1875
*291. John Roscoe[8] Raynor, b. 22 Oct 1877, d. 18 Jan 1944

153. HERRICK JAGGER[7] RAYNOR (John Cook[6], Elihu[5], Nathan[4], Jonathan[3], Jonathan[2], Thurston[1]), b. 8 Dec 1838, Westhampton, d. 16 May 1909; m. 23 Dec 1870 at Jamesport, Maria Woodhull Payne, b. 7 Oct 1845, Jamesport, d. 22 Feb 1927, d/o Samuel Payne. Herrick was a farmer. He and Maria are bur. in Westhampton. Herrick's will, dated 9 May 1909, was proved 26 May 1909 (Liber 52, p. 57, Suffolk County Surrogate's Court).
Issue:
292. Thurston Herrick[8] Raynor, b. 19 Dec 1874, d. 13 Jan 1961, bur. Westhampton Cemetery; had a dairy farm on South Country Road, Westhampton.

154. OSCAR BINGLEY[7] RAYNOR (Herrick[6], Elihu[5], Nathan[4], Jonathan[3], Jonathan[2], Thurston[1]), b. 9 Oct 1828, Westhampton Beach, d. 18 Feb 1900, Westhampton; m. 30 Nov 1853, Sarah Jane ("Sally") Cook, b. 12 May 1829, d. 12 Sept 1908,

32

d/o Luther and Mary (Hoctor) Cook; both bur.
Westhampton Cemetery.
Issue:

*293. Charles Luther[8] Raynor, b. 5 June 1855, d.
16 Dec 1904

*294. Mary C.[8] Raynor, b. 1857, d. 1926, bur.
Remsenburg

295. Harriet Halsey[8] Raynor, b. 16 Mar 1860, d.
25 Mar 1916, unmarried, bur. Westhampton
Cemetery. Harriet owned and operated
the Grassmere Hotel on Beach Lane,
Westhampton Beach.

*296. John Everett[8] Raynor, b. 2 Dec 1864, d. 19
Mar 1917

297. Addison O.[8] Raynor, b. 10 Aug 1867, d. 23
Dec 1933, Hempstead, L.I., ae 66 yrs.,
unmarried; was a physician, but did not
practice because of deafness.

155. HARRIET[7] RAYNOR (Herrick[6], Elihu[5], Nathan[4],
Jonathan[3], Jonathan[2], Thurston[1]), b. 23 Dec
1833, d. 31 Jan 1912, ae 78 yrs., 1 mo., 8 days,
bur. Northville Cemetery, Riverhead; m. 15 Dec
1852, James Harvey Benjamin of Northville, d. 8
May 1896, ae 73 yrs., 1 mo., 4 days, bur.
Northville Cemetery, Riverhead, s/o Rev. William
F. and Amelia (Hallock) Benjamin.
Issue:

298. Mary Amelia[8] Benjamin, b. 15 Feb 1854,
Northville, d. 4 Apr 1856, ae 2 yrs., 1
mo., 12 days, bur. Northville Cemetery

299. Harriet H. ("Hettie")[8] Benjamin, b. 23 Oct
1856, d. 22 Mar 1857, ae 1 yr., 5 days,
bur. Northville Cemetery

300. Nancy W.[8] Benjamin, b. 28 Dec 1857; m. 6
Apr 1895, Alfred Rigby; no issue.

301. Amelia H.[8] Benjamin, b. 25 Aug 1860; with
Salvation Army in Amity County, Ohio.

302. Henrietta[8] Benjamin, b. 7 Apr 1863, d. 5
Aug 1863, ae 5 mos., bur. Northville
Cemetery

303. William H.[8] Benjamin, b. 25 Dec 1865,

Northville, d. 1928; m. 1 Jan 1891,
Florence M. Downs, b. 1865, d. 1943, d/o
Sheldon and Matilda Keziah (Hallock)
Downs; both bur. Northville Cemetery.

157. JACOB A.[7] **RAYNOR** (Caleb S.[6], Josiah
Woodhull[5], William[4], Jonathan[3], Jonathan[2],
Thurston[1]), b. 1 July 1834, d. 17 Jan 1914; m.
Mary A. Halsey, b. 16 June 1839, d. 29 Oct 1909,
d/o Oliver Halsey; both bur. Remsenburg
Cemetery. Jacob was a carpenter.
Issue:
*304. Oliver Jacob[8] Raynor, b. 1861, d. 1927,
       bur. Remsenburg Cemetery
*305. Frederick Caleb[8] Raynor, b. 26 July 1868
       (or 1869), Speonk, d. 1936, bur.
       Remsenburg Cemetery

158. JOSEPH[7] **RAYNOR** (Caleb S.[6], Josiah
Woodhull[5], William[4], Jonathan[3], Jonathan[2],
Thurston[1])
Issue:
 306. Hannah[8] Raynor

159. MIRIAM WICKES[7] **RAYNOR** (William R.[6],
William[5], William[4], Jonathan[3], Jonathan[2],
Thurston[1]), b. 15 Jan 1815, Westhampton, d. 5
Oct 1861, Aquebogue, bur. Riverhead Cemetery; m.
9 Jan 1837 at Wading River, Henry Wickham
Corwin, b. 2 June 1809, Aquebogue, d. 15 Dec
1895, Riverhead, bur. Riverhead Cemetery, s/o
Benjamin and Sarah (Vail) Corwin. Henry was a
building contractor.
Issue:
 307. Harriet Elizabeth[8] Corwin, b. 29 (or 20)
       Dec 1837, d. 3 May 1867, unmarried, bur.
       Riverhead Cemetery
*308. Henry Harrison[8] Corwin, b. 17 Sept 1840,
       Aquebogue, d. 8 Sept 1935, bur.
       Riverhead Cemetery
 309. William Wickham[8] Corwin, b. 17 June 1847,
       d. 22 Apr 1872, unmarried, bur.

Riverhead Cemetery

310. Mary Minetta[8] Corwin, b. 15 June 1849,
     Aquebogue; m. 16 Dec 1875, Dr. J. Frank
     Davis; no issue; resided in NYC.

311. Helen Florence[8] Corwin, b. 18 June 1850,
     d. 24 Aug 1877, unmarried, bur.
     Riverhead Cemetery

160. WILLIAM JAGGER[7] RAYNOR (William R.[6],
William[5], William[4], Jonathan[3], Jonathan[2],
Thurston[1]), b. 20 (or 19) Dec 1816, d. 11 Jan
1882, ae 65 yrs., 22 days; m. 21 Mar 1844, Mary
Jane Hawkins, b. 12 May 1818 at Port Jefferson,
d. 2 Oct 1899 (or 13 Jan 1882), ae 81 yrs., 4
mos., 20 days, d/o Zachary and Charry
(Yarrington) Hawkins. William and Mary resided
in Westhampton, where William was a carpenter.
Both are bur. Westhampton Cemetery. The 1850
U.S. Census listed William J. Raynor as a farmer
in Southampton Town along with his wife, Mary,
and daughters, Antoinette, 5, and Harriet, 1.
They were listed in the 1860 U.S. Census as well
along with William's mother, Harriet, 71, and
dau, Sarah, 6.
Issue:

*312. Antoinette ("Nettie") Hawkins[8] Raynor, b.
      26 Sept 1845, d. 11 Sept 1931
 313. Harriet Jagger[8] Raynor, b. 11 Sept 1849,
      probably d. before 1882
 314. Sarah Louise[8] Raynor, b. 7 May 1854, d. 31
      July 1882; m. 8 May 1875, **277.** ERASTUS
      W.[8] RAYNOR, b. 9 Mar 1855, Westhampton,
      d. 10 Mar 1923, s/o # 146. Elihu[7] and
      Hannah Maria (Tuttle) Raynor; no issue.
 315. Eliza Kate[8] Raynor, b. 22 May 1856, d. 19
      Aug 1856, bur. Westhampton Cemetery

161. ELIZABETH[7] RAYNOR (William R.[6], William[5],
William[4], Jonathan[3], Jonathan[2], Thurston[1]), b. 4
Mar 1820, d. 17 Dec 1893, ae 73 yrs., 9 mos., 13
days; m. Lester G. Rogers, b. 18 (or 14) Sept
1822, d. 4 (or 1) Oct 1895, ae 73 yrs., 16 days,

s/o Thomas Nicholl and Elizabeth (Halsey) Rogers. Both Elizabeth and Lester are bur. Westhampton Cemetery.
Issue:

316. Mary G.[8] Rogers, d. at 1 yr. and 2 mos.

*317. David Roswell[8] Rogers, b. ca 1845

*318. Frances Harriet[8] Rogers, b. 6 June 1847, Westhampton, d. 29 Apr 1939, ae 91 yrs.

*319. Jennie B.[8] Rogers

*320. Susan Halsey[8] Rogers, b. 7 Apr 1851, d. 12 Oct 1944, Westhampton, ae 93 yrs., 6 mos., 5 days, bur. Westhampton Cemetery

*321. Millicent Brewster[8] Rogers, b. 4 Oct 1858, d. 9 Dec 1934

322. John N.[8] Rogers, b. 10 Jan 1860, d. 10 Feb 1861, bur. Westhampton Cemetery

? Larsan (or Larson)[8] Rogers

162. SUSAN[7] RAYNOR (William R.[6], William[5], William[4], Jonathan[3], Jonathan[2], Thurston[1]), b. 1824, d. 6 Mar 1873; m. 2 June 1849, as his 2nd wife, Lindley Benton Tyler of Water Mill, L.I., b. 30 Nov 1813 (or 1814) at St. George Manor, d. 24 Dec 1875, s/o Nathaniel and Nancy (Stockwell) Tyler of Northfield, CT. Lindley m. (1) 28 Jan 1835, Beulah Robinson, b. 16 Apr 1817, d. 18 Apr 1848; m. (3) 1873, Esther (Robinson) Hulse, b. 5 Aug 1819, d. 16 Mar 1888. After Lindley's death, Esther m. (2) 1880, Davis Robinson.
Issue:

323. William Lindley[8] Tyler, b. 20 Apr 1850, d. 18 Aug 1856, ae 6 yrs., 5 mos., bur. Robinson Cemetery, Manorville

324. John Lester[8] Tyler, b. 1854, d. 4 Mar 1909; m. Elanora Edwards, b. 24 July 1856, d. 31 July 1930.

325. Harriet Lucretia[8] Tyler, b. 25 Sept 1858, d. 15 Nov 1875, unmarried

326. Roscoe Conklin[8] Tyler, of Eastport, b. 8 May 1861, d. 12 Sept 1883 (drowned); unmarried.

327. Susan Frances ("Fanny")[8] Tyler, b. 30 Sept

1864, d. 5 Nov 1944; m. Perry Tuttle, b.
17 Feb 1856, d. July 1933

163. NANCY P.[7] **RAYNOR** (William R.[6], William[5],
William[4], Jonathan[3], Jonathan[2], Thurston[1]), b. 5
Mar 1827, d. 21 Feb 1869; m. Rogers Bishop, b. 7
Mar 1827, d. 3 July 1881. Rogers Bishop m. (2)
Jennie Browning, b. 16 Nov 1828, d. 1 Mar 1906,
widow of William Browning of Scotland.
Issue:

328. Ida May[8] Bishop, b. 4 Aug 1858, d. 6 Oct
1893; m. 18 May 1881 by Rev. E.K.
Fanning, **293.** CHARLES LUTHER[8] RAYNOR,
b. 5 June 1855, d. 16 Dec 1904, s/o
154. Oscar Bingley[7] and Sarah Jane
("Sally")(Cook) Raynor.
Issue: See **293.** CHARLES LUTHER[8] RAYNOR.

329. Stanton Rogers[8] Bishop, of Westhampton, b.
11 July 1863, d. 20 Dec 1911, bur.
Westhampton Cemetery; unmarried.

165. ELIJAH PIERSON[7] **RAYNOR** (William R.[6],
William[5], William[4], Jonathan[3], Jonathan[2],
Thurston[1]), b. 21 Oct 1833, d. 30 May 1911; m.
(1) 19 Nov 1850 in Greenport by John Reid,
Pastor of the Franklinville Church, Harriet N.
Carpenter of Greenport, b. ca 1836, d/o Enoch
and Mary C. Carpenter of Greenport; m. (2) 14
Nov 1856, Harriett N. Golder (or Goulder), b.
1839 in Newtown, L.I., d. 23 Feb 1904, d/o James
and Mary Goulder. Both Elijah and Harriett
(Golder) Raynor are bur. Westhampton Cemetery.
Elijah lived in the homestead, built by either
his father or grandfather, on the Southeast
corner of Library Avenue and Main Street,
Westhampton Beach; the homestead was moved much
later to the East side of Seafield Lane, 950'
North of Sunswyck Lane. Elijah, a carpenter,
founded E. Raynor's Sons, Building Contracting
and Real Estate, in 1875. The 1850 U.S. Census
listed Elijah as 17 yrs. old, a carpenter, in
the home of Richard Benjamin of Southold Town.
Elijah was listed in the 1860 U.S. Census as a

ship's carpenter and resident of Greenport, along with his wife, Harriet, and sons, Franklin and Charles. The family was also listed in the 1865 Southampton Town Census; Elijah P.[7] Raynor, his wife, Harriet, and their children, Franklin C., Charles H., Augustus H., and William, were living in the household of Elijah's brother, William[7] Raynor, at that time. The will of Elijah Pierson[7] Raynor, dated 27 Apr 1911, proved 5 Sept 1911, left $2,405 in personal property and $7,600 in real property to his sons, Charles E. of Westhampton Beach, Frank C. of Southampton, William S. of Westhampton Beach, Augustus H. of Westhampton Beach, John M. of Westhampton Beach, Dwight E. of Westhampton Beach, and Fred W. of Sag Harbor (Liber 55; p. 498).

Issue Wife (1):

*330. Franklin Carpenter[8] Raynor, b. 26 Sept 1856 in Greenport, d. 22 Nov 1920, Southampton, bur. North End Burying Ground, Southampton

Issue Wife (2):

*331. Charles Edward[8] Raynor, b. 1 Jan 1859 in Greenport, d. 12 Apr 1929, bur. Westhampton Cemetery

332. William S. ("Bachelor Bill")[8] Raynor, b. 1862, d. 1915, unmarried, bur. Westhampton Cemetery; he was a carpenter.

*333. Augustus Hiram ("Gus")[8] Raynor, b. 1864, d. 1943

*334. Frederick Woodhull[8] Raynor, b. 14 (or 11) Nov 1866, Westhampton Beach, d. 17 June 1945, Westhampton Beach, bur. Westhampton Cemetery

*335. John Mitchell Burns[8] Raynor, b. 15 Sept 1872, d. 18 Nov 1960, bur. Westhampton Cemetery

336. Dwight Elijah ("Doc")[8] Raynor, b. 1876 (or 1878), d. 1946; m. 1 Nov 1900 in the Sag Harbor Presbyterian Church, Nellie L. White, b. ca 1878, d/o William White of

Sag Harbor. Dwight was a carpenter.

169. MULFORD T.[7] RAYNOR (Nathaniel Woodhull[6], William[5], William[4], Jonathan[3], Jonathan[2], Thurston[1]), m. Ann Persall; removed to Rockville Center, L.I. and to Brooklyn.
Issue:
*337. Charles[8] Raynor, b. 1844, d. 1912
338. George[8] Raynor
339. Rachel[8] Raynor

173. EGBERT[7] JESSUP (Susannah[6], William[5], William[4], Jonathan[3], Jonathan[2], Thurston[1]), b. 16 (or 30) June 1818, Quogue, d. 22 Mar 1876, ae 57 yrs., 9 mos., 6 days; m. 14 Dec 1843, Nancy Wells, b. 16 June 1821, d. 25 June 1883, d/o Christopher Wells of Southold; both bur. Quogue Cemetery.
Issue:
*340. Susan Mary[8] Jessup, b. 21 Apr 1846, Quogue, d. 4 Jan 1918, Patchogue, bur. Patchogue
341. Fannie J.[8] Jessup, b. 4 Mar 1851, d. 26 July 1919
342. Silas Egbert[8] Jessup, b. 14 Sept 1855, d. 27 Jan 1900; m. 18 May 1880, **235.** FLORENCE[8] BISHOP, b. 1860; d. 1941, d/o William and # 131. Mary Jane[7] (Penny) Bishop.
Issue: See **235.** FLORENCE[8] BISHOP.

174. WILLIAM HENRY[7] JESSUP (Susannah[6], William[5], William[4], Jonathan[3], Jonathan[2], Thurston[1]), b. 21 Nov 1819, d. 30 Apr 1852, ae 32 yrs., 5 mos., 22 days; m. 22 Nov 1842 by Rev. Charles Knowles, Huldah Homan, b. 31 Mar 1816, d. 13 Feb 1896, ae 79 yrs., 11 mos., 14 days. Huldah m. (2) Jesse Halsey, b. 1835, d. 1892. William and Huldah lived in Quogue.
Issue:
343. Silas B.[8] Jessup, b. 2 Mar 1845, d. 23

Sept 1845, ae 6 mos., 21 days
344. William H.[8] Jessup, b. 3 Mar 1848, d. 11
     Aug 1848, ae 5 mos., 8 days
345. George Hildreth[8] Jessup, b. 27 Nov 1849,
     d. 1912; m. 27 Jan 1871, <u>318.</u> FRANCES
     HARRIET[8] ROGERS, b. 6 June 1847,
     Westhampton, d. 29 Apr 1939, ae 91 yrs.,
     d/o Lester G. and # 161. Elizabeth[7]
     (Raynor) Rogers.
     Issue: See <u>318.</u> FRANCES HARRIET[8] ROGERS.

<u>177.</u> MARY FRANCES[7] RAYNOR (Elijah[6], William[5],
William[4], Jonathan[3], Jonathan[2], Thurston[1]), b.
17 Oct 1846, d. 24 Feb 1930; m. 4 June 1868 at
Quogue by Rev. M. R. Reeve, Nathaniel Miller
Talmage, b. 1 Mar 1834 at Springs, L.I., d. 12
Sept 1912, s/o David and Mary A. (Miller)
Talmage; both bur. Baiting Hollow Cemetery.
Nathaniel was a Lieutenant in the Civil War.
Issue:
346. Anna Miller[8] Talmage, b. Oct 1869; m.
     Frank H. Corwin.
347. Henry Raynor[8] Talmage, b. 28 Dec 1871,
     Westhampton; m. 26 July 1895, Ellen
     Ernestine Wells, d/o Goldsmith and
     Phile (Corwin) Wells.
348. Caroline Bishop[8] Talmage, b. 20 Mar 1882;
     m. Aug 1902, Everett Hulse, s/o Samuel
     Hulse.

<u>184.</u> CYRUS TIMOTHY[7] RAYNOR (James Hewitt[6],
James[5], Hugh[4], Jonathan[3], Jonathan[2], Thurston[1]),
b. 1842.
Issue:
349. Henry William[8] Raynor, b. 1874
350. Lester James Huit[8] Raynor
351. Charles F.[8] Raynor
352. Cyrus Timothy[8] Raynor, Jr.
353. Robert Whittemore[8] Raynor

193. NANCY[7] HAWKINS (Elizabeth[6], Henry[5], Hugh[4], Jonathan[3], Jonathan[2], Thurston[1]), b. 26 Apr 1811, d. 25 Mar 1890; m. Walter Hawkins, b. 26 Feb 1808 at South Haven, L.I., d. 16 Jan 1888, s/o Samuel and Phebe (Rose) Hawkins; both bur. at South Haven. Residence: South Haven. Walter, a farmer, was also a Justice of the Peace.
Issue:

*354. Phebe Rose[8] Hawkins, b. 27 Oct 1832, South Haven, d. 27 Jan 1818

*355. Elizabeth[8] Hawkins, b. 8 Sept 1835, South Haven, d. 17 Apr 1907

*356. Samuel Augustus[8] Hawkins, b. 8 Sept 1838, Fireplace, L.I., d. 17 Nov 1914

*357. James Henry[8] Hawkins, b. 9 Nov 1840, South Haven, d. 31 Dec 1911

*358. William Prescott[8] Hawkins, b. 19 May 1852, South Haven, d. 13 Jan 1915

194. ELMIRA[7] HAWKINS (Elizabeth[6], Henry[5], Hugh[4], Jonathan[3], Jonathan[2], Thurston[1]), b. 15 Aug 1815, d. 20 Feb 1912; m. 4 Dec 1832 at Speonk, Lewis Hawkins, b. 1 Dec 1804, d. 1 Oct 1887, s/o Selah and Rachel (Rose) Hawkins; both bur. Woodland Cemetery, Bellport, L.I. Residence: Brookhaven. Lewis was a farmer.
Issue:

*359. Henry Egbert[8] Hawkins, b. 24 July 1835, Brookhaven, d. 19 July 1923, Brookhaven, bur. Woodland Cemetery, Bellport

*360. Selah[8] Hawkins, b. 13 June 1838, Brookhaven, d. 9 July 1919, Brookhaven, bur. Woodland Cemetery, Bellport

*361. Chauncey Lewis[8] Hawkins, b. 23 May 1844, Brookhaven, d. 10 July 1909, Brookhaven, bur. Woodland Cemetery, Bellport

195. SYLVESTER[7] HAWKINS (Elizabeth[6], Henry[5], Hugh[4], Jonathan[3], Jonathan[2], Thurston[1]), b. 1818, Brookhaven, d. 1882; m. Isabella Goldsmith, b. 2 Jan 1833, Peconic, d. 22 Jan

1913, Southold; both bur. at Southold.
Residence: Southold. Sylvester was a laborer.
Issue:
362. George Frank[8] Hawkins, b. 29 July 1851; m.
Mrs. Azalia Verity of Peconic.
363. Mary[8] Hawkins, b. 1853, d. 1855
364. Gilbert Rose[8] Hawkins, b. 1855, d. 1886
*365. Herbert Monroe[8] Hawkins, b. 18 Feb 1870

196. WILLIAM HENRY[7] HAWKINS (Elizabeth[6], Henry[5],
Hugh[4], Jonathan[3], Jonathan[2], Thurston[1]), b. 24
Apr 1829, Brookhaven, d. 1 Aug 1907; m. Ellen
Louise Homan, b. 1 Nov 1830, d. 28 Sept 1897,
d/o Thomas and Christian Homan; both bur.
Greenfield Cemetery, Hempstead, L.I. Residence:
Hempstead. William was a carpenter and
contractor.
Issue:
366. Theodore Judson[8] Hawkins
367. Ella C.[8] Hawkins

198. ANGELINE CECELIA[7] ROGERS (Hannah[6], Henry[5],
Hugh[4], Jonathan[3], Jonathan[2], Thurston[1]), b. 24
Sept 1825, d. 27 Jan 1897, bur. Cedar Grove
Cemetery, Patchogue; m. (1) 30 Dec 1845 at
Westhampton Presbyterian Church, Phineas
Robinson, b. 1816, East Patchogue, d. 1857, bur.
Cedar Grove Cemetery, Patchogue; m. (2) David F.
Conklin, b. 1830, d. 1910.
Issue Husband (1):
368. Georgiana[8] Robinson, b. 28 Feb 1848, E.
Patchogue, d. 17 Nov 1954, bur. Cedar
Grove Cemetery, Patchogue; m. 28 Feb
1871 in E. Patchogue, Edward Eugene
Hawkins, b. 19 Sept 1845, d. 4 Dec 1930.
369. Sally A.[8] Robinson, b. 24 Mar 1850, d. 30
Mar 1850
370. Charles Henry[8] Robinson, b. 1852, d. 6 Apr
1878 (lost at sea)
Issue Husband (2):
371. Howard S.[8] Conklin, b. 1863, d. 14 Oct
1925; m. Elizabeth ("Lizzie") F. Newins,

b. 1867, d. 1950.
372. Hattie M.[8] Conklin, b. Dec 1864
373. Alena[8] Conklin, b. 28 May 1871, d. 21 Nov
     1953; m. Dr. Frank Overton, b. 29 Dec
     1867, d. 9 Oct 1953.

Eighth Generation

200. MARY ELIZABETH[8] BREESE, dau. of Silas
Gildersleeve[7] and Anna (Heath) Breese, b. 15 Apr
1827, NJ; m. 2 Oct 1855, Seth Solomon Sage, b. 2
Aug 1816, d. June 1873.
Issue:
*374. Ellis Douglas[9] Sage, b. 29 Mar 1863

201. JOHN HEATH[8] BREESE, son of Silas
Gildersleeve[7] and Anna (Heath) Breese, b. 20 Oct
1830, NJ; m. 16 Nov 1859, Elizabeth Lewis, b. 20
Apr 1842.
Issue:
375. Nellie Virginia[9] Breese, b. 2 Sept 1861,
     d. 27 Dec 1863
376. Ellis Eugene[9] Breese, b. 14 Apr 1867
377. Elmer Ellsworth[9] Breese, b. 28 June 1869,
     d. 25 Jan 1881
*378. Cora May[9] Breese, b. 19 Sept 1871
*379. Nora Bell[9] Breese, b. 11 Mar 1874, d.
     1 Jan 1910
*380. Will Louis[9] Breese, b. 25 Oct 1876
*381. Walter Douglas[9] Breese, b. 24 Dec 1878

202. LUCILLA LARWILL[8] BREESE, dau. of Silas
Gildersleeve[7] and Henrietta Rosina (Larwill)
Breese, b. 28 Jan 1839, Newark, NJ; m. 26 Nov
1857 in LaSalle County, IL, James Wheeler
Conard, b. 23 Mar 1838, Ohio.
Issue:
382. Clara Rosina[9] Conard, b. 28 Aug 1858,
     Somonauk, IL; m. 8 June 1887 in Arkansas
     City, KS, James Franklin Beecher,

43

b. 11 Jan 1861, Miami County, IN; no issue.

*383. George Theron[9] Conard, b. 23 Feb 1860, LaSalle County, IL

*384. Mabel Isadora[9] Conard, b. 20 Aug 1861, LaSalle County, IL

*385. Viola Ernestine[9] Conard, b. 10 Sept 1864, Blackhawk County, IA

386. Edna Lucilla[9] Conard, b. 11 Feb 1866, Blackhawk County, IA; unmarried.

*387. Waldo Llewellyn[9] Conard, b. 28 May 1867, Blackhawk County, IA

*388. Nettie Florence[9] Conard, b. 19 Sept 1868, Blackhawk County, IA

389. Bessie Oriana[9] Conard, b. 16 Aug 1870, LaSalle County, IL; unmarried.

390. Hattie Ella[9] Conard, b. 17 Apr 1873, Atchinson County, MO; m. 23 June 1909 at St. Louis, MO, William Essex.

391. Burton Leslie[9] Conard, b. 16 June 1876, Atchinson County, MO

203. HENRIETTA ROSINA[8] BREESE, dau. of Silas Gildersleeve[7] and Henrietta Rosina (Larwill) Breese, b. 31 Jan 1841, Serena, IL, d. 12 June 1911, Heaton, ND; m. 14 Jan 1865, Wilson Lee Smith, b. 12 Apr 1824, d. 15 Oct 1885. Issue:

*392. Rosina Jane[9] Smith, b. 30 June 1866

393. Dill Ellsworth[9] Smith, b. 28 July 1868, d. 17 Oct 1877

394. Elton Lee[9] Smith, b. 22 Sept 1870; m. 8 June 1899, Carrie Elizabeth Goodrich, b. 16 Sept 1877; no issue.

395. Leon Ruber[9] Smith, b. 26 Feb 1874, d. 7 Sept 1875

396. Cyril Glenn[9] Smith, b. 22 Aug 1877; m. 14 June 1905, Mary Elizabeth McMahon, b. 28 June 1881.

397. Gertrude Brooks[9] Smith, b. & d. 21 Dec 1875

204. SILAS HOWARD[8] BREESE, son of Silas Gildersleeve[7] and Henrietta Rosina (Larwill) Breese, b. 10 Mar 1843, Serena, IL; m. 8 July 1869, Sarah Jeantee Inman, b. 23 July 1852, Ladi, OH.
Issue:
*398. Minnie Bell[9] Breese, b. 6 Oct 1870
399. Edwin Augustus[9] Breese, b. 7 Oct 1879, d. 12 June 1892

206. HARRIET MARIA[8] BREESE, dau. of Silas Gildersleeve[7] and Henrietta Rosina (Larwill) Breese, b. 22 Mar 1851 at Serena, IL; m. 9 Dec 1880, Irving Graves.
Issue:
400. Worth[9] Graves, b. 9 Nov 1882, IA
401. Grace[9] Graves, b. 24 Mar 1887, IA

207. ELLA FLORENCE[8] BREESE, dau. of Silas Gildersleeve[7] and Henrietta Rosina (Larwill) Breese, b. 11 Oct 1854, Serena, IL; m. 26 Mar 1879, Thomas McAtee, b. VA.
Issue:
402. Clinton Clyde[9] McAtee, b. 19 Jan 1880
403. Rollo Dale[9] McAtee, b. 27 Aug 1884; m. 11 Feb 1909 at Serena, IL, Mary Elizabeth Arntzen, b. 13 May 1884.
404. Hettie Essie Pearl[9] McAtee, b. 20 May 1888
405. Thomas Cecil[9] McAtee, b. 31 July 1891

208. EUGENIA ARTILISA[8] BREESE, dau. of Silas Gildersleeve[7] and Henrietta Rosina (Larwill) Breese, b. 9 Apr 1857, Serena, IL, d. 8 Dec 1910, Ottawa, IL; m. 9 Jan 1883, Alphin Herbert Whitmore, b. 15 Dec 1856 at North Vernon, IN.
Issue:
406. Ora Rosina[9] Whitmore, b. 8 Nov 1883 near Ottawa, IL, d. 6 Sept 1964 at Richmond, VA; m. 1917 at Berrien Springs, MI, Durward Swingle Williams, d. 30 July

1930 at Chias Ten Djen, Kiangsee
Province, China; no issue.
*407. Maude Decelle[9] Whitmore, b. 26 Oct 1884
near Ottawa, IL, d. 14 Aug 1965 in CA
*408. Bernice Breese[9] Whitmore, b. 22 May 1887
near Ottawa, IL, d. 25 Apr 1963 at
Ottawa, IL
409. Helen Herberta[9] Whitmore, b. 10 May 1892,
Ottawa, IL, d. 7 Aug 1979, Fresno, CA;
m. 14 Nov 1927 at Madera, CA, Arthur
Prentice Harwood, b. 24 July 1881 near
Streater, IL.

209. **THURLOW ELLSWORTH**[8] **BREESE**, son of Silas
Gildersleeve[7] and Henrietta Rosina (Larwill)
Breese, b. 29 June 1861 at Serena, IL, d. 12 Apr
1933; m. (1) 16 Jan 1883 at Blackstone, IL, Rose
Tompkins, b. 5 May 1862 at Marseilles, IL, d. 4
Oct 1917; m. (2) Laura Brown, d. 5 Apr 1933.
Issue Wife (1):
*410. Ellsworth Chase[9] Breese, b. 15 Feb 1884 at
Ottawa, IL, d. Feb 1960
*411. Verne Gildersleeve[9] Breese, b. 24 May 1885
in Serena, IL, d. 20 May 1955 at Ottawa,
IL
412. Alma Lucina[9] Breese, b. 21 Feb 1887 at
Buckley, IL, d. 23 Apr 1913 at
Fairfield, IL
413. Larwill Wilsey[9] Breese, b. 26 May 1889, d.
Sept 1959
414. Ernest Arthur[9] Breese, b. 28 Dec 1891, d.
15 Feb 1961
415. LaRue Floyd[9] Breese, b. 15 Apr 1898, d.
Aug 1968
416. Minnie Elizabeth[9] Breese, b. 23 Nov 1903,
d. 11 Apr 1984

215. **AUGUSTIN**[8] **BREESE**, son of David Raynor[7] and
Hannah (Vail) Breese, m. Marian _____
Issue:
417. Karl[9] Breese

217. AGNES[8] BREESE, dau. of David Raynor[7] and Hannah (Vail) Breese, m. Eugene _____
Issue:
  418. Grace[9] _____

220. LIZZIE[8] BREESE, dau. of Augustus[7] and Susan (   ) Breese, m. Dean DeGrass.
Issue:
  419. Ellen Dean[9] DeGrass

222. EMMA[8] BREESE, dau. of Augustus[7] and Susan (   ) Breese, m. Will Mitchell.
Issue:
  420. Ella[9] Mitchell
  421. Ernest[9] Mitchell
  422. Garfield Arthur[9] Mitchell

226. ANNA[8] CLARK, dau. of Thomas and Sarah Naomi[7] (Breese) Clark, m. Henry Leonard.
Issue:
  423. Edith[9] Leonard

233. LILLIE[8] WADE, dau. of Benajmin[7] and Sarah (Pierson) Wade, b. 11 Feb 1850, d. 12 Feb 1917; m. 22 Dec 1880, Emmett Van Wyck(e) Filer, b. 6 Nov 1851, d. 10 June 1919. Emmett was a druggist. The family moved from Sag Harbor, L.I. to Lexington, NE, and then, to Dayton, OR, where Emmett owned and operated a general store. Both Lillie and Emmett are bur. in Dayton, OR.
Issue:
  *424. Emmett Sylvanus[9] Filer, b. 10 Mar 1883, d. 18 Mar 1952

235. FLORENCE[8] BISHOP, dau. of William and Mary Jane[7] (Penny) Bishop, b. 1860, d. 1941; m. 18 May 1880, #342. Silas Egbert[8] Jessup, b. 14 Sept 1855, d. 27 Jan 1900, bur. Quogue, s/o #173. Egbert[7] and Nancy (Wells) Jessup.
Issue:
  *425. Florence B.[9] Jessup, b. 24 Apr 1882, d.

*426. George Penny[9] Jessup, twin, b. 29 Feb
    1884, Quogue

427. Nancy W.[9] Jessup, twin, b. 29 Feb 1884,
    Quogue; m. 5 July 1923 at Quogue by Rev.
    Thomas Coyle, William H. Wilson, b. ca
    1884 at Coxsackie, NY, s/o William J.
    and Ada G. (Pierson) Wilson. Residence:
    Noyac, L.I. William was a carpenter.

238. GEORGE W.[8] RAYNOR, son of William[7] and
Sarah Ann (Robinson) Raynor, b. 16 Dec 1847,
Westhampton, d. 30 Oct 1873, ae 25 yrs., 10
mos., 14 days, bur. Westhampton Cemetery; m. 24
Dec 1869, Hannah R. ("Annie") Stevens, b. 17 Feb
1849, Westhampton, d. 1936, bur. Westhampton
Cemetery, d/o Abraham Stevens. Hannah m. (2)
Israel Monroe Rose, b. 1837, d. 1909, bur.
Westhampton Cemetery.
Issue:

*428. Clarence Russell[9] Raynor, b. 23 Feb 1872,
    Westhampton, d. 2 Jan 1947, Southampton
    (Half siblings: Albert Edward, James
    Monroe, Millicent, and John Mitchell
    Rose)

244. JOHN MITCHELL[8] STEVENS, son of Abraham and
Hannah[7] (Raynor) Stevens, b. 25 June 1840, d. 1
Feb 1922, Germantown, PA; m. 26 Nov 1868, Laura
Blackburn Hawkins, b. 25 Oct 1846 at Moriches,
d. 19 May 1925, d/o William Sidney and Ann
(Wines) Hawkins. Both John and Laura are bur.
Westhampton Cemetery.
Issue:

429. Abram Howell[9] Stevens, b. 5 Sept 1871; m.
    20 Apr 1899, Lugenia Kaler of Sayville,
    L.I.

430. Mabel Blackburn[9] Stevens, b. 3 July 1874;
    m. 10 Oct 1900, Edwin Forrest Williams

254. WILLIAM CLARK[8] RAYNOR, son of Nathan[7] and
Sarah Jane (Carter) Raynor, b. 10 Sept 1839, d.
1921; m. 10 Dec 1864, Eliza O'Bryan (or

O'Brien), b. Feb 1844, d. 1924; both bur.
Westhampton Cemetery.
Issue:

*431. Elizabeth ("Lizzie") Halsey[9] Raynor, b.
Mar 1870 (or 1868)

*432. William Fletcher[9] Raynor, b. 12 Mar 1875,
d. 6 Dec 1959

255. **JOHN GILBERT[8] RAYNOR**, son of Nathan[7] and
Sarah Jane (Carter) Raynor, b. 12 Oct 1841, d.
17 May 1916, bur. Westhampton Cemetery; m. (1)
Ellen Grace Robinson, b. 15 June 1844, d. 12 Feb
1907, bur. Westhampton Cemetery, d/o Timothy and
Jerusha (Halsey) Robinson; m. (2) at Southold by
Rev. J. A. Swann, Henrietta M. Youngs, b. 1857,
d. 1920, widow of Franklin W. Phillips, and d/o
Jobin H. and Mary (Miller) Youngs. John was a
fisherman.
Issue Wife (1):

*433. Arthur Halsey[9] Raynor, b. 1868,
Westhampton, d. 27 June 1947, bur.
Westhampton Cemetery

*434. Frederic Conklin[9] Raynor, b. 4 Aug 1871,
Westhampton, d. 11 June 1940

*435. Frances Helene[9] Raynor, b. 1875, d. 31 Oct
1950

*436. John Gilbert[9] Raynor, Jr., b. 10 Aug 1876,
d. 1 Dec 1958

437. Walter[9] Raynor, b. 24 Oct 1878, d. 21 May
1879

256. **GEORGE CLINTON[8] RAYNOR**, son of Nathan[7] and
Sarah Jane (Carter) Raynor, b. 30 Aug 1843 (or
1842), d. 17 May 1901, ae 57 yrs., 8 mos., 17
days, bur. Westhampton Cemetery; m. Mary
Elizabeth Raynor, b. 23 May 1848, d. 13 Jan
1916, East Moriches, aged 67 yrs., bur.
Westhampton Cemetery, d/o of Laban and Elizabeth
(Robinson) Raynor, Sr.
Issue:

438. Ella Mae ("Polly")[9] Raynor, b. 21 May
1880, Westhampton, d. 27 Dec 1955,
Riverhead; m. 21 May 1910, Silas Abram

Stevens, b. 25 Oct 1879, Westhampton
Beach, d. 20 Jan 1955, Westhampton, s/o
Hubert F. and Susan Margaret (Tuttle)
Stevens; both bur. Westhampton Cemetery;
no issue. Silas, a carpenter, was one
of the first police commissioners in
Westhampton Beach, in 1929.

257. MILLICENT[8] RAYNOR, dau. of Nathan[7] and
Sarah Jane (Carter) Raynor, b. ca 1846; m. 14
Jan 1865, James T. Robinson, b. ca 1842/3.
Issue:
439. Jessie[9] Robinson, b. Sept 1869
440. Wesley[9] Robinson

258. NATHAN SIDNEY[8] RAYNOR, son of Nathan[7] and
Sarah Jane (Carter) Raynor, b. 15 Oct 1848, d.
13 Nov 1904; m. (1) 25 Jan 1868, Eliza H.
Jessup, b. 9 Sept 1850, d. 14 Apr 1871,
Westhampton, aged 20 (or 21) yrs., 7 mos., 5
(or 4) days, d/o Timothy P. and Mary M. Jessup;
m. (2) Annie A. Fleet, b. 15 July 1855, d. 28
Dec 1924; all bur. Westhampton Cemetery.
Issue:
*441. Archie W.[9] Raynor, b. 4 Dec 1875,
       Westhampton, d. 1950
*442. Chester Sidney[9] Raynor, b. 28 May 1885, d.
       28 July 1961, Riverhead

259. CHARLOTTE ELIZABETH[8] RAYNOR, dau. of
Nathan[7] and Sarah Jane (Carter) Raynor, b. 3
June 1852, Westhampton; m. 27 Dec 1871, Nathan
Henry Gordon, b. 27 July 1852, d. 26 Sept 1908,
s/o Baldwin Cook and Jerusha (Raynor) Gordon.
Issue:
*443. Minnie J.[9] Gordon, b. 6 May 1874
444. George Homan[9] Gordon, b. 15 June 1879,
       Westhampton, d 1953; m. Josephine H.
       Gordon, b. 1879, d. 1939, d/o Robert and
       Lydia A. (Griffing) Gordon.

260. CHARLES WESLEY[8] RAYNOR, son of Nathan[7] and
Sarah Jane (Carter) Raynor, b. 28 Nov 1856,

Westhampton, d. 18 May 1943, White Haven, MD; m.
15 Dec 1883 in White Haven, MD, Betty Ann Dolbey
(widow Goodman), b. 15 Oct 1858, White Haven,
MD, d. 29 Jan 1932, White Haven, MD, d/o Stephen
Wesley and Henrietta J. (Simpkins) Dolbey; both
bur. Dolbey Cemetery, White Haven, MD. Charles
Wesley was Captain of a fishing vessel out of
Perryville, VA; later, he owned and operated a
farm in White Haven, MD.
Issue:

*445. Russell Wesley[9] Raynor, M.D., b. 23 July
1886, White Haven, MD, d. 20 Jan 1939,
Pikeville, KY, bur. Pikeville
Cemetery

*446. Clark Sidney[9] Raynor, b. 5 Oct 1893, White
Haven, MD, d. 13 Sept 1966, bur. Dolbey
Cemetery, White Haven, MD

261. HETTIE JANE[8] RAYNOR, dau. of Nathan[7] and
Sarah Jane (Carter) Raynor, b. 29 Jan 1858, d.
24 July 1941; m. Christopher William Nichols, b.
3 Jan 1855, d. 2 Dec 1911; both bur. Westhampton
Cemetery.
Issue:

*447. Adolph E.[9] Nichols, b. 1877, d. 4 Dec 1939
448. Lillian R.[9] Nichols, b. 1879, d. 1962,
bur. Westhampton Cemetery; unmarried.
449. Louis W.[9] Nichols, b. 25 Nov 1885, d. 20
June 1976; m. 1913, Mabel Blackburn.

262. SARAH RUPELL[8] RAYNOR, dau. of Nathan[7] and
Sarah Jane (Carter) Raynor, b. ca 1859; m. John
Ketcham; lived near Atlantic City, NJ.
Issue:
*450. Aleta (or Lecta)[9] Ketcham

263. WALTER SCOTT[8] RAYNOR, son of Nathan[7] and
Sarah Jane (Carter) Raynor, b. 20 Aug 1860 (or
1862 or 1864), Westhampton, d. 8 Feb 1921, ae 59
yrs.; m. 22 Nov 1888 by Rev. H. B. Holmes, Mary
Frances Benjamin, b. 17 Mar 1866, East Moriches,
d. 28 (or 29) Dec 1923, ae 57 yrs., d/o Mitchell
and Margaret (   ) Benjamin. Walter was a

commercial fisherman.
Issue:

?451. Deborah (or Beulah)[9] Raynor, b. 28 Apr
       1890(?), d. 27 June 1903
 452. Walter Benjamin[9] Raynor, b. 8 Jan 1890, d.
       10 Jan 1971 (or 1921); m. 18 Feb 1917,
       Amanda Gould Hawkins, b. 7 Aug 1892, d.
       27 Aug 1965, d/o George Raynor and
       Isabella L. Raynor (Edwards) Hawkins; no
       issue. Residence: Patchogue.
*453. Ruby LeMay[9] Raynor, b. 17 June 1896,
       Westhampton, d. 23 (or 24) Mar 1975
*454. Pearl[9] Raynor, b. 20 Aug 1901, Moriches,
       d. 23 May 1988

266. WILLIAM[8] RAYNOR, son of Daniel[7] and Laura
P. (   ) Raynor, b. 1840; m. Beulah Tuthill,
b. 12 July 1842, Speonk, d/o Noah and Elizabeth
("Eliza") (Raynor) Tuthill.
Issue:

 455. Lillian[9] Raynor, b. ca 1862; m. William
       Hutch
 456. Ernest Preston[9] Raynor, b. ca 1866

271. SARAH TUTHILL[8] RAYNOR, dau. of Uriah[7] and
Mary (Foster) Raynor, b. ca 1852; m. Henry
Warren Overton.
Issue:

 457. Florence M.[9] Overton, b. 3 Mar 1893, Good
       Ground, d. 28 Nov 1975, Southampton; m.
       7 Nov 1914, Guy Lancelot Carter, b. 9
       Jan 1889, d. 14 Dec 1954, s/o John Edwin
       and Phoebe Rachel (Ruland) Carter.

272. JOHN FLETCHER[8] RAYNOR, son of Uriah[7] and
Mary (Foster) Raynor, b. 26 Nov 1855, d. 8 May
1913; m. 13 June 1874, Sarah M. Bellows, b. 24
Sept 1864 (or 1857), d. 10 Mar 1934. Sarah m.
(2) 14 June 1920, Orville Benjamin Tuthill.
Issue:

*458. Charles Bupton[9] Raynor, b. 28 Feb 1876,
       Good Ground, d. 8 Feb 1928
 459. Walter Austin[9] Raynor, d. 28 Aug 1892, ae

4 yrs., 4 mos., 19 days
460. Minnie M.[9] Raynor, d. 5 May 1889 in
   infancy

273. WILLIAM ANDERSON[8] RAYNOR, son of Uriah[7] and
Mary (Foster) Raynor, b. ca 1861, d. 20 Jan
1934, Hampton Bays; m. (1) Emma Lenora Raynor,
b. 11 May 1862, Calverton, d. 3 Jan 1931,
Sanford, FL, ae 66 yrs., d/o Clark Oliver and
Anne Eliza (Edwards) Raynor; m. (2) 1932, Lulu
Moseley Gerard, b. 26 July 1869, d. 2 Jan 1952.
William Anderson Raynor, a farmer, and his wife,
Emma, spent the winter months in Sanford,
Florida, where William was a successful
vegetable and citrus fruit grower. Emma was a
school teacher.
Issue Wife (1):
*461. William Uriah[9] Raynor, b. 8 Jan 1896,
   Hampton Bays, d. 27 Feb 1922, Sanford FL
   (typhoid fever), ae 26 yrs., bur.
   Sanford, FL
*462. Mary Alida ("Lyda")[9] Raynor, b. 5 (or 6)
   June 1881, d. 21 Feb 1960
*463. Hattie Ainsley[9] Raynor, b. 10 Nov 1884,
   Hampton Bays, d. 11 Sept 1966
*464. Ethel Emma[9] Raynor, b. 15 Jan 1889, d.
   1969, bur. Hampton Bays
*465. Isabel Matilda[9] Raynor, b. Hampton Bays,
   d. Aug 1952

274. ELIJAH (OR ELIHU)[8] HUBBARD, son of Erastus
and Elizabeth[7] (Raynor) Hubbard, b. ca 1847
Issue:
466. Robert[9] Hubbard, a Town Trustee

275. WILLIAM[8] HUBBARD, son of Erastus and
Elizabeth[7] (Raynor) Hubbard
Issue:
467. Charles[9] Hubbard, b. 1891

277. ERASTUS W.[8] RAYNOR, son of Elihu[7] and
Hannah Maria (Tuttle) Raynor, b. 9 Mar 1853,

53

Westhampton, d. 10 Mar 1923, bur. Westhampton
Cemetery; m. (1) 8 May 1875, #314. Sarah Louise[8]
Raynor, b. 7 May 1854, d. 31 July 1882, d/o
#160. William Jagger[7] and Mary Jane (Hawkins)
Raynor; m. (2) Harriet ("Hattie") Emily Carter,
b. 21 June 1854 (or 1856), d. 1 July 1935, bur.
Westhampton Cemetery, d/o Mitchel and Mary
Cornelia (Raynor) Carter. Erastus was a farmer.
Issue Wife (2):

468. Ralph L.[9] Raynor, b. 27 (or 3) June 1889,
Westhampton, d. 5 Mar 1973, Riverhead,
ae 83 yrs., bur. Westhampton Cemetery;
m. (1) 6 June 1914, Westhampton, Ellen
Olsen, b. 26 Feb 1886, d. 7 Apr 1962; m.
(2) Bertha Blackwood, b. 22 Oct 1899, d.
17 May 1970; no issue. Ralph was a
teamster.

278. ELIHU JOTHAM[8] RAYNOR, son of Elihu[7] and
Hannah Maria (Tuttle) Raynor, b. 19 Jan 1855, d.
19 Feb 1938; m. 30 Mar 1874 (or 1873) by Rev.
John D. Stokes, Ida (or Idawella) Johnson Young,
b. 8 Sept 1854 (or 1855), East Hampton, d. 24
June 1929, Westhampton. Elihu was a farmer.
Issue:

*469. Mary Ellen (or Ella)[9] Raynor, b. 3 Nov
1874, d. 21 Sept 1938 in the hurricane
470. William Corwin[9] Raynor, b. 28 Oct 1880, d.
1 Nov 1963
471. Lusie[9] Raynor

279. KATE[8] RAYNOR, dau. of Charles[7] and Anna M.
(Dungan) Raynor, m. Anthony M. Gilbert
Issue:
472. Anna[9] Gilbert
473. Emily[9] Gilbert
474. Mary[9] Gilbert

290. MARY JAGGER[8] RAYNOR, dau. of John Morrison[7]
and Frances J. (Robinson) Raynor, b. 10 Sept
1875; m. 26 Oct 1896 at Greenport by Rev. Loren
A. Rowley, Herbert Germond Vail, b. 5 May 1874,
s/o Daniel Terry and Sarah (Germond) Vail.

Issue:
475. Daniel Morrison[9] Vail, b. 26 Aug 1897, d. 29 Aug 1898, ae 1 yr.
476. Clifford Robinson[9] Vail, b. 26 July 1900, d. 26 Dec 1901, East Marion, ae 1 yr., 5 mos., 6 days
477. Roscoe Philip[9] Vail, b. Jan 1901
478. Kenneth A.[9] Vail, b. 4 Aug 1912

291. JOHN ROSCOE[8] RAYNOR, son of John Morrison[7] and Frances J. (Robinson) Raynor, b. 22 Oct 1877, d. 18 Jan 1944; m. 12 Jan 1906 in NYC by Rev. Philip Germund, Helen Deemer, of New Jersey. John Roscoe was a marine engineer.
Issue:
*479. Mildred Frances[9] Raynor, b. 13 Dec 1909, d. 20 Aug 1984, ae 74 yrs., Norwich, NY, bur. Sterling Cemetery, Greenport
480. Ralph Morrison[9] Raynor, b. 6 Nov 1906; residence: Lynbrook, L.I.

293. CHARLES LUTHER[8] RAYNOR, son of Oscar Bingley[7] and Sarah Jane (Cook) Raynor, b. 5 June 1855, d. 16 Dec 1904; m. 18 May 1881 by Rev. E. K. Fanning, #328. Ida May[8] Bishop, b. 4 Aug 1858, d. 6 Oct 1893, aged 35 yrs., 2 mos., 2 days, d/o Rogers and #163. Nancy P.[7] (Raynor) Bishop. Charles built and operated the Apaucuck Point House in Westhampton.
Issue:
481. Oscar Bishop[9] Raynor, b. 5 Jan 1884, d. 27 Nov 1902 in Trenton, NJ; a student at Lawrenceville School, Lawrenceville, NJ, he was crushed between two trolley cars.
*482. Laura Vincent[9] Raynor, b. 6 Oct 1887, Westhampton, d. 17 Apr 1938
483. Woodhull[9] Raynor
484. Charles Luther[9] Raynor, Jr.

294. MARY C.[8] RAYNOR, dau. of Oscar Bingley[7] and Sarah Jane (Cook) Raynor, b. 1857, d. 1926; m. 28 Nov 1877 at the Westhampton Presbyterian

Church, Gilbert D. Rogers, b. 8 Oct 1853,
Speonk, d. 1921, s/o Capt. John and Maria R.
(Smith) Rogers. Both Mary and Gilbert are bur.
in Remsenburg.
Issue:

485. J. Dwight[9] Rogers, b. 30 Sept 1879; lived
in Big Stone Gap, VA in 1933.

*486. Helen Cook[9] Rogers, b. 14 June 1886,
Remsenburg, d. 5 Dec 1984, Southampton,
bur. Westhampton Cemetery

487. Oscar B.[9] Rogers, b. 26 Dec 1889, d. 1945,
bur. Remsenburg Cemetery; m. Lillie F.
_____, b. 1891, d. 1976, bur. Remsenburg
Cemetery; resided in Queens Village,
L.I. in 1933.

296. JOHN EVERETT ("BIG JOHN")[8] RAYNOR, son of
Oscar Bingley[7] and Sarah Jane (Cook) Raynor, b.
2 Dec 1864, Westhampton, d. 19 Mar 1917,
Westhampton; m. 26 Jan 1910 at Riverhead, Mabel
Eliza Black, b. 18 Dec 1874, DeWitt, NY, d. 10
Nov 1963, Westhampton. John Everett and his
sister, Harriet, operated the Apaucuck Point
House in Westhampton from the time of their
brother, Charles's death (1904) until John
Everett's marriage in 1910, after which John
Everett and his wife, Mabel, operated the
Apaucuck Point House until John Everett's death
in 1917.
Issue:

488. Sarah Vincent ("Sally")[9] Raynor, b. 23
June 1911, Westhampton; m. (1) 29 Mar
1964 in Westhampton, Allen J. Black, d.
27 Sept 1974, bur. Syracuse, NY; m. (2)
27 Sept 1987 in Southampton, Martin W.
Lind, d. 24 June 1989.

489. Elizabeth ("Betty")[9] Raynor, b. 5 Mar
1916, Westhampton; m. 16 Sept 1958,
Richard Neuffer, d. 30 Sept 1989,
Seaford, L.I.

304. OLIVER JACOB[8] RAYNOR, son of Jacob A.[7] and
Mary A. (Halsey) Raynor, b. 1861, d. 1927, bur.
Remsenburg Cemetery; m. Ann McLoughlin, b. 1862,

d. 1948, bur. Remsenburg Cemetery. Oliver was a farmer.
Issue:

*490. Kathryn E.[9] Raynor, b. ca 1889, d. 10 Dec 1976, ae 87 yrs.

*491. Hubert I.[9] Raynor, b. 25 Aug 1892, d. 18 Dec 1965

492. John W.[9] Raynor, b. 1893, d. 1966, bur. Remsenburg Cemetery; m. Lillian _____. John was a highway foreman.

*493. Elizabeth[9] Raynor

?494. Oliver Jacob[9] Raynor, d. 23 Aug 1897, ae 3 mos.

305. **FREDERICK CALEB[8] RAYNOR**, son of Jacob A.[7] and Mary A. (Halsey) Raynor, b. 26 July 1868 (or 1869), Speonk, d. 1936, bur. Remsenburg Cemetery; m. 3 June 1891, Edith Rogers, b. 3 Aug 1872, Eastport, d. 5 Dec 1955, Remsenburg, aged 83 yrs., bur. Remsenburg Cemetery, d/o Harrison Rogers of Eastport. Frederick was a farmer.
Issue:

495. Harrison Strong[9] Raynor, b. 30 Apr 1893 (or 1892), d. 30 Apr 1978, bur. Remsenburg Cemetery; m. Louise Lenz, b. 28 Mar 1897, d. 1982, d/o E. Preston Raynor.

*496. Halsey Jacob[9] Raynor, b. 11 Feb 1895; d. 14 Sept 1941, bur. Westhampton Cemetery

308. **HENRY HARRISON[8] CORWIN**, son of Henry Wickham and Miriam Wicks[7] (Raynor) Corwin, b. 17 Sept 1840, Aquebogue, d. 8 Sept 1935, bur. Riverhead Cemetery; m. 20 Dec 1866 at Riverhead, Sarah Ellen Terrell, b. 30 Nov 1848 at Manorville, d. 21 Sept 1935 (cancer) at home, in Riverhead, bur. Riverhead Cemetery, d/o Allen Townsend and Phebe Ann (Robinson) Terrell. Henry, a Civil War Veteran, was a contractor and builder-carpenter. With his brother-in-law, George M. Vail, H. Harrison (he didn't like the name, Henry) founded Corwin and Vail Lumber Co., a business in Riverhead and Southampton. He was

a large landowner.
Issue:
*497. Miriam Grant[9] Corwin, b. 19 Feb 1868,
    Riverhead, d. 30 May 1969, Riverhead
*498. Dwight Townsend[9] Corwin, b. 11 Aug 1870,
    Riverhead, d. 1960
*499. Hubert Florence[9] Corwin, b. 1876, d. 2
    Sept 1959
500. Percy[9] Corwin, b. 1884, d. 15 July 1886,
    bur. Riverhead Cemetery

312. ANTOINETTE ("NETTIE") HAWKINS[8] RAYNOR, dau.
of William Jagger[7] and Mary Jane (Hawkins)
Raynor, b. 26 Sept 1845, d. 11 Sept 1931; m. 22
Dec 1870 at the Westhampton Methodist Episcopal
Church by Rev. O. C. Lane, Edward Charles Smith
of Moriches, b. 10 Feb 1846, d. 23 Apr 1908, s/o
John K. C. and Esther (Bishop) Smith.
Issue:
*501. Elizabeth[9] Smith

317. DAVID ROSWELL[8] ROGERS, son of Lester G. and
Elizabeth[7] (Raynor) Rogers, b. ca 1845; m. Sarah
Culver.
Issue:
*502. Sophia[9] Rogers
*503. Daisy[9] Rogers
*504. Thomas[9] Rogers

318. FRANCES ("FANNIE") HARRIET[8] ROGERS, dau. of
Lester G. and Elizabeth[7] (Raynor) Rogers, b. 6
June 1847, Westhampton, d. 29 Apr 1939, ae 91
yrs.; m. 27 Jan 1871, #345. George Hildreth[8]
Jessup, b. 27 Nov 1849, d. 1912, s/o #174.
William Henry[7] and Huldah (Homan) Jessup.
Issue:
505. Lester R.[9] Jessup
506. Dr. William H.[9] Jessup, d. 30 Apr 1941
*507. Isabel Browning[9] Jessup, d. 24 Feb 1958

319. JENNIE B.[8] ROGERS, dau. of Lester G. and

Elizabeth[7] (Raynor) Rogers, m. George Baker;
lived in East Moriches.
Issue:
508. Bess[9] Baker
*509. Leila[9] Baker

320. SUSAN HALSEY[8] ROGERS, dau. of Lester G. and
Elizabeth[7] (Raynor) Rogers, b. 7 Apr 1851, d. 12
Oct 1944, Westhampton, ae 93 yrs., 6 mos., 5
days, bur. Westhampton Cemetery; m. Enoch H.
Pierson, b. 10 Nov 1842, d. 12 Jan 1903.
Issue:
*510. C. Floyd[9] Pierson, b. 1875, d. 1962
511. Mary[9] Pierson, d. 16 Mar 1880, ae 4 mos.,
2 days
512. Helen B.[9] Pierson, b. 1884, d. 1971
513. Lee[9] Pierson

321. MILLICENT BREWSTER[8] ROGERS, dau. of Lester
G. and Elizabeth[7] (Raynor) Rogers, b. 4 Oct
1858, d. 9 Dec 1934; m. 19 Feb 1879, Isaac
Davidson Gildersleeve, b. 7 June 1849, d. 10 Jan
1944, s/o William H. and Mehitable (Ward)
Gildersleeve.
Issue:
*514. Hettie Rogers[9] Gildersleeve, b. 30 Mar
1880, d. 10 June 1930
515. DeWitt[9] Gildersleeve, b. 9 May 1882, d. 31
May 1961; unmarried
*516. Effie[9] Gildersleeve, b. 9 Apr 1885, d. 18
Aug 1978
*517. Clara L.[9] Gildersleeve, b. 25 May 1889, d.
31 Jan 1988
518. Bertha Halsey[9] Gildersleeve, b. 9 July
1891, d. 23 Aug 1891
*519. Raymond Scudder[9] Gildersleeve, b. 29 Apr
1896 (or 24 Apr 1895), d. 30 Mar 1952
520. Gladys Marie[9] Gildersleeve, b. 8 Mar 1898,
d. 8 Sept 1983; m. (1) Philip Gordon, b.
1903, d. 1967; m. (2) Symes Burtsell,
b. 1882, d. 1967.

<u>330.</u> FRANKLIN ("FRANK") CARPENTER[8] RAYNOR, son
of Elijah Pierson[7] and Harriet N. (Carpenter)
Raynor, b. 26 Sept 1856, Greenport, d. 22 Nov
1920, Southampton, ae 64 yrs., bur. No. End
Cemetery, Southampton; m. 11 Oct 1881 at the
bride's residence in Southampton by Rev. Platt,
Amy Louise White, b. 1862 (or 1864),
Southampton, d. 1918, d/o Capt. William and
Phebe A. (Proud) White (William White was a sea
captain). Franklin and his family moved to
Southampton after the Ketchabonack House, a
boarding house he built and operated on Beach
Lane, Westhampoton Beach, was destroyed by fire
about 1892. Franklin was a carpenter in
Southampton.
Issue:
  521. Julia C. (or G.)[9] Raynor, b. 1884, d. 15
       Aug 1910, Southampton, ae 26 yrs.
       (cancer), bur. North End Burying
       Ground, Southampton; unmarried.
 *522. Lester White[9] Raynor, b. 7 Feb 1886,
       Southampton; d. 25 Feb 1975
 *523. Henry Proud[9] Raynor, b. ca 1889,
       Westhampton Beach
  524. Frank Lawrence (or Laurence)[9] Raynor, b.
       1890, d. 1965; m. 30 May 1921 in
       Brooklyn, as her second husband, Eva
       (Bishop) Wiltshire, b. 1881, d. 1971,
       widow of _____ Wiltshire and d/o Samuel
       and Emily (Drake) Bishop. Frank served
       in France in World War I, and later
       owned and operated a gas station in
       Southampton, where the family resided.
       Eva had a son from her first marriage.
 *525. Wilmun ("Flip") Halsey[9] Raynor, b. 31 Jan
       1893, d. 15 Jan 1952, bur. Jefferson
       Barracks National Cemetery, St.
       Louis, MO.
 *526. Edith McKay[9] Raynor, b. 7 Apr 1895,
       Southampton, d. 12 Apr 1982
 *527. Harriet Jagger[9] Raynor, b. 23 July 1904,
       d. 30 Dec 1984

331. CHARLES EDWARD[8] RAYNOR, son of Elijah Pierson[7] and Harriett N. (Golder) Raynor, b. 1 Jan 1859, Greenport, d. 12 Apr 1929 (heart attack), bur. Westhampton Cemetery; m. 1 Nov 1882 at Westhampton by Rev. E. K. Fanning, Helen Elizabeth Youngs, b. 15 Oct 1864, East Hampton, d. 31 Jan 1956, d/o John Haynes and Mary Elizabeth (Miller) Youngs. In 1880, Charles E. Raynor built and operated a general store, which was at first located in a small building on Main Street, near the corner of Beach Lane, Westhampton Beach; the store also contained the Post Office and telegraph office. He later sold the store to Ernest H. Bishop. Charles E. Raynor was also in the insurance business, which he sold in 1909 to William H. Winters. Charles E. Raynor was the first Postmaster in Westhampton Beach, receiving the appointment from President Chester A. Arthur.
Issue:

*528. Elijah Pierson[9] Raynor, b. 16 Dec 1883, Westhampton Beach, d. 23 Sept 1955

*529. Charlotte Elizabeth[9] Raynor, b. 6 Mar 1890, Westhampton Beach, d. 9 Jan 1974, Riverhead

530. Lydia Young[9] Raynor, b. 6 Dec 1900, d. 11 Apr 1983, bur. Westhampton Cemetery; m. 26 May 1945 in Westhampton Beach, as his second wife, Henry Hough. Lydia, a graduate of St. Luke's Hospital School of Nursing in NYC, was the Westhampton Beach School Nurse for many years; no issue.

333. AUGUSTUS HIRAM ("GUS")[8] RAYNOR, son of Elijah Pierson[7] and Harriett N. (Golder) Raynor, b. 1864, d. 1943; m. at Westhampton, 9 Sept 1890 (or 1889), Grace Alice Tuttle, b. 16 Feb 1868, Speonk, d. 3 Jan 1969, Center Moriches, d/o Joshua W. and Christiana Tamazenia (Howell) Tuttle. Both Augustus and Grace are bur. Westhampton Cemetery. Augustus was a carpenter in 1910-11. He operated a lumber and coal

company founded by his father in 1880, and he
started Raynor's Garage on Library Avenue,
Westhampton Beach. Although Grace (Tuttle)
Raynor weighed less than two lbs. at birth, she
lived to be 100 years old.
Issue:
  531. Eliott Joshua[9] Raynor, d. 5 Feb 1892, ae 5
       mos., 13 days
 *532. Clifford Tuttle[9] Raynor, b. 22 Feb 1893,
       Westhampton Beach, d. 9 Nov 1953
  533. Amy B.[9] Raynor, b. 11 Nov 1895, d. 14 Jan
       1979, ae 83 yrs.; m. 26 Oct 1929 at the
       Westhampton Presbyterian Church, Edward
       G. B. Miller of New Jersey and West Palm
       Beach, Florida. Amy was the first Clerk
       and Treasurer of the incorporated
       village of Westhampton Beach. She later
       was a social worker and marriage
       counselor in Dade County, FL; no issue.
 *534. Elsa E.[9] Raynor, b. 5 Aug 1900,
       Westhampton Beach, d. 25 Feb 1991 in
       Ohio
 *535. Norman Hiram[9] Raynor, b. 25 Mar 1903, d.
       23 Nov 1980, ae 77 yrs.

334. FREDERICK ("FRED") WOODHULL[8] RAYNOR, son of
Elijah Pierson[7] and Harriett N. (Golder) Raynor,
b. 14 (or 11) Nov 1866, Westhampton Beach, d. 17
June 1945, Westhampton Beach; m. 11 Nov 1885 in
Sayville, Marguerite DeForrest Tyler, b. 6 July
1868, Brooklyn, d. 6 Dec 1927, NYC, d/o Capt.
William S. and Sarah C. (Horton) Tyler. Both
Frederick and Marguerite are bur. Westhampton
Cemetery. F. W. Raynor was a building and
painting contractor and realty operator at
Westhampton Beach and Baldwin, L.I. At one
time, he owned the Islip Mustard and Pickle Co.
in Islip and Clam Bullion Factory in Bay Shore
and Sag Harbor. He lived for a time at W. 66th
Street, NYC when he was a salesman for a clam
factory.
Issue:
 *536. William Frederick[9] Raynor, b. 16 Jan 1887,
       Sayville, d. 10 Sept 1957, Westhampton

Beach

537. Harold Hastings[9] Raynor, b. 9 (or 19) Feb
     1889, Sayville, d. 5 Feb 1936,
     Southampton, bur. Westhampton Cemetery;
     m. 15 Sept 1909 at the bride's residence
     in Richmond Hill, L.I., Lila Grace
     Morris, b. 1893, d/o G. G. Morris,
     formerly of Sayville.

*538. Carrie Marguerite[9] Raynor, b. 13 Sept
     1890, d. 13 Feb 1970

*539. Kenneth Alan[9] Raynor, b. 9 Apr 1897, d. 19
     Oct 1983

540. Kingsley[9] Raynor, d. at 3 or 4 yrs. of age

541. Kevin[9] Raynor, d. in infancy

542. Roger[9] Raynor, d. young, bur. in Bay Shore

543. Frederick[9] Raynor, bur. as a child in
     Cypress Hills Cemetery, Brooklyn

335. JOHN MITCHELL ("MITCH") BURNS[8] RAYNOR, son
of Elijah Pierson[7] and Harriett N. (Golder)
Raynor, b. 15 Sept 1872, Westhampton Beach, d.
18 Nov 1960; m. 17 Nov 1892 in East Hampton,
Elizabeth Miller Strong, b. 9 June 1872 (or
1873), d. 30 July 1955, d/o James Madison and
Mary Agatha (Young) Strong. Both J. Mitchell
and Elizabeth ("Lib") are bur. Westhampton
Cemetery. J. Mitchell was a carpenter and
building contractor and operated E. Raynor's
Sons for many years.
Issue:

*544. James Madison[9] Raynor, b. 18 Feb 1894,
      Westhampton Beach, d. 31 Aug 1973,
      Westhampton Beach, bur. Westhampton
      Cemetery

*545. Emerson Mitchell[9] Raynor, b. 11 Oct 1898,
      Westhampton Beach, d. 13 May 1979,
      Bradenton, FL

337. CHARLES[8] RAYNOR, son of Mulford T.[7] and Ann
(Persall) Raynor, b. 1844, d. 1912
Issue:

*546. Townsend Richard[9] Raynor, b. 1865

63

547. Charles D.[9] Raynor, b. 1870
548. Alice C.[9] Raynor, b. 1872
549. Frederick M.[9] Raynor, b. 1875
550. George W.[9] Raynor, b. 1878

340. SUSAN MARY[8] JESSUP, son of Egbert[7] and Nancy (Wells) Jessup, b. 21 Apr 1846, Quogue, d. 4 Jan 1918, Patchogue, bur. Patchogue; m. 22 Nov 1865 in Quogue, Isaac Terry Moore, b. 13 Sept 1838, Cutchogue, d. 31 Jan 1927, Patchogue, bur. Patchogue, s/o Calvin and Mary Ann (Tuthill) Moore.
Issue:
  551. Fannie Mae[9] Moore, b. 17 Nov 1874, d. 16 Apr 1943; unmarried.
  552. Egbert Jessup[9] Moore, b. 10 July 1877, d. 1 Feb 1944; m. 2 Sept 1903, Georgia Anna Holley.
 *553. Helen Christine[9] Moore, b. 6 Mar 1883, Middletown, NY, d. 27 Jan 1978, Patchogue, bur. Patchogue
  554. Howard Raymond[9] Moore, b. 4 June 1891, d. 6 Oct 1918; unmarried.

354. PHEBE ROSE[8] HAWKINS, dau. of Walter and Nancy[7] (Hawkins) Hawkins, b. 27 Oct 1832, South Haven, d. 27 Jan 1918; m. 26 Nov 1856, Joseph L. Bishop. Residence: Patchogue. Joseph was head of a lace mill in Patchogue.
Issue:
  555. William[9] Bishop, resided in Eastport
  556. Frank[9] Bishop, resided in Patchogue

355. ELIZABETH[8] HAWKINS, dau. of Walter and Nancy[7] (Hawkins) Hawkins, b. 8 Sept 1835, South Haven, d. 17 Apr 1907; m. (1) 16 Aug 1854, Frederick S. Wilkinson, a seaman, who was lost at sea; m. (2) _____ Fahy. Residence: Eureka, CA.
Issue Husband (1):
  557. William[9] Wilkinson, resided in Oakland, CA

356. SAMUEL AUGUSTUS[8] HAWKINS, son of Walter and Nancy[7] (Hawkins) Hawkins, b. 8 Sept 1838, Fireplace, L.I., d. 17 Nov 1914; m. 11 Jan 1866, Adeline Burns, b. 9 Apr 1846, d. 29 Mar 1926, d/o John and Susannah Burns of Riverhead. Samuel, a Civil War Veteran, was a contractor and builder. Residence: Greenport.
Issue:

558. Evelyn B.[9] Hawkins, b. 12 Nov 1866, unmarried

559. Robert W.[9] Hawkins, b. 11 Sept 1870, unmarried

560. Leonard Vernon[9] Hawkins, b. 15 May 1872; m. Mary L. Wells

561. Albert E.[9] Hawkins, b. 26 Mar 1874, d. 6 Jan 1875

562. Susan R.[9] Hawkins, b. 15 May 1877, d. 2 July 1878

563. Forest Foster[9] Hawkins, b. 7 Dec 1878; m. (1) Ida May Smith; m. (2) Ada A. Stone.

564. Elsie A.[9] Hawkins, b. 12 Mar 1882, unmarried

565. John Shirley[9] Hawkins, b. 22 Sept 1883; m. Grace Compton.

566. Leah E.[9] Hawkins, b. 8 Jan 1887, d. 30 Mar 1916; unmarried

357. JAMES HENRY[8] HAWKINS, son of Walter and Nancy[7] (Hawkins) Hawkins, b. 9 Nov 1840, South Haven, d. 31 Dec 1911; m. Huldah J. Robinson, b. 10 June 1846. Residence: East Haven, CT. James was a miller.
Issue:

567. Frederick L.[9] Hawkins, b. 12 Oct 1865; m. Bertha M. Andrews.

568. Eleanor T.[9] Hawkins, b. 9 May 1867, d. 31 Dec 1872

358. WILLIAM PRESCOTT[8] HAWKINS, son of Walter and Nancy[7] (Hawkins) Hawkins, b. 19 May 1852, South Haven, d. 13 Jan 1915; m. (1) Fannie

Lovsey, d. 1882, bur. East Haven, CT; m. (2)
Elizabeth Brown. Removed to Boston, MA and
later, to Minneapolis, MN. William was a
merchant.
Issue Wife (1):

569. Fannie C.[9] Hawkins, b. 4 Apr 1882

359. HENRY EGBERT[8] HAWKINS, son of Lewis and
Elmira[7] (Hawkins) Hawkins, b. 24 July 1835,
Brookhaven, d. 19 July 1923, Brookhaven; m. Sept
1871, Henrietta Louise Barteau, b. 2 Apr 1852,
d. 8 July 1930, d/o William Marshall Barteau;
both bur. Woodland Cemetery, Bellport.
Residence: Brookhaven.
Issue:

570. Nettie[9] Hawkins

571. Elizabeth C.[9] Hawkins, b. 30 Apr 1875, a
school teacher in NY; resided in
Brookhaven.

572. William Sherman[9] Hawkins, b. 16 July 1878;
m. Ethel Newey.

360. SELAH[8] HAWKINS, son of Lewis and Elmira[7]
(Hawkins) Hawkins, b. 13 June 1838, Brookhaven,
d. 9 July 1919, Brookhaven; m. 30 Jan 1875, Alma
Parks, b. 12 Jan 1852, d. 6 May 1921, d/o Henry
and Maria (Hicks) Parks of Patchogue; both bur.
Woodland Cemetery, Bellport. Residence:
Brookhaven. Selah was a farmer, sailor, and
later, a coal dealer.
Issue:

573. Ella Rose[9] Hawkins, b. 19 July 1877; a
school teacher in Brooklyn.

361. CHAUNCEY LEWIS[8] HAWKINS, son of Lewis and
Elmira[7] (Hawkins) Hawkins, b. 23 May 1844,
Brookhaven, d. 10 July 1909, Brookhaven; m. 28
Nov 1866, at Mason City, IL, Almira Mosslander,
b. 1 May 1840, d. 16 Aug 1888, Brookhaven; both
bur. Woodland Cemetery, Bellport. Residence:
Brookhaven. Chauncey was a farmer.
Issue:

574. George Lewis[9] Hawkins, b. 17 Apr 1870; m.

Ida Hollis.

365. HERBERT MONROE[8] HAWKINS, son of Sylvester[7] and Isabella (Goldsmith) Hawkins, b. 18 Feb 1870; m. (1) Emma Goldsmith Wood, b. 22 Jan 1871, d. 12 Apr 1914; m. (2) Harriette Pearl Stout, b. 25 Aug 1877. Residence: Greenport. Herbert was a painter and, also, editor of the *Greenport Watchman*.
Issue Wife (1):
575. Mildred Lydia[9] Hawkins, b. 15 Dec 1892; residence: Southold.
Issue Wife (2):
576. Ralph Stout[9] Hawkins, b. 17 June 1917

Ninth Generation

374. ELLIS DOUGLAS[9] SAGE, son of Seth Solomon and Mary Elizabeth[8] (Breese) Sage, b. 29 Mar 1863; m. 5 Mar 1884, Rose Cynthia Barnes, b. 22 Jan 1865.
Issue:
577. Charity Edenia[10] Sage, b. 8 June 1891

378. CORA MAY[9] BREESE, dau. of John Heath[8] and Elizabeth (Lewis) Breese, b. 19 Sept 1871; m. 10 May 1899, Robert W. Wilson, b. 7 Aug 1867.
Issue:
578. Blanche Elizabeth[10] Wilson, b. 1 Mar 1901
579. Hollace Margretta[10] Wilson, b. 12 Oct 1902
580. Robert Gerald[10] Wilson, b. 5 July 1904
581. Violet Jeanette[10] Wilson, b. 14 Feb 1907
582. Edith May[10] Wilson, b. 31 May 1910

379. NORA BELL[9] BREESE, dau. of John Heath[8] and Elizabeth (Lewis) Breese, b. 11 Mar 1874, d. 1 Jan 1910; m. 25 Dec 1893, Lowell Highland Hoxie, b. 22 Oct 1869.
Issue:
583. Charles Wilson[10] Hoxie, b. 27 Feb 1899

380. WILL LOUIS[9] BREESE, son of John Heath[8] and Elizabeth (Lewis) Breese, b. 25 Oct 1876; m. 20 Aug 1905, Nellis Elizabeth Heath, b. 7 Aug 1878.
Issue:

584. Marion Lewis[10] Breese, b. 23 June 1907

585. Mathew Lewis[10] Breese, b. 22 Aug 1909, d. 1977

586. Kathryn Elizabeth[10] Breese, b. & d. 29 Aug 1912

381. WALTER DOUGLAS[9] BREESE, son of John Heath[8] and Elizabeth (Lewis) Breese, b. 24 Dec 1878; m. 12 June 1906, Edith F. Lawrence, b. 19 May 1882.
Issue:

587. Howard Lawrence[10] Breese, b. 19 May 1908

383. GEORGE THERON[9] CONARD, son of James Wheeler and Lucilla Larwill[8] (Breese) Conard, b. 23 Feb 1860, LaSalle County, IL; m. 18 Feb 1883 in IL, Emma Althea Dominy.
Issue:

*588. Ida May[10] Conard, b. 17 Nov 1885, d. 15 Aug 1909

589. Lorenzo Dominy[10] Conard, b. 11 June 1887, d. 13 Oct 1892

590. Sarah Lucilla[10] Conard, b. 30 Jan 1889, d. 3 Oct 1892, OK

591. George Theron[10] Conard, b. 2 Nov 1895

384. MABEL ISADORA[9] CONARD, dau. of James Wheeler and Lucilla Larwill[8] (Breese) Conard, b. 20 Aug 1861, LaSalle County, IL; m. 1 Mar 1884 in Vancouver, WA, William Allen Mercer, b. 18 Feb 1857 in Randolph County, IN.
Issue:

*592. Clarence Alva[10] Mercer, b. 17 Nov 1884, Vancouver, WA

*593. William Elmer[10] Mercer, b. 5 Sept 1886, Atchinson County, MO

594. Marica[10] Mercer, twin, b. 9 June 1898, Logan County, OK

595. Rhetta[10] Mercer, twin, b. 9 June 1898,
Logan County, OK, d. 9 Dec 1908 in KS.

385. VIOLA ERNESTINE[9] CONARD, dau. of James
Wheeler and Lucilla Larwill[8] (Breese) Conard, b.
10 Sept 1864, Blackhawk County, IA; m. 24 Sept
1885 in Winfield, KS, Alexander Wood, b. 18 Aug
1856 in Scotland.
Issue:
596. Jennie Mable[10] Wood, b. 19 June 1886,
Arkansas City, KS
597. Fred Alexander[10] Wood, b. 18 July 1888,
Arkansas City, KS, d. 17 Apr 1896,
Newkirk, OK
*598. Clara Hazel[10] Wood

387. WALDO LLEWELLYN[9] CONARD, son of James
Wheeler and Lucilla Larwill[8] (Breese) Conard, b.
28 May 1867, Blackhawk County, IA; m. Nellie M.
Shepard.
Issue:
599. Lucian Chester[10] Conard, b. 8 Mar 1888
600. Byron[10] Conard, b. 28 July 1889
601. Irene[10] Conard, b. 28 Apr 1891
602. Frank Remsen[10] Conard, b. 16 Feb 1905
603. Ruby[10] Conard, b. Feb 1908, Harrison
County, AR

388. NETTIE FLORENCE[9] CONARD, dau. of James
Wheeler and Lucilla Larwill[8] (Breese) Conard, b.
19 Sept 1868, Blackhawk County, IA; m. 20 Mar
1890, William H. Lydamore, b. 28 Dec 1863.
Issue:
604. Leslie Everett[10] Lydamore, b. 17 Mar 1898
605. Milton Charles[10] Lydamore, b. 17 Jan 1900

392. ROSINA JANE[9] SMITH, dau. of Wilson Lee and
Henrietta Rosina[8] (Breese) Smith, b. 30 June
1866; m. 16 Feb 1887, William Harrison Thurston,
b. 4 Apr 1861.
Issue:

606. Galen Curtis[10] Thurston, b. 13 Dec 1896
607. Ruth Henrietta[10] Thurston, b. 31 Jan 1899
608. Vivian Elizabeth[10] Thurston, b. 11 Nov
     1900

398. MINNIE BELL[9] BREESE, dau. of Silas Howard[8]
and Sarah Jeantee (Inman) Breese, b. 6 Oct 1870;
m. 22 Mar 1892, Fred Doderer, b. 23 Mar 1877 in
Dorchester, Suva, England.
Issue:
609. Bernice Breese[10] Doderer, b. 27 Sept 1893,
     d. Aug 1894
610. Doris Minnie[10] Doderer, b. 30 Apr 1905

407. MAUDE DECELLE[9] WHITMORE, dau. of Alphin
Herbert and Eugenia Artilisa[8] (Breese) Whitmore,
b. 26 Oct 1884 near Ottawa, IL, d. 14 Aug 1965
in CA; m. 26 Dec 1914 at Ottawa, IL, Dwight
Percy Henders.
Issue:
611. Norman Arthur[10] Henders, b. 7 Nov 1915; m.
     16 Feb 1940 at Las Vegas, Nevada, Ruth
     Tranberg, b. 26 Dec 1912.

408. BERNICE BREESE[9] WHITMORE, dau. of Alphin
Herbert and Eugenia Artilisa[8] (Breese) Whitmore,
b. 22 May 1887 near Ottawa, IL, d. 25 Apr 1963
at Ottawa, IL; m. 21 Oct 1911 at Ottawa, IL,
Arthur Henry Simmons, b. 10 Aug 1881, d. 25 Jan
1970 at Mendota, IL.
Issue:
*612. Virginia Breese[10] Simmons, b. 22 Sept
     1912, Marseilles, IL
*613. Russell Terry[10] Simmons, b. 4 Oct 1915,
     Marseilles, IL

410. ELLSWORTH CHASE[9] BREESE, son of Thurlow
Ellsworth[8] and Rose (Tompkins) Breese, b. 15 Feb
1884, Ottawa, IL, d. Feb 1960; m. 16 Dec 1908 in
Winnipeg, Canada, Christine ("Tina") Graham, b.
2 Nov 1878 in Toronto, Canada.
Issue:

*614. Ralph Graham[10] Breese, b. 10 Nov 1910,
      Winnipeg, Canada
*615. Flora I.[10] Breese, b. 9 Feb 1913 in
      Winnipeg, Canada

411. VERNE GILDERSLEEVE[9] BREESE, son of Thurlow
Ellsworth[8] and Rose (Tompkins) Breese, b. 24 May
1885, Serena, IL, d. 20 May 1955, Ottawa, IL; m.
7 June 1906 at Ottawa, IL, Bessie Rae Sinclair,
b. 18 Sept 1885, d. 6 Jan 1959, Villa Park, IL,
d/o William and Susan (Miller) Sinclair of
Serena. Verne was an officer in the U.S. Army
during World War I and later became Assistant
Postmaster in Marseilles, IL.
Issue:
*616. Treva May[10] Breese, b. 4 Dec 1907, Serena,
      IL
*617. Thelma Joyce[10] Breese, b. 2 Jan 1909,
      Serena, IL
*618. Roma Adele[10] Breese, b. 21 Dec 1913,
      McPherson, KS, d. 15 July 1973
 619. Robert Verne[10] Breese, b. 22 July 1922,
      Ottawa, IL, d. Apr 1923
 620. Lloyd Ellsworth[10] Breese, b. 1 Dec 1925,
      Ottawa, IL, d. 19 Feb 1944, Lafayette,
      IN from complications while in the U.S.
      Marine Corps.

424. EMMETT SYLVANUS[9] FILER, son of Emmett Van
Wyck and Lillie[8] (Wade) Filer, b. 10 Mar 1883,
d. 18 Mar 1952; m. 5 Sept 1920, Lena Dower, b.
16 Oct 1892, Dayton, OR, d. 24 Apr 1988; both
bur. in Dayton, OR. Emmett owned and operated a
general store in Dayton, OR.
Issue:
 621. Charlotte[10] Filer, b. 7 Mar 1932

425. FLORENCE B.[9] JESSUP, dau. of Silas Egbert[8]
and Florence[8] (Bishop) Jessup, b. 24 Apr 1882,
d. 1961; m. at Quogue, 2 Sept 1905, Bertram
Frederic Pierson, formerly of Sag Harbor.
Issue:

622. Katherine Jessup[10] Pierson, m. Elmer
      Warner

426. **GEORGE PENNY[9] JESSUP**, son of Silas Egbert[8]
and Florence[8] (Bishop) Jessup, twin, b. 29 Feb
1884, Quogue; m. Mannie L. Dealy, b. 1895.
Issue:
   623. Mary S.[10] Jessup, b. 1919; m. Thomas G.
      McCawley, b. 1913
   624. Nancy Wells[10] Jessup
   625. George Penny[10] Jessup
?626. Florence Bishop[10] Jessup

428. **CLARENCE RUSSELL ("RUSS")[9] RAYNOR**, son of
George W.[8] and Hannah R. (Stevens) Raynor, b. 23
Feb 1872, Westhampton, d. 2 Jan 1947,
Southampton; m. 12 July 1898, Pauline Webber, b.
27 Feb 1872, New York City, d. 1950, d/o Philip
and Frederico M. (Palmer) Webber; both bur.
Westhampton Cemetery. They resided in
Westhampton Beach, where "Russ" Raynor was a
clockmaker and inventor.
Issue:
*627. Anna Millicent[10] Raynor, b. 30 Aug 1899,
      d. 27 Sept 1976
  628. Philip Russell[10] Raynor, b. 6 Aug 1901,
      d. 19 Feb 1943, bur. Quogue; m. Eunice
      Helm; no issue. Eunice m. (2)
      Charles Stevens of Quogue.
*629. Clarence Elisha[10] Raynor, b. 8 Apr 1904,
      Westhampton
*630. David Lester[10] Raynor, b. 27 May 1908,
      Westhampton Beach, d. 15 Jan 1989
?631. Mary[10] Raynor, b. 29 May 1912

431. **ELIZABETH ("LIZZIE") HALSEY[9] RAYNOR**, dau.
of William Clark[8] and Eliza (O'Bryan) Raynor, b.
Mar 1870 (or 1868), Westhampton; m. 20 Dec 1888,
Wallace Alfred Raynor, b. Apr 1865 (or 1868),
Manorville, d. 7 Feb 1931, s/o Clark Oliver and
Anne Eliza (Edwards) Raynor. Wallace was a
sturgeon fisherman, and later, was Captain in

the U.S. Coast Guard, on Long Island.
Issue:
*632. Blanche A.[10] Raynor, b. June 1892
633. Mildred E.[10] Raynor, b. ca 1901; m. _____
     Peck.

432. WILLIAM FLETCHER[9] RAYNOR, son of William
Clark[8] and Eliza (O'Bryan) Raynor, b. 12 Mar
1875, d. 6 Dec 1959; m. 24 Dec 1896 (or 1897),
Louisa Raynor Benjamin, b. 29 Aug 1880, East
Moriches, d. 31 Oct 1958, d/o Hiram Francis and
Laura Cordelia[8] (Benjamin) Benjamin. William
Fletcher and his family resided in Westhampton.
He was a sturgeon fisherman prior to 1918, and
was a Southampton Town Trustee for many years.
Issue:
634. William Clifford[10] Raynor, b. 7 June 1897,
    d. 1 Dec 1986; m. Elizabeth Laube of
    Jamaica, d. 1975; no issue.
*635. Everett Clark[10] Raynor, b. 24 Sept 1900,
    d. 2 (or 3) Dec 1943
636. Beatrice Albertine[10] Raynor, a nurse,
    Westhampton Beach High School Class of
    1923, b. 9 Dec 1903, d. 12 Feb 1984;
    m. Harold Dinton Luce, b. 1905, d. 1983;
    both bur. Westhampton Cemetery; no
    issue.
637. Sidney Fletcher[10] Raynor, b. 19 (or 9) Mar
    1906, d. 13 Nov 1991; m. 13 Nov 1948,
    Marian Scudder (Hallock) Raynor, b. 10
    Jan 1900, d/o Arthur Hallock, Jr. and
    widow of #635. Everett Clark[10] Raynor,
    Sidney Fletcher Raynor's brother.
*638. Louis Benjamin[10] Raynor, b. 4 Mar 1917,
    Westhampton
639. Louise Preston[10] Raynor, twin, b. 26 Feb
    1920
640. Elsie Faye[10] Raynor, twin, b. 26 Feb 1920,
    d. 10 June 1925 (appendicitis)
*641. Charles Marvin[10] Raynor, b. 28 Apr 1922

433. ARTHUR HALSEY[9] RAYNOR, son of John Gilbert[8]

and Ellen Grace (Robinson) Raynor, b. 1868,
Westhampton, d. 27 June 1947, bur. Westhampton
Cemetery; m. (1) 20 Nov 1892, Helen Louise
Fournier, b. 6 Oct 1871, Good Ground, d. 1 May
1943, bur. Westhampton Cemetery, d/o Sheldon
Mercator and Marietta (Ketcham) Fournier; m. (2)
Nettie Smith, widow of the East Hampton Station
agent. Arthur was a commercial fisherman.
Issue Wife (1):

642. Halsey Gilbert[10] Raynor, b. ca 1894, d. 22
     Dec 1935; m. (1) Hannah Zaharis; m. (2)
     Maude McCoy.

*643. Daniel Tuttle[10] Raynor, b. 22 Apr 1895, d.
      15 Apr 1978, Los Angeles, CA, ae 83
      yrs.

644. Abbie Louise[10] Raynor, b. 1896, d. 1965;
     m. Charles Bell Whited.

645. Mary[10] Raynor, d. 22 Oct 1897, ae 1 mo.

434. FREDERIC CONKLIN[9] RAYNOR, son of John
Gilbert[8] and Ellen Grace (Robinson) Raynor, b. 4
Aug 1871, Westhamnpton, d. 11 June 1940; m. 13
May 1892, Lottie T. Reardon, b. 1873, East
Moriches, d. 1953, d/o Thomas F. and Louisa
(Robinson) Reardon (or William H. and Annie L.
(Robinson) Reardon); both bur. Westhampton
Cemetery. Frederic was a brick mason.
Issue:

646. Olin Shepherd[10] Raynor, b. 1894, d. 1986,
     bur. Westhampton Cemetery; unmarried.
     Olin, a bank clerk, lived with his
     sister, Clara, on the east side of
     Baycrest Avenue, Westhampton; he was a
     devout member of the Independent
     order of Odd Fellows.

647. Clara Gertrude[10] Raynor, b. 1 July 1906,
     d. 30 Mar 1980, bur. Westhampton
     Cemetery; unmarried.

435. FRANCES HELENE[9] RAYNOR, dau. of John
Gilbert[8] and Ellen Grace (Robinson) Raynor, b.
1875, d. 31 Oct 1950; m. 9 Mar 1898 at the
bride's home in Westhampton by Rev. Barnabus

Reeve, William Sherman Grimshaw, b. 1 Feb 1862 at Hay Ground, East Hampton, d. 1952, s/o Francis E. and Fanny (Cullum) Grimshaw. William Grimshaw owned and operated plumbing and heating and hardware businesses in Westhampton Beach.
Issue:
648. Wesley Sherman[10] Grimshaw, b. 10 Jan 1899, d. 22 Feb 1969; m. Geraldine _____; no issue.
*649. Florence Jerusha[10] Grimshaw, b. 22 Mar 1900, d. 1987
650. Roger William[10] Grimshaw, b. 6 Jan 1902, d. 10 Oct 1905 (lockjaw)
*651. Rose Helene[10] Grimshaw, b. 12 Feb 1903, d. 15 Aug 1977
*652. Lilla Madelyn[10] Grimshaw, b. 16 Sept 1904, d. 1989
*653. Leah Frances[10] Grimshaw, b. 5 Oct 1908, d. 1985

436. **JOHN GILBERT ("LITTLE JOHN")**[9] **RAYNOR, JR.** son of John Gilbert[8] and Ellen Grace (Robinson) Raynor, b. 10 Aug 1876, d. 1 Dec 1958; m. 23 Dec 1908, Phoebe (or Phebe) Genevieve Hawkins, b. 20 Sept 1886 (or 1877), d. 17 Apr 1962, d/o Nathaniel Brewster and Ida M. (Terrell) Hawkins. John was a sturgeon fisherman prior to 1918.
Residence: Westhampton.
Issue:
*654. Walter Raleigh[10] Raynor, b. 30 Jan 1910, d. 21 May 19__
*655. George Lafayette[10] Raynor, b. 4 May 1916, Westhampton, d. 29 Apr 1983, Riverhead

441. **ARCHIE W.**[9] **RAYNOR,** son of Nathan Sidney[8] and Eliza H. (Jessup) Raynor, b. 4 Dec 1875, Westhampton, d. 1950; m. 23 Nov 1898 at the bride's home in Center Moriches, Grace H. Hawkins, b. 15 July 1877, d. Jan 1940, Westhampton, ae 62 yrs., d/o Edwin and Emma R. (Terry) Hawkins; both bur. Westhampton Cemetery. Archie was a poultry farmer.
Issue:

656. Virginia[10] Raynor, b. 18 June 1904,
     Westhampton; m. (1) 4 Apr 1928, Howard
     E. Hembury, b. 1893, d. 1932, bur.
     Westhampton Cemetery; m. (2) C. Irving
     Foster, b. 1893, d. 1963, bur.
     Westhampton Cemetery; no issue.
*657. Robert A.[10] Raynor, b. 22 Apr 1908,
     Westhampton, d. 1963
658. Roscoe[10] Raynor, b. 1910, d. 1911, bur.
     Westhampton Cemetery, in plot with
     parents.
659. Harold Wilson[10] Raynor, b. 10 July 1913;
     m. 19 Apr 1940, Helen Elizabeth Ehlers,
     b. 19 June 1916, d/o Ludvig D. and Meta
     Christine (Petersen) Ehlers of Denmark;
     no issue.

442. CHESTER SIDNEY[9] RAYNOR, son of Nathan
Sidney[8] and Eliza H. (Jessup) Raynor, b. 28 May
1885, d. 28 July 1961, Riverhead; m. 12 Sept
1912 in Islip by Rev. Daniel H. Overton, Louise
Rushmore Raynor, b. 9 (or 8) Nov 1884, d. 22
Feb 1962, d/o Henry D. and Lucy (Jagger) Raynor
of Manorville. Lucy was d/o George C. Jagger,
who was s/o Enoch F. Jagger. Chester Sidney
Raynor was a duck farmer.
Issue:
*660. Frances Jean[10] Raynor, b. 22 June 1914
*661. Chester Sidney ("Bud")[10] Raynor, Jr., b.
     17 Sept 1916

443. MINNIE J.[9] GORDON, dau. of Nathan Henry and
Charlotte Elizabeth[8] (Raynor) Gordon, b. 6 May
1874; m. Elbert ("Bud") Van Cott.
Issue:
*662. Clifford[10] Van Cott

445. RUSSELL WESLEY[9] RAYNOR, M.D., son of
Charles Wesley[8] and Betty Ann (Dolbey) Raynor,
b. 23 July 1886, White Haven, MD, d. 20 Jan
1939, Pikeville, KY, bur. Pikeville Cemetery; m.
(1) 16 Nov 1910 at Deal Island, MD, Lola

Edgerton Wilson, b. 25 Apr 1891, Wenona, Deal Island, MD, d. 13 Mar 1926, Pikeville, KY, bur. Dolbey Cemetery, White Haven, MD, d/o Edgerton Granville and Winifred Helen (Windsor) Wilson; m. (2) Sarah Williamson of Pikeville, KY. Russell Wesley graduated from the University of Maryland Medical College in 1908 and became an EENT specialist. Following service with the Public Health Department, he established a private practice in Pikeville, KY and later, formed the Pikeville Clinic.
Issue Wife (1):

*663. Virginia Mae[10] Raynor, twin, b. 14 Feb 1922, Pikeville, KY

*664. Helen Elizabeth[10] Raynor, twin, b. 14 Feb 1922, Pikeville, KY

446. CLARK SIDNEY[9] RAYNOR, son of Charles Wesley[8] and Betty Ann (Dolbey) Raynor, b. 5 Oct 1893, White Haven, MD, d. 13 Sept 1966, bur. Dolbey Cemetery, White Haven, MD; m. Audrey Sommers, b. 27 Jan 1901, d. 27 June 1977.
Issue:

*665. Holmes[10] Raynor, b. in MD

447. ADOLPH ("DOPH") E.[9] NICHOLS, son of Christopher William and Hettie Jane[8] (Raynor) Nichols, b. 1877, d. 4 Dec 1939; m. Tealie Lillian King, d/o Charles and Martha (Pedrick) King of Wading River.
Issue:

*666. Wilson ("Pete")[10] Nichols

667. Eugene[10] Nichols

*668. Elizabeth[10] Nichols

450. ALETA (OR LECTA)[9] KETCHAM, dau. of John and Sarah Rupell[8] (Raynor) Ketcham, m. Albert Sommers; lived in Atlantic City, NJ.
Issue:

669. Frank[10] Sommers

670. Marjorie[10] Sommers

671. Douglas[10] Sommers

453. RUBY LEMAY[9] RAYNOR, dau. of Walter Scott[8] and Mary Frances (Benjamin) Raynor, b. 17 June 1896, Westhampton, d. 23 (or 24 Mar) 1975; m. 9 Aug 1919 at Patchogue, Edward Chamier, b. 31 Oct 1888, Westhampton, d. 10 Apr 1973, bur. Cedar Grove Cemetery, Patchogue, s/o Edward and Elizabeth (Smith) Chamier. Edward was an auto mechanic.
Issue:

*672. Edward Walter[10] Chamier, b. 17 Jan 1921 at Patchogue, d. 4 Jan 1981, Smithtown, L.I., bur. Cedar Grove Cemetery, Patchogue

*673. Claire LeMay[10] Chamier, b. 10 Nov 1925 at Patchogue

*674. Scott Lemont[10] Chamier, b. 19 Oct 1929, Patchogue

454. PEARL[9] RAYNOR, dau. of Walter Scott[8] and Mary Frances (Benjamin) Raynor, b. 20 Aug 1901, Moriches, d. 23 May 1988; m. (1) Richard Farrow, d. 22 Mar 1963; m. (2) Lee Johnson.
Issue Husband (1):

675. Richard[10] Farrow

458. CHARLES BUPTON[9] RAYNOR, son of John Fletcher[8] and Sarah M. (Bellows) Raynor, b. 28 Feb 1876, Good Ground (or Westhampton), d. 8 Feb 1928; m. 12 Mar 1898, Charlotte M. Tuthill, b. 20 Jan 1880, Good Ground, d. 16 Dec 1932, d/o William and Martha (Culbert) Tuthill. Residence in 1910-11: Good Ground, where Charles Bupton worked at the Life Saving Station. He also served at the Potunk Life Saving Station, in Westhampton.
Issue:

*676. Joseph Fletcher[10] Raynor, b. 20 Dec 1902 at the Potunk Life Saving Station, Westhampton

677. Christine M.[10] Raynor, b. ca 1908

461. WILLIAM URIAH[9] RAYNOR, son of William

Anderson[8] and Emma Lenora (Raynor) Raynor, b. 8
Jan 1896, Hampton Bays, d. 27 Feb 1922 at the
age of 26 yrs. (typhoid fever), Sanford, FL,
bur. old graveyard, Sanford, FL; m. 1914, Ramona
McLain of Geneva, FL. William was a farmer and
mechanic. Residence: Sanford, FL.
Issue:
*678. William Thomas[10] Raynor, b. 4 Oct 1915,
    Sanford, FL

462. MARY ALIDA ("LYDA")[9] RAYNOR, dau. of
William Anderson[8] and Emma Lenora (Raynor)
Raynor, b. 5 (or 6) June 1881, d. 21 Feb 1960;
m. Clarence F. Benjamin, b. 31 July 1882, s/o
Franklin Howell and Dora Belle (Raynor)
Benjamin. Mary Alida was a school teacher for
over thirty years.
Issue:
  679. Leonard[10] Benjamin
  680. Alta[10] Benjamin

463. HATTIE AINSLEY[9] RAYNOR, dau. of William
Anderson[8] and Emma Lenora (Raynor) Raynor, b. 10
Nov 1884, Hampton Bays, d. 11 Sept 1966; m. 18
Sept 1907 at Good Ground by Rev. J. H. Swann,
Harold Leroy Carter, Commander, U.S. Coast
Guard, b. 23 Dec 1886, d. 3 Nov 1972,
Westhampton, s/o Theodore Henry and Emma Estelle
(Corwin) Carter; both Hattie Ainsley and Harold
Leroy are bur. Westhampton Cemetery.
Issue:
*681. Emma Ainsley[10] Carter, b. 30 July 1908, d.
    3 Mar 1994
  682. Genevieve Estelle[10] Carter, b. 2 Feb 1921,
    d. 5 Feb 1921
*683. Norma Theodora[10] Carter, b. 9 Feb 1925,
    Quiogue

464. ETHEL EMMA[9] RAYNOR, dau. of William
Anderson[8] and Emma Lenora (Raynor) Raynor, b. 15
Jan 1889, d. 1969, bur. Hampton Bays; m. 17 Oct
1908 at Good Ground by Rev. C. S. Gillispie,

Donald Remson Penny, b. 20 June 1888, d. 1980, s/o Alexander Harris and Emmeline Althea (Foster) Penny. Ethel was a graduate of Claghorn's Bryant Stratton Business College in Brooklyn, NY, and she was a talented pianist.
Issue:

684. William A.[10] Penny, b. 24 June 1909, d. 27 Jan (or Dec) 1941, ae 31 yrs.

*685. Emma Laverne[10] Penny, b. 11 May 1914, Good Ground

686. Isabelle[10] Penny, b. 1916; m. 1933, Russel H. Creef.

465. ISABEL MATILDA[9] RAYNOR, dau. of William Anderson[8] and Emma Lenora (Raynor) Raynor, b. Hampton Bays, d. Aug 1952; m. William D. Rowe.
Issue:

687. Alonzo Dial[10] Rowe, b. 11 Aug 19__, d. at 17 yrs. of age (pernicious anemia)

*688. Emma Katherine ("Kay")[10] Rowe, b. 12 Mar 1924

689. Isabelle Virginia ("Belle")[10] Rowe, b. 26 May 1926; m. Henry Harris.

690. William Lawrence[10] Rowe, d. ca 42 yrs. of age in Arcadia, FL

*691. Mamie Aleen ("Eileen")[10] Rowe, b. 16 Dec 1930, d. ca 1984

469. MARY ELLEN (OR ELLA)[9] RAYNOR, dau. of Elihu Jotham[8] and Ida Johnson (Young) Raynor, b. 3 Nov 1874, d. 21 Sept 1938 in the hurricane; m. 15 Nov 1892, William Jacob Jarvis, b. 1872, d. 21 Sept 1938 in the hurricane; both bur. Westhampton Cemetery.
Issue:

692. Roscoe W.[10] Jarvis, b. 11 July 1893, d. 14 Oct 1893, aged 3 mos., 8 days (gravestone), bur. Westhampton Cemetery, with parents

*693. Helen L.[10] Jarvis, b. 1895, d. 1984, bur. Westhampton Cemetery

694. Ida M.[10] Jarvis, b. 6 Jan 1898, d. 8 June

1898, aged 5 mos., 2 days, bur. Westhampton Cemetery, with parents

695. Gertrude E.[10] Jarvis, b. 15 Dec 1901, d. 1981; m. Glentis F. Dean, b. 7 Sept 1908, d. 27 May 1983; both bur. Westhampton Cemetery.

*696. Leonard Prescott[10] Jarvis, b. 15 Dec 1903, Southampton, d. 2 Jan 1976, bur. Westhampton Cemetery

479. MILDRED FRANCES[9] RAYNOR, dau. of John Roscoe[8] and Helen (Deemer) Raynor, b. 13 Dec 1909, d. 20 Aug 1984, Norwich, NY, ae 74 yrs., bur. Sterling Cemetery, Greenport; m. LeGrant Chapman; resided in Greenport in 1954.
Issue:
697. John[10] Chapman

482. LAURA VINCENT[9] RAYNOR, dau. of Charles Luther[8] and Ida May[8] (Bishop) Raynor, b. 6 Oct 1887, Westhampton, d. 17 Apr 1938; m. 26 Nov 1910 by Rev. Thomas Coyle, as his 2nd wife, Stephen Fanning Griffing, b. 6 June 1872, Westhampton Beach, d. 3 Sept 1954, bur. Westhampton Cemetery, s/o Charles E. and Mary Ann (Raynor) Griffing. Stephen F. Griffing owned and operated the Hampton Inn in Westhampton Beach.
Issue:
698. Stephen Fanning[10] Griffing, Jr., b. 29 June 1920, d. 1988; m. (1) Patricia Selden Roberts; m. (2) Margaret Clifton, widow of Charles Clifton. Stephen graduated from Columbia University Law School in 1948.

486. HELEN COOK[9] ROGERS, dau. of Gilbert D. and Mary C.[8] (Raynor) Rogers, b. 14 June 1886, Remsenburg, d. 5 Dec 1984, Southampton, bur. Westhampton Cemetery; m. 23 Oct 1909, Richard Fowler Culver, b. 16 Sept 1885, Westhampton, d. 7 Apr 1959, Westhampton Beach, s/o Eckford Fowler and Lillie (Gildersleeve) Culver.

Issue:
*699. Richard Dwight[10] Culver of Kenilworth, IL

490. KATHRYN E.[9] **RAYNOR**, dau. of Oliver Jacob[8]
and Ann (McLoughlin) Raynor, b. ca 1889, d. 10
Dec 1976, ae 87 yrs.; m. Michael J. Parlato.
Kathryn was a nurse.
Issue:
  700. Elizabeth[10] Parlato, b. before 1910; m.
     Samuel Cross; no issue. Elizabeth was a
     school teacher; Samuel, an engineer,
     was also Westhampton Beach Village
     Historian.
  701. Louis Oliver[10] Parlato, b. 27 Jan 1910
*702. Katherine Marian[10] Parlato, b. 12 Apr 1911

491. HUBERT I.[9] **RAYNOR**, son of Oliver Jacob[8] and
Ann (McLoughlin) Raynor, b. 25 Aug 1892,
Remsenburg, d. 18 Dec 1965; m. Estelle M.
Arnold, b. 19 Feb 1900, d. July 1983. Hubert
was Remsenburg Postmaster.
Issue:
*703. Mary Ann[10] Raynor
*704. Hubert I.[10] Raynor, Jr., b. 1922

493. ELIZABETH[9] **RAYNOR**, dau. of Oliver Jacob[8]
and Ann (McLoughlin) Raynor, m. (1) Baylis
Reeve; m. (2) Walter Klaus; residence:
Hauppauge, L.I.
Issue Husband (1):
  705. Rodney[10] Reeve

496. HALSEY JACOB[9] **RAYNOR**, son of Frederick
Caleb[8] and Edith (Rogers) Raynor, b. 11 Feb
1895, d. 14 Sept 1941; m. Eloise M. Rogers, d.
15 Nov 1992, ae 95 yrs., d/o George H. and Edith
Rogers; both bur. Westhampton Cemetery.
Residence: Remsenburg.
Issue:
*706. Lois Halsey[10] Raynor, b. 1 Sept 1922,
     Remsenburg
*707. Jean Edith[10] Raynor, b. 12 Feb 1924,

497. MIRIAM GRANT[9] CORWIN, dau. of Henry Harrison[8] and Sarah Ellen (Terrell) Corwin, b. 19 Feb 1868, Riverhead, d. 30 May 1969, Riverhead, ae 101 yrs.; m. 27 Dec 1888, Riverhead, Arthur Milton Tyte, Sr., a professor of music, b. 14 July 1852, NYC, d. 3 Jan 1940, Riverhead; both bur. Riverhead Cemetery.
Issue:

*708. Harrison Edmund[10] Tyte, b. 9 Apr 1891, Riverhead, d. 10 May 1979

*709. Stephen Alexander[10] Tyte, b. 1 Jan 1893, Riverhead, d. 6 Jan 1981

*710. Mary Althea Terrell[10] Tyte, b. 29 June 1901, Riverhead, d. 28 Dec 1981

*711. Arthur Milton[10] Tyte, Jr., b. 15 May 1904, Riverhead

*712. Wickham Corwin[10] Tyte, b. 6 Mar 1911, Riverhead

498. DWIGHT TOWNSEND[9] CORWIN, son of Henry Harrison[8] and Sarah Ellen (Terrell) Corwin, b. 11 Aug 1870, Riverhead, d. 1960; m. 14 Sept 1892, Arrene Wise, b. 1871, d. 28 Sept 1956, Southampton; both bur. Riverhead Cemetery.
Issue:

713. Edith Evangeline[10] Corwin, b. 17 Aug 1895, d. 29 Nov 1988, bur. Riverhead Cemetery; m. 30 Nov 1918, Shermanton Baisden; no issue.

499. HUBERT FLORENCE[9] CORWIN, son of Henry Harrison[8] and Sarah Ellen (Terrell) Corwin, b. 1876, d. 2 Sept 1959; m. 11 June 1902 at Laurel, L.I., Minnie Cornelia Woodhull, b. 1876, d. 1953, d/o Zophar M. and Cornelia Abigail (Brown) Woodhull; Hubert and Minnie are both bur. Riverhead Cemetery. Hubert ran the Corwin and Vail Lumber Company after his father's death.
Issue:

*714. Leone Woodhull[10] Corwin, b. 2 Nov 1903
*715. Florence ("Flossie") Miller[10] Corwin, b. 2
     Sept 1909
 716. Cornelia[10] Corwin, b. 12 Mar 1912, d. 30
     July 1985, bur. Riverhead; unmarried.
*717. Muriel[10] Corwin, b. 13 June 1917

501. ELIZABETH[9] SMITH, dau. of Edward Charles
and Antoinette Hawkins[8] (Raynor) Smith, m.
Halsey Clark.
Issue:
*718. Antoinette[10] Clark

502. SOPHIA[9] ROGERS, dau. of David Roswell[8] and
Sarah (Culver) Rogers, m. Theophilus Brouwer.
Issue:
 719. son[10] Brouwer

503. DAISY[9] ROGERS, dau. of David Roswell[8] and
Sarah (Culver) Rogers, m. Earle Bishop.
Issue:
 720. Caroline[10] Bishop
 721. Earldine[10] Bishop
 722. Patricia[10] Bishop

504. THOMAS[9] ROGERS, son of David Roswell[8] and
Sarah (Culver) Rogers, m. Carrie Townsen (of
Pawling, NY), a teacher in Remsenburg.
Issue:
 723. May[10] Rogers
 724. Constance[10] Rogers
 725. Elinor[10] Rogers
 726. Charles[10] Rogers
 727. Thomas[10] Rogers

507. ISABEL BROWNING[9] JESSUP, dau. of George
Hildreth[8] and Frances Harriet[8] (Rogers) Jessup,
d. 24 Feb 1958; m. 28 Jan 1902 at Westhampton
Presbyterian Church, Alanson Pierson Rogers, b.
16 May 1864, Westhampton, s/o Noel Byron and

Virginia L. D. (Pierson) Rogers of Westhampton.
Isabel was a graduate of the New England
Conservatory of Music.
Issue:
  728. Alanson Noel[10] Rogers, b. 17 Feb 1911; m.
    Elizabeth ("Betty") Carman.

509. LEILA[9] BAKER, dau. of George and Jennie B.[8]
(Rogers) Baker, m. George Journey (?).
Issue:
  *729. Dorothy[10] Journey (?)

510. C. FLOYD[9] PIERSON, son of Enoch H. and
Susan Halsey[8] (Rogers) Pierson, b. 1875, d.
1962; m. Lena B. _____, b. 1878, d. 1949.
Issue:
  730. Marian[10] Pierson, m. Bernard Van Popering
    of Greenport.

514. HETTIE ROGERS[9] GILDERSLEEVE, dau. of Isaac
Davidson and Millicent Brewster[8] (Rogers)
Gildersleeve, b. 30 Mar 1880, d. 10 June 1930;
m. Alexander Soyars, d. 1961. Residence:
Riverhead.
Issue:
  731. Vinton[10] Soyars, b. 1900, d. 1974
  732. George[10] Soyars, b. 1907, d. 1992

516. EFFIE[9] GILDERSLEEVE, dau. of Isaac Davidson
and Millicent Brewster[8] (Rogers) Gildersleeve,
b. 9 Apr 1885, d. 18 Aug 1978; m. Fred M.
Phillips, b. 1888, d. 1949. Residence: Hampton
Bays.
Issue:
  733. Murray G.[10] Phillips, b. 1920, d. 1982
  734. Jeannette M.[10] Phillips, b. 1923

517. CLARA L.[9] GILDERSLEEVE, dau. of Isaac
Davidson and Millicent Brewster[8] (Rogers)
Gildersleeve, b. 25 May 1889, d. 31 Jan 1988; m.
Lewis W. Satterly, b. 12 Mar 1877, d. 13 Oct
1961, s/o Thomas and Isabelle F. (Rowland)

Satterly.
Issue:

735. Geraldine[10] Satterly, b. 24 July 1915; m. _____ Morgan.

*736. Margaret I.[10] Satterly, b. 9 Nov 1920

519. RAYMOND SCUDDER[9] GILDERSLEEVE, son of Isaac Davidson and Millicent Brewster[8] (Rogers) Gildersleeve, b. 29 Apr 1896 (or 24 Apr 1895), d. 30 Mar 1952; m. Ida Reeve, b. 1892, d. 1980.
Issue:

737. Shirley[10] Gildersleeve, b. 1919
738. Richard[10] Gildersleeve, b. 1920, d. 1987
739. Betsy[10] Gildersleeve, b. 1922, d. 1972
740. Wilbur[10] Gildersleeve, b. 1928, d. 1987

522. LESTER WHITE[9] RAYNOR, son of Franklin Carpenter[8] and Amy Louise (White) Raynor, b. 7 Feb 1886, Southampton, d. 25 Feb 1975; m. 25 Oct 1922 at Lynbrook, L.I., Marie Frances Lee, b. 3 Sept 1895, Brooklyn, d. 12 Jan 1949, d/o Philo A. and _____ (Bell) Lee. Lester was a carpenter and active member of the First Presbyterian Church of Southampton. Marie was a teacher.
Issue:

741. Rexford Lee[10] Raynor, b. 27 Mar 1925, d. 19 Nov 1944; unmarried. He served in World War II.
*742. Louise Wanda[10] Raynor, b. 20 Feb 1929

523. HENRY PROUD[9] RAYNOR, son of Franklin Carpenter[8] and Amy Louise (White) Raynor, b. ca 1889, Westhampton Beach; m. (1) 5 Oct 1912 in Islip, Laura Eldridge Williams, b. ca 1889, Brattleboro, VT, d/o W. S. and Charlotte (Eldridge) Williams; m. (2) Lulu Edwards. Residence: Bridgehampton, L.I. At the time of his first marriage, in 1912, Henry Proud was a carpenter in Bay Shore.
Issue Wife (1):

743. child[10] Raynor
744. child[10] Raynor

745. child[10] Raynor
746. child[10] Raynor

525. WILMUN ("FLIP") HALSEY[9] RAYNOR, son of Franklin Carpenter[8] and Amy Louise (White) Raynor, b. 31 Jan 1893, d. 15 Jan 1952, bur. Jefferson Barracks National Cemetery, St. Louis, MO; m. Dolly Eleanor Crawford. Wilmun was wounded in action in France in World War I. After his discharge, he traveled the country as a journeyman plasterer.
Issue:
*747. Douglas C.[10] Raynor, b. 4 May 1930

526. EDITH MCKAY[9] RAYNOR, dau. of Franklin Carpenter[8] and Amy Louise (White) Raynor, b. 7 Apr 1895, Southampton (or Westhampton), d. 12 Apr 1982; m. 21 Oct 1921 in Southampton, Percy Leroy Dunwell, b. 1 Nov 1893, d. 18 June 1955, s/o Fred L. and Dora (Kent) Dunwell. Percy was a civil engineer. Residence: Southampton.
Issue:
*748. LeRoy Raynor[10] Dunwell, b. 16 Oct 1926
*749. Dorothy Seely[10] Dunwell, b. 24 July 1931, Southampton

527. HARRIET JAGGER[9] RAYNOR, dau. of Franklin Carpenter[8] and Amy Louise (White) Raynor, b. 23 July 1904, d. 30 Dec 1984; m. June 19__, Philo Stephen Lee, b. 29 Apr 1903, d. 6 Apr 1959. Known as "Babe" to her brothers, Harriet was an artist and school teacher. Philo was a policeman. Residence: Malverne, L.I.
Issue:
750. Philo William[10] Lee, b. 12 Aug 1936
751. Harriet Virginia[10] Lee, b. 27 Sept 1938
752. Barbara Joy[10] Lee, b. 21 July 1943

528. ELIJAH PIERSON[9] RAYNOR, son of Charles Edward[8] and Helen Elizabeth (Youngs) Raynor, b. 16 Dec 1883, Westhampton Beach, d. 23 Sept 1955; m. 14 Oct 1908 in Remsenburg by Rev. Teller,

Blanche Rogers Learie, b. 14 Feb 1883, Moriches,
d. 22 Feb 1979, d/o John Legrand and Harriet
Frances (Tuthill) Learie; both bur. Westhampton
Cemetery. Elijah was Postmaster in Westhampton
Beach, 5 Oct 1908 to 24 Jan 1918. He was also a
builder and carpenter.
Issue:
   753. Harriet Helen[10] Raynor, b. 23 May 1910, d.
        1964
*754. Pierson Tuthill[10] Raynor, b. 7 Mar 1912
*755. Charles Homer[10] Raynor, b. 12 July 1919

529. CHARLOTTE ELIZABETH[9] RAYNOR, dau. of
Charles Edward[8] and Helen Elizabeth (Youngs)
Raynor, b. 6 Mar 1890, Westhampton Beach; d. 9
Jan 1974, Riverhead; m. 30 Dec 1916 at the
Westhampton Presbyterian Church, William
Theodore Hulse, b. 28 Dec 1889, Calverton, L.I.,
d. 25 Oct 1930, Southampton, s/o Theodore Orren
and Jessie Alice (Randall) Hulse. Both
Charlotte and William are bur. Westhampton
Cemetery. Charlotte was a teacher. William was
a 1914 graduate of the Syracuse University Law
School and was an Army officer in World War I.
He was a lawyer and businessman and the first
Mayor of the incorporated village of Westhampton
Beach.
Issue:
*756. William Theodore[10] Hulse, Jr., b. 16 June
       1918
*757. Theodore Orren[10] Hulse, b. 17 Jan 1923, d.
       30 May 1989, bur. Westhampton Cemetery

532. CLIFFORD TUTTLE[9] RAYNOR, son of Augustus
Hiram[8] and Grace Alice (Tuttle) Raynor, b. 22
Feb 1893, Westhampton Beach, d. 9 Nov 1953; m.
10 Apr 1918 at Southampton by Rev. Charles S.
Gray, Genevieve Adele Halsey, b. 12 Apr 1890,
Brooklyn, d. 13 Nov 1969, Westhampton Beach, d/o
Benjamin Griffin(g) and Josephine (Jagger)
Halsey. Both Clifford and Genevieve are bur.
Westhampton Cemetery. Shortly after Clifford
and his brother, Norman, were released from the

Armed Forces following World War I, Raynor's
Garage on Library Avenue, Westhampton Beach was
founded by them, in 1919. Clifford was a
Westhampton Beach Village Trustee and long time
School Board member; he was President of the
School Board at the time of his death. He was
also President of the Long Island Dodge Dealers
Association.
Issue:
*758. Marion Genevieve[10] Raynor, b. 29 June
    1921, Quiogue, Westhampton Beach
*759. Dorothy Halsey[10] Raynor, b. 17 Mar 1924,
    Quiogue, Westhampton Beach
760. Sidney Eliot[10] Raynor, d. at birth

534. ELSA E. ("ELSIE")[9] RAYNOR, dau. of Augustus
Hiram[8] and Grace Alice (Tuttle) Raynor, b. 5 Aug
1900, Westhampton Beach, d. 25 Feb 1991, in
Ohio; m. 25 Dec 1924 in Westhampton Beach by
Rev. Thomas Coyle, Seth Wells Hulse, b. ca 1902,
Maryland, d. 14 Apr 1967, s/o Charles R. and
Ella (Ramsey) Hulse. Both Elsa and Seth are
bur. Westhampton Cemetery.
Issue:
*761. Jean M.[10] Hulse
*762. Floyd[10] Hulse

535. NORMAN HIRAM[9] RAYNOR, son of Augustus
Hiram[8] and Grace Alice (Tuttle) Raynor, b. 25
Mar 1903, Westhampton Beach, d. 23 Nov 1980,
Port Jefferson Station, ae 77 yrs.; m. Carol
Affron, b. 25 Dec 1901, Sag Harbor, d. 5 May
1979, Port Jefferson Station, ae 77 yrs., d/o
Thomas W. and Bernice (Preston) Affron; both
bur. Westhampton Cemetery. Shortly after Norman
and his brother, Clifford, were released from
the Armed Forces following World War I, the
Raynor's Garage on Library Avenue, Westhampton
Beach was founded by them, in 1919. Carol was a
school teacher.
Issue:
763. William[10] Raynor, m. 4 May 1969, Kathy
    _____, of Ft. Lauderdale, Florida.

536. WILLIAM FREDERICK[9] RAYNOR, son of Frederick Woodhull[8] and Marguerite DeForrest (Tyler) Raynor, b. 16 Jan 1887, Sayville, d. 10 Sept 1957, Westhampton Beach; m. 2 July 1910, Helen Page Scribner, b. 11 July 1889, Sag Harbor, d. 10 Mar 1984, Center Moriches, d/o Edgar W. and Fannie M. (Page) Scribner of Sag Harbor. William F. Raynor was Postmaster in Westhampton Beach from 22 Dec 1921 to 25 Mar 1929. Both William and Helen are bur. Westhampton Cemetery. Issue:

764. Laurens Tyler ("Bing")[10] Raynor, b. 23 Oct 1911, Sag Harbor, d. 26 July 1935, Southampton (appendicitis), bur. Riverhead Cemetery; m. 22 June 1934 at Riverhead, Lavinia H. Pugsley of Riverhead, d/o William Frederick and Annie (Perico) Pugsley. Lavinia m. (2) 22 Nov 1939, Idos F. Mercer.

*765. Helen Louise[10] Raynor, b. 19 Feb 1916

*766. Marcia Page[10] Raynor, b. 21 June 1923, d. 25 Mar 1991, bur. Westhampton Cemetery

538. CARRIE MARGUERITE[9] RAYNOR, dau. of Frederick Woodhull[8] and Marguerite DeForrest (Tyler) Raynor, b. 13 Sept 1890, Westhampton Beach, d. 13 Feb 1970, Westhampton Beach, bur. Westhampton Cemetery; m. 11 Jan 1913, Stuart Payne Howell, b. 11 Jan 1892, Brooklyn, d. 8 Mar 1977, s/o Frank Norton and Ella Stuart (Payne) Howell. Issue:

767. Ella Marguerite[10] Howell, b. 16 Nov 1913, East Hampton, d. 19 Nov 1913

768. Ruth Marguerite[10] Howell, b. 28 Nov 1914, Westhampton Beach, d. 30 June 1922, bur. Westhampton Cemetery

769. Lucile Elizabeth[10] Howell, b. 11 July 1925, Westhampton Beach; m. 22 Mar 1954, George C. Frey, of Eastport.

*770. Stuart Payne[10] Howell, Jr., b. 8 Dec 1928, Southampton

539. KENNETH ALAN[9] RAYNOR, son of Frederick Woodhull[8] and Marguerite DeForrest (Tyler) Raynor, b. 9 Apr 1897, d. 19 Oct 1983; m. 26 Apr 1918, Catherine Isabel Jessup, b. 24 Apr 1899, Westhampton Beach, d. 23 Sept 1969, d/o Winfield French and Catharine Jerusha (Corwin) Jessup. Kenneth, a World War I Navy Veteran, was a painting contractor. Both Kenneth and Catherine are bur. Westhampton Cemetery.
Issue:

*771. Margery DeForrest[10] Raynor, b. 29 June 1919

*772. Elizabeth Ellison[10] Raynor, b. 20 July 1920

*773. Catherine Isabel[10] Raynor, b. 9 Feb 1922, d. 12 Oct 1978

*774. Winifred Ann[10] Raynor, b. 4 Dec 1927

*775. Barbara Jane[10] Raynor, b. 14 Sept 1933

544. JAMES MADISON[9] RAYNOR, son of John Mitchell Burns[8] and Elizabeth Miller (Strong) Raynor, b. 18 Feb 1894, Westhampton Beach, d. 31 Aug 1973, Westhampton Beach; m. 26 July 1921, Gertrude Blair, of Clinton, NY, b. 19 Feb 1898, d. 4 Sept 1988; both bur. Westhampton Cemetery. J. Madison graduated from Syracuse University in 1917. The contracting and building division of E. Raynor's Sons was in the hands of the third generation, J. Madison[9] Raynor.
Issue:

*776. Jeannette[10] Raynor, b. 2 Mar 1925, d. 10 Apr 1993, Tallahassee, FL, bur. Hosford, FL

*777. James Madison[10] Raynor, Jr., b. 10 Jan 1930, Westhampton Beach, d. 28 Feb 1985, ae 55 yrs.

545. EMERSON MITCHELL[9] RAYNOR, son of John Mitchell Burns[8] and Elizabeth Miller (Strong) Raynor, b. 11 Oct 1898, Westhampton Beach, d. 13 May 1979, Bradenton, FL; m. 1 June 1922 in

Syracuse, NY, Ruth Carol Haviland, of
Pittsfield, MA, b. 23 Dec 1898, White Plains,
NY, d/o Benjamin and Mary Mathison (Stevens)
Haviland. Emerson graduated from Syracuse
University in 1921. Emerson was the first
Trustee of the incorporated village of
Westhampton Beach (Nov 1928); he was also Mayor
of Westhampton Beach from 1946 to 1949. The
real estate and insurance division of E.
Raynor's Sons, founded in 1923, was run by
Emerson Raynor. Later, he was owner of E.
Raynor Sons Real Estate, Inc. After retirement
from his real estate business, Emerson was First
Vice President of the Riverhead Savings Bank,
where he had been a Trustee for several years.
Issue:

*778. Carol Elizabeth[10] Raynor, b. 2 June 1924

*779. Priscilla[10] Raynor, b. 27 Aug 1928

546. TOWNSEND RICHARD[9] RAYNOR, son of Charles[8]
Raynor, b. 1865; m. Luranna Jimmerson.
Issue:

  780. Isabelle[10] Raynor, b. 1893; m. Clarence
      Stowe.

*781. Harold J.[10] Raynor, b. 1896

  782. Royal Wade[10] Raynor, b. 1900, d. 1944; m.
      Doris Mold

  783. Kenneth D.[10] Raynor, b. 1900, d. 1902

553. HELEN CHRISTINE[9] MOORE, dau. of Isaac Terry
and Susan Mary[8] (Jessup) Moore, b. 6 Mar 1883,
Middletown, NY, d. 27 Jan 1978, Patchogue, bur.
Patchogue; m. 6 Sept 1910 in Patchogue by Rev.
Sherman Havens, Herbert Case Woodhull, b. 3 Mar
1885, Sayville, L.I., d. 27 Dec 1966, Patchogue,
bur. Patchogue, s/o Charles Herbert and Harriett
Newell (Case) Woodhull.
Issue:

*784. John Robert[10] Woodhull, b. 27 June 1918,
      Patchogue, d. 23 May 1975, Baldwin, NY

*785. Richard Moore[10] Woodhull, b. 30 Aug 1922,
      Patchogue

Tenth Generation

588. IDA MAY[10] CONARD, dau. of George Theron[9] and Emma Althea (Dominy) Conard, b. 17 Nov 1885, d. 15 Aug 1909; m. 12 Sept 1904 in Sapulpa Indian Territory, John Charles Henry Kerr, b. 29 Jan 1882, Morrisonville, IL.
Issue:
786. Carlyle A.[11] Kerr, b. 9 Nov 1906
787. Ruth Elaine[11] Kerr, b. 18 Feb 1909, d. 18 July 1909

592. CLARENCE ALVA[10] MERCER, son of William Allen and Mabel Isadora[9] (Conard) Mercer, b. 17 Nov 1884, Vancouver, WA; m. 29 June 1909 at Seward, OK, Grace Edna Watson, b. 19 Nov 1891.
Issue:
788. Eunice Lucilla[11] Mercer, b. 24 Sept 1910, OK

593. WILLIAM ELMER[10] MERCER, son of William Allen and Mabel Isadora[9] (Conard) Mercer, b. 5 Sept 1886 in Atchinson County, MO; m. 1 Feb 1908, Olive Emmaline Nadterhoff, b. 22 Feb 1890.
Issue:
789. Hazel Elizabeth[11] Mercer, b. 24 Oct 1909, d. 2 Nov 1909
790. _____[11] Mercer, b. Oct 1910

598. CLARA HAZEL[10] WOOD, dau. of Alexander and Viola Ernestine[9] (Conard) Wood, m. 3 June 1910 at Guthrie, OK, Luther Samuel Lovell, b. 3 Aug 1889 in IL.
Issue:
791. Mary Ernestine[11] Lovell, b. 9 Apr 1911, OK

612. VIRGINIA BREESE[10] SIMMONS, dau. of Arthur Henry and Bernice Breese[9] (Whitmore) Simmons, b. 22 Sept 1912, Marseilles, IL; m. (1) 31 July 1940 at Marseilles, IL, Wesley Hastings Wright, b. 5 July 1910, d. 25 July 1970, Mendota, IL; m.

(2) 18 May 1974 at Mendota, IL, Louis Ernest
Farrell, b. 18 July 1911, Marseilles, IL.
Issue Husband (1):
   792. Janet Evelyn[11] Wright, b. 21 June 1942,
      Mendota, IL
   793. Carol Jean[11] Wright, b. 31 Mar 1945,
      Mendota, IL; m. 26 Apr 1975 in Pontiac,
      MI, Lawrence James Tischler, b. 21 June
      1942.

613. RUSSELL TERRY[10] SIMMONS, son of Arthur
Henry and Bernice Breese[9] (Whitmore) Simmons, b.
4 Oct 1915, Marseilles, IL; m. (1) 10 June 1941
at Decatur, IL, Jean Annette Terhune, b. 16 Aug
1912, Olney, IL, d. 10 Oct 1969, Morrison, IL;
m. (2) 22 Sept 1973 at Morrison, IL, Ruth Smith
Gronner, b. 29 Dec 1914, Morrison, IL.
Issue Wife (1):
*794. Jeffrey Terhune[11] Simmons, b. 28 Feb 1946,
      Oak Park, IL
*795. Stephen Arthur[11] Simmons, b. 18 June 1950,
      Oak Park, IL

614. RALPH GRAHAM[10] BREESE, son of Ellsworth
Chase[9] and Christine (Graham) Breese, b. 10 Nov
1910, Winnipeg, Canada; m. 21 Apr 1939 in
Toronto, Canada, Margaret Cardwell.
Issue:
   796. Peter Ralph[11] Breese, b. 17 Nov 1941

615. FLORA I.[10] BREESE, dau. of Ellsworth Chase[9]
and Christine (Graham) Breese, b. 9 Feb 1913,
Winnipeg, Canada; m. 26 June 1942, John J. Love,
b. 6 Oct 1913.
Issue:
   797. Peter Michael[11] Love, b. 27 Oct 1943, d.
      17 Sept 1964 in an automobile accident
   798. Joy[11] Love, twin, b. 11 Nov 1944
   799. Jay[11] Love, twin, b. 11 Nov 1944

616. TREVA MAY[10] BREESE, dau. of Verne
Gildersleeve[9] and Bessie Rae (Sinclair) Breese,

b. 4 Dec 1907, Serena, IL; m. 24 Sept 1932 in
Chicago, IL, Orville Wayne Thogmartin, b. 5 May
1907, d. 5 Dec 1979.
Issue:
*800. Janice Ray[11] Thogmartin, b. 15 Sept 1933,
      Morris, IL, d. 20 Apr 1990
*801. Vern Mac[11] Thogmartin
*802. Wayne Kent[11] Thogmartin
*803. Jon Brees[11] Thogmartin

617. THELMA JOYCE[10] BREESE, dau. of Verne
Gildersleeve[9] and Bessie Rae (Sinclair) Breese,
b. 2 Jan 1909, Serena, IL; m. 26 Dec 1929 at
Joliet, IL, Merle A. Rhines, b. 20 Oct 1902,
Marseilles, IL, d. 29 July 1984.
Issue:
*804. Marlene Ann[11] Rhines, b. 26 Dec 1935,
      Ottawa, IL

618. ROMA ADELE[10] BREESE, dau. of Verne
Gildersleeve[9] and Bessie Rae (Sinclair) Breese,
b. 21 Dec 1913, McPherson, KS, d. 15 July 1973;
m. 14 Mar 1937, Warren Singer, b. 5 Oct 1912.
Issue:
*805. James[11] Singer, b. 24 Apr 1951
 806. Thomas[11] Singer, b. 1 July 1953

627. ANNA MILLICENT[10] RAYNOR, dau. of Clarence
Russell[9] and Pauline (Webber) Raynor, b. 30 Aug
1899, d. 27 Sept 1976; m. 18 Sept 1917 at the
Southampton Methodist Church, George Corey
Beckwith, b. 30 May 1893, d. 29 Oct 1979.
Issue:
*807. Richard Corey[11] Beckwith, b. 23 Apr 1922,
      Quogue
 808. Herman Douglas[11] Beckwith, b. 23 June
      1924, Quogue; m. 8 Jan 1961 at Center
      Moriches, Helen Krupski, b. 17 Jan
      1923; no issue.

629. CLARENCE ELISHA ("RUSS")[10] RAYNOR, son of

Clarence Russell[9] and Pauline (Webber) Raynor, b. 8 Apr 1904, Westhampton; m. 30 Oct 1926 in the Eastport Gospel Church, Lucretia Irene Thode, b. 24 Feb 1908, Brooklyn, d. 25 Oct 1990, Riverhead, bur. Westhampton Cemetery.
Issue:

*809. Herbert Clarence[11] Raynor, b. 19 Apr 1927, Westhampton
*810. George Davis[11] Raynor, b. 4 Apr 1929, Westhampton, d. 9 Apr 1968, Westhampton Beach
*811. Lillian Ann[11] Raynor, b. 28 Dec 1931, Westhampton Beach
*812. Cora Lee[11] Raynor, b. 9 Jan 1935, Westhampton Beach
*813. Milton Ernest[11] Raynor, b. 1 Oct 1940, Westhampton Beach
*814. Clarence Henry[11] Raynor, b. 1 June 1943, Southampton
*815. Richard Robert[11] Raynor, b. 7 Oct 1946

630. DAVID LESTER[10] RAYNOR, son of Clarence Russell[9] and Pauline (Webber) Raynor, b. 27 May 1908, Westhampton Beach, d. 15 Jan 1989; m. 24 Oct 1936, Marguerite Josephine Keck, b. 29 May 1912, Eastport, d. 6 Jan 1987, d/o Camille Keck. David was a carpenter and Marguerite was cook at the Quogue School. They resided at Quogue.
Issue:

*816. David Eugene[11] Raynor, b. 10 Mar 1943
*817. Faith Millicent[11] Raynor, b. 1 Apr 1946

632. BLANCHE A.[10] RAYNOR, dau. of Wallace Alfred and Elizabeth Halsey[9] (Raynor) Raynor, b. June 1892; m. 10 June 1910, Carl E. Lindgren, of Stockholm, Sweden.
Issue:

818. Wilhelmina Elizabeth[11] Lindgren, m. Fred A. Cools.

635. EVERETT CLARK[10] RAYNOR, son of William

Fletcher[9] and Louisa Raynor (Benjamin) Raynor,
b. 24 Sept 1900, d. 2 (or 3) Dec 1943,
Southampton, bur. Westhampton Cemetery; m. 30
Oct 1920 at the Westhampton Methodist Church,
Marian Scudder Hallock, b. 10 Jan 1900, d/o
Arthur Jonah and Julia Ward (Tuttle) (or
Tuthill) Hallock. Marian m. (2) 13 Nov 1948,
#637. Sidney Fletcher[10] Raynor, brother of
Everett Clark[10] Raynor. Up until the time of
his death, in 1931, at the age of 62 yrs.,
Marian (Hallock) Raynor's father, Arthur J.
Hallock, was owner of Atlantic Farms, the
largest duck farm in the world. He was a
pioneer of mass production and processing of
Long Island ducks. He was also head of FCH,
Inc. and the L.I. Duck Growers Assn., President
of the Center Moriches Bank, a Director of the
Seaside Bank, Westhampton Beach, Eastport
National Bank, and the Long Island State Bank
and Trust Co. of Riverhead. Everett Clark[10]
Raynor was co-owner (with Herbert R. Culver) of
the C. & R. Duck Farm in Westhampton.
Issue:
    819. Everett Clark[11] Raynor, Jr., b. 28 Feb
         1923, Speonk
  *820. Julia Emma[11] Raynor, b. 19 Nov 1925,
         Speonk
    821. Priscilla C.[11] Raynor, b. 14 Mar 1929,
         Speonk; m. David Sparks; no issue.
  *822. Karen Louisa[11] Raynor, b. 24 Sept 1938,
         Southampton

638. LOUIS BENJAMIN[10] RAYNOR, son of William
Fletcher[9] and Louisa Raynor (Benjamin) Raynor,
b. 4 Mar 1917, Westhampton; m. (1) 6 Mar 1942 at
Alfred, NY, Mary Emily Zude, of Seattle, WA; m.
(2) Sherry _____. Residence: Michigan.
Issue Wife (1):
    823. Raymond Louis[11] Raynor, b. 1942
    824. Fletcher[11] Raynor
Issue Wife (2):
    825. Ebba[11] Raynor

826. Nels[11] Raynor
827. Beatrice[11] Raynor

641. CHARLES MARVIN[10] RAYNOR, son of William
Fletcher[9] and Louisa Raynor (Benjamin) Raynor,
b. 28 Apr 1922; m. 5 Sept 1942 at the
Westhampton Presbyterian Church, Marian Louise
Payne, b. 31 May 1922, d/o Joseph Phillips and
Ruth (Smith) Payne.
Issue:
*828. Ruth Louise[11] Raynor, b. 20 June 1945,
    Southampton
*829. Beatrice Eileen[11] Raynor, b. 16 Nov 1949,
    Southampton

643. DANIEL TUTTLE[10] RAYNOR, son of Arthur
Halsey[9] and Helen Louise (Fournier) Raynor, b.
22 Apr 1895, d. 15 Apr 1978, Los Angeles, CA, ae
83 yrs.; m. 1919, Irene Marie Cody, of Brooklyn,
b. 10 Dec 1895, Brooklyn, d. 21 May 1985,
Patchogue, d/o Thomas L. and Mary E. (Murphy)
Cody. Daniel was an auto mechanic and a World
War I Veteran.
Issue:
*830. Arthur Daniel[11] Raynor, b. 30 May 1920,
    Brooklyn, NY
*831. Frances Louise[11] Raynor, b. 21 June 1923

649. FLORENCE JERUSHA[10] GRIMSHAW, dau. of
William Sherman and Frances Helene[9] (Raynor)
Grimshaw, b. 22 Mar 1900, d. 1987; m. 7 May 1925
in Westhampton Beach by Rev. Thomas B. Miller,
Frank Datson Gould, Sr., b. 1901, d. 1950, s/o
Frank Lamphere and Lillian (Datson) Gould of
Westerly, RI.
Issue:
 832. Frank Datson[11] Gould, Jr.
*833. Thomas Lamphere[11] Gould
 834. Florence Helene[11] Gould, b. 1927, d. in
    infancy

651. ROSE HELENE[10] GRIMSHAW, dau. of William

Sherman and Frances Helene[9] (Raynor) Grimshaw, b. 12 Feb 1903, d. 15 Aug 1977; m. 26 Mar 1922 at Westhampton Beach by Rev. Thomas B. Miller, Harry Arnold Pugh, Sr., b. 1899, Westerly, RI, d. 1986.
Issue:

*835. Harry Arnold[11] Pugh, Jr.

*836. Rodney William[11] Pugh

837. Rose Marie[11] Pugh, b. 1929, d. 1979

652. LILLA MADELYN[10] GRIMSHAW, dau. of William Sherman and Frances Helene[9] (Raynor) Grimshaw, b. 16 Sept 1904, d. 1989; m. (1) Fred Gould Palmer, Sr., b. 1901, d. 23 Feb 1934; m. (2) 1946, Paul Nevins, of Providence, RI, b. 1916. Issue Husband (1):

*838. Fred Gould[11] Palmer, Jr.

653. LEAH FRANCES[10] GRIMSHAW, dau. of William Sherman and Frances Helene[9] (Raynor) Grimshaw, b. 5 Oct 1908, d. 1985; m. James Francis Coady, b. 16 May 1900, Ireland, d. 3 Apr 1972. Issue:

839. Michael James[11] Coady, b. 1927, d. 1990

840. Leah Mae[11] Coady

841. Edwin Francis[11] Coady, m. Grace Frick Hamor, widow of Scott Hamor. Grace Frick had three sons by her first husband, Scott Hamor.

654. WALTER RALEIGH[10] RAYNOR, son of John Gilbert[9] and Phoebe Genevieve (Hawkins) Raynor, Jr., b. 30 Jan 1910, d. 21 May 19__; m. 28 Oct 1939, Martha E. Fenn, b. 21 Sept 1915, CT. Issue:

*842. Marleigh Anne[11] Raynor, b. 31 July 1941

843. Frances Ellen[11] Raynor, b. 9 May 1943; m. 7 Nov 1970, Michael Ross.

655. GEORGE LAFAYETTE ("LET")[10] RAYNOR, son of John Gilbert[9] and Phoebe Genevieve (Hawkins)

Raynor, Jr., b. 4 May 1916, Westhampton, d. 29
Apr 1983, Riverhead; m. 16 Aug 1956 at the
Westhampton Methodist Church as her second
husband, Lorraine Irene Lavelle, b. 6 May 1919,
Center Moriches, d. 2 Nov 1987, d/o Joseph and
Grace (Loper) Lavelle.
Issue:

*844. Rachel Lorraine^{11} Raynor, b. 10 Sept 1961

657. ROBERT A.^{10} RAYNOR, son of Archie W.^{9} and
Grace H. (Hawkins) Raynor, b. 22 Apr 1908,
Westhampton, d. 1963; m. 5 Aug 1932, Mildred
Skidmore, b. 1911, d. 1984; both bur.
Westhampton Cemetery.
Issue:

*845. Terry Lynn^{11} Raynor
  846. Herbert Lynn^{11} Raynor, b. 7 July 1936,
      Southampton
  847. son^{11} Raynor, b. 16 July 1940, Southampton
*848. Sandra Virginia^{11} Raynor, b. 25 June 1941,
      Southampton

660. FRANCES JEAN^{10} RAYNOR, dau. of Chester
Sidney^{9} and Louise Rushmore (Raynor) Raynor, b.
22 June 1914; m. 7 Sept 1940, Charles Henry
Halsey, b. 6 Apr 1911, St. Anthony,
Newfoundland, Canada, d. 7 Aug 1993,
Southampton, s/o Rev. Jesse and Helen (Quass)
Halsey of Southampton. Residence: Westhampton.
Issue:

*849. Wilmun Jesse^{11} Halsey, b. 3 Nov 1943,
      Southampton

661. CHESTER SIDNEY ("BUD")^{10} RAYNOR, JR. son of
Chester Sidney^{9} and Louise Rushmore (Raynor)
Raynor, b. 17 Sept 1916; m. 18 July 1937 at
Newburgh, NY, Lorraine Irene Lavelle, b. 6 May
1919, Center Moriches, d. 2 Nov 1987, d/o Joseph
and Grace (Loper) Lavelle. Lorraine m. (2)
#655. George Lafayette^{10} Raynor.
Issue:

*850. Chester Sidney ("Sid")^{11} Raynor III, b. 21

June 1939, Southampton

851. Jeanne Grace[11] Raynor, b. 16 May 1944; resides in a house in Westhampton formerly owned by Art Raynor's grandfather, Arthur Halsey[9] Raynor.

662. CLIFFORD[10] VAN COTT, son of Elbert and Minnie J.[9] (Gordon) Van Cott, m. Leona _____.
Issue:

852. Leona ("Noni")[11] Van Cott, m. William ("Bill") Allen; residence: Westhampton Beach.

663. VIRGINIA MAE[10] RAYNOR, dau. of Russell Wesley[9] and Lola Edgerton (Wilson) Raynor, twin, b. 14 Feb 1922, Pikeville, KY; m. Oct 1944 at Pikeville Methodist Church, William Francis Clark, M.D. Virginia Mae is a graduate of the University of Kentucky with a B.S. degree in Medical Technology.
Issue:

*853. Judith Ann[11] Clark, b. 27 June 1946

*854. Susan Elizabeth[11] Clark, b. 24 Feb 1949

*855. John Russell[11] Clark, b. 11 Jan 1953

664. HELEN ELIZABETH[10] RAYNOR, dau. of Russell Wesley[9] and Lola Edgerton (Wilson) Raynor, twin, b. 14 Feb 1922, Pikeville, KY; m. 20 Oct 1951 in Pikeville, KY, Buford Allen Short, b. 5 Oct 1921, Lexington, KY, d. 15 Jan 1993, Beattyville, KY, bur. Riverview Cemetery, Beattyville, KY, s/o Hardin Charles and Louise (Allen) Short. Residence: Beattyville, KY. Helen is a graduate of the University of Kentucky with a B.S. degree in Medical Technology; she was subsequently employed in hospitals, physicians' offices, and a health department. Buford Allen Short, a graduate of the University of Kentucky Law School, was a partner in the Rose and Short Law Firm in Beattyville. He was the Beattyville City Attorney, on the Board of Directors of the People's Exchange Bank, and in 1992, was named

"Man of the Year" by the Beattyville Chamber of
Commerce.
Issue:
856. Elizabeth Raynor[11] Short, b. 28 Jan 1953,
      Lexington, KY; she is an attorney with
      the Rose and Short Law Firm in
      Beattyville, KY.
*857. Buford Allen[11] Short, Jr., b. 30 Mar 1955,
      Lexington, KY
*858. Virginia-Earl Wilson[11] Short, b. 17 Dec
      1957, Lexington, KY

665. HOLMES[10] RAYNOR, son of Clark Sidney[9] and
Audrey (Sommers) Raynor, b. in MD; m. Irene
Whayland, d. 1991 or 1992. Residence:
Salisbury, MD.
Issue:
859. Melodie Ann[11] Raynor, m. _____ Triplett
860. Sharon Leigh[11] Raynor, m. _____ Warren
861. Michael Jay[11] Raynor, m. Connie Peterman
862. Franklin Scott[11] Raynor, m. Sandra Deal

666. WILSON ("PETE")[10] NICHOLS, son of Adolph
E.[9] and Tealie Lillian (King) Nichols
Issue:
863. Wilson[11] Nichols, a dentist

668. ELIZABETH[10] NICHOLS, dau. of Adolph E.[9] and
Tealie Lillian (King) Nichols
Issue:
864. David[11] Nichols

672. EDWARD WALTER[10] CHAMIER, son of Edward and
Ruby LeMay[9] (Raynor) Chamier, b. 17 Jan 1921 at
Patchogue, d. 4 Jan 1981, Smithtown, L.I., bur.
Cedar Grove Cemetery, Patchogue; m. (1) 8 Apr
1945 in Hawthorne, Passaic County, NJ, Charlotte
Frances Bouma, b. 28 July 1924, Patterson,
Passaic County, NJ, d/o Albert Hayes and
Charlotte Frances (Phelps) Bouma; m. (2) 15 Sept
1951 at East Patchogue, Marian Elizabeth (Hulse)
Monroe.

Issue Wife (1):

*865. Edward Robert[11] Chamier, b. 4 June 1947,
     Patterson, NJ
Issue Wife (2):

*866. Kevin[11] Chamier, b. 21 Apr 1954

*867. William[11] Chamier, b. 12 Dec 1957

673. CLAIRE LEMAY[10] CHAMIER, dau. of Edward and
Ruby LeMay[9] (Raynor) Chamier, b. 10 Nov 1925 at
Patchogue; m. 16 Sept 1950, Charles Joseph
("Chuck") Gutman, b. 5 Jan 1926, d. 5 Dec 1981.
Issue:

868. Brian[11] Gutman, b. 28 Apr 1952, Riverdale,
     NY

869. Keith[11] Gutman, b. 18 Oct 1958, Riverdale,
     NY

674. SCOTT LEMONT[10] CHAMIER, son of Edward and
Ruby LeMay[9] (Raynor) Chamier, b. 19 Oct 1929,
Patchogue; m. 17 June 1958, Joan Cinquemani(e).
Issue:

870. Colin[11] Chamier, b. 15 Jan 1959

871. Craig[11] Chamier, b. 3 July 1960

872. Aimee Michelle[11] Chamier, b. 29 Sept 1961;
     m. 19 May 1990 at Patchogue, John Joseph
     Gremmo III

873. Courtney[11] Chamier, b. 1 Sept 1967; m.
     _____ _____.

676. JOSEPH FLETCHER[10] RAYNOR, son of Charles
Bupton[9] and Charlotte M. (Tuthill) Raynor, b. 20
Dec 1902 at the Potunk Life Saving Station,
Westhampton; m. in North Carolina, Marguerite L.
White, b. 20 Feb 1910, d. 4 Dec 1989, d/o
Leonidous R. and Maggie Baxter (Cowell) White.
Joseph Served with the U.S. Coast Guard during
World War II; while stationed on the North
Carolina coast, he met and married Marguerite
White.
Issue:

*874. Alice June[11] Raynor, b. 8 Feb 1943

875. John F.[11] Raynor, b. 30 Oct 1947; a
     graduate of Hampton Bays High School, he
     served in the U.S. Army Military
     Police, Hampton Bays Police Department,
     and Suffolk County Police Department.
     Residence: Hampton Bays.

678. WILLIAM THOMAS[10] RAYNOR, son of William
Uriah[9] and Ramona (McLain) Raynor, b. 4 Oct 1915
in Sanford, FL; m. in Centerville, MD, Margaret
Elizabeth Hudson, b. 5 Apr 1917 in Ocean View,
DE, d/o Clarence R. and Sarah E. Hudson.
William Thomas Raynor had a career in the U.S.
Coast Guard. Residence: Nokomis, FL.
Issue:
*876. Ellen Ramona[11] Raynor, b. 17 May 1937,
     Lewes, DE
*877. William Thomas[11] Raynor, Jr., b. 30 June
     1942, Lewes, DE
*878. Robert Hudson[11] Raynor, b. 16 July 1946,
     Norfolk, VA

681. EMMA AINSLEY[10] CARTER, dau. of Harold Leroy
and Hattie Ainsley[9] (Raynor) Carter, b. 30 July
1908, d. 3 Mar 1994 in VA, ashes interred
Westhampton Cemetery; m. 22 Oct 1930 at her
parents' residence in East Moriches, Walter
Reginald Hill. Emma was a Registered Nurse.
Walter worked at the Brooklyn Navy yard. Emma's
residence: Manassas, VA.
Issue:
879. Aileen Jeanette[11] Hill, b. 23 Oct 1931,
     Brooklyn, d. 25 Aug 1934, Bay Shore,
     bur. Westhampton Cemetery
*880. Walter Leroy[11] Hill, b. 10 Mar 1934,
     Brooklyn
*881. Robert Reginald[11] Hill, b. 30 Sept 1938,
     Brooklyn
*882. Elizabeth Ainsley[11] Hill, b. 19 Oct 1943,
     Brooklyn

683. NORMA THEODORA[10] CARTER, dau. of Harold

Leroy and Hattie Ainsley[9] (Raynor) Carter, b. 9
Feb 1925, Quiogue; m. (1) 24 May 1947 at the
Hampton Bays Methodist Church, Lawrence Evermond
Raynor, b. 17 Mar 1923, d. 9 May 1991, s/o
Augustus Evermond and Marian F. (Carter) Raynor;
m. (2) 10 Dec 1960 in the East Moriches United
Methodist Church, Arthur Raymond Fechtmann, b.
25 July 1921, Roosevelt, L.I., s/o Reinhart F.
and Emily Margaretta (Koch) Fechtmann.
Issue Husband (1):
*883. William Lawrence[11] Raynor, b. 16 Sept
      1949, Southampton
 884. Carol Susan[11] Raynor, b. 22 July 1953,
      Port Jefferson; employed at
      Manufacturers Hanover Bank, and resides
      in East Elmhurst, L.I.
Issue Husband (2):
 885. Paul Reinhart[11] Fechtmann, b. 24 Sept
      1961, E. Patchogue; m. 21 Sept 1991 at
      the United Methodist Church,
      Westhampton, Susan Bannon, b. 13 June
      1961, Riverhead, d/o John Joseph and
      Anna (Malits) Bannon of Manorville.
      Paul is in business with his father in
      Speonk and Susan is a nurse. Residence:
      Manorville.
*886. Esther Marie[11] Fechtmann, b. 12 Oct 1963,
      E. Patchogue

685. EMMA LAVERNE[10] PENNY, dau. of Donald Remson
and Ethel Emma[9] (Raynor) Penny, b. 11 May 1914,
Good Ground (Hampton Bays); m. 3 Nov 1933 at the
East Moriches Methodist Church, Charles Gerald
Mades, b. 26 Jan 1913, d. 18 Apr 1960 after a
prolonged illness, s/o John and Mary Catherine
(Whitehurst) Mades of Beaufort, NC. At the time
of the 1938 hurricane, Charles Mades was
stationed at the Shinnecock Coast Guard Station
in Hampton Bays. With a wind velocity of
approximately 100 mph and tides 10 to 15 feet
above normal, along with 15 foot breakers, the
Coast Guard Station, including the watch house,
was swept away; a new inlet was formed just west
of the Coast Guard Station. Charles Mades and

the Coast Guard crew barely escaped with their
lives. Charles participated in maneuvers at
Camp Le Jeune, NC shortly before going overseas
on a troop ship in 1942 to the South Pacific and
helped to land the 1st Marine Division on Tulagi
and Guadalcanal in the Solomon Islands. He was
engaged in the Battles of both Guadalcanal and
Coral Sea. He retired in 1947 with a Service
connected disability after 17 years of service
in the Coast Guard.
Issue:
*887. C. Kenneth[11] Mades, b. 18 Apr 1938,
       Southampton
 888. Donald John[11] Mades, b. 20 Sept 1951,
       Southampton; resides in Hampton Bays.

688. EMMA KATHERINE ("KAY")[10] ROWE, dau. of
William D. and Isabel Matilda[9] (Raynor) Rowe, b.
12 Mar 1924; m. (1) 9 Apr 1952 in Compton, CA,
Daniel M. Ziemer; m. (2) _____ Schultz. Daniel
Ziemer was a surveyor with the Sanitation
Department in Compton, CA.
Issue Husband (1):
*889. Eric[11] Ziemer, b. 20 Sept 1953
*890. Mark[11] Ziemer, b. 8 Sept 1958

691. MAMIE ALEEN ("EILEEN")[10] ROWE, dau. of
William D. and Isabel Matilda[9] (Raynor) Rowe, b.
16 Dec 1930, d. ca 1984; m. _____ Brooker.
Issue:
*891. Sylvia[11] Brooker, b. 20 Jan 19__
*892. Ginnie[11] Brooker, b. 11 June 19__

693. HELEN L.[10] JARVIS, dau. of William Jacob
and Mary Ellen[9] (Raynor) Jarvis, b. 1895, d.
1984; m. Lyance G. Littlejohn, Sr., of North
Carolina, b. 1889, d. 1966; both bur.
Westhampton Cemetery.
Issue:
 893. Lorraine[11] Littlejohn, m. _____ Homan
 894. Lyance G.[11] Littlejohn, Jr.
 895. William L.[11] Littlejohn, d. 27 Aug 1921,

aged 2 days, bur. Westhampton Cemetery, with parents

696. LEONARD PRESCOTT[10] JARVIS, son of William Jacob and Mary Ellen[9] (Raynor) Jarvis, b. 15 Dec 1903, Southampton, d. 2 Jan 1976; m. 25 Dec 1928 at Cortland, NY, Catherine Bennett Reed, b. 27 Feb 1905, Syracuse, NY, d. 4 Mar 1987, Portland, OR; both bur. Westhampton Cemetery.
Issue:

*896. Reed Warren[11] Jarvis, b. 8 Nov 1932, NYC
 897. Nan Mary[11] Jarvis, b. 1 Sept 1940, Southampton, d. 25 Aug 1992, Portland, OR; m. 15 Sept 1979, Luther Jerstad. No issue.

699. RICHARD DWIGHT[10] CULVER, son of Richard Fowler and Helen Cook[9] (Rogers) Culver, of Kenilworth, IL
Issue:

 898. Richard Dwight[11] Culver, Jr.
 899. Deborah Ann[11] Culver
 900. Benson Rixon[11] Culver
 901. Lynn Rogers[11] Culver

701. LOUIS OLIVER[10] PARLATO, son of Michael J. and Kathryn E.[9] (Raynor) Parlato, b. 27 Jan 1910; m. Estelle Bouvier, of Buffalo, NY.
Issue:

 902. John[11] Parlato
 903. Robert[11] Parlato

702. KATHERINE MARIAN[10] PARLATO, dau. of Michael J. and Kathryn E.[9] (Raynor) Parlato, b. 12 Apr 1911; m. 24 June 1938, Thomas Henry Stevens, Jr., s/o Thomas Henry and Charlotte (Poole) Stevens.
Issue:

*904. Barbara Ann[11] Stevens, b. 14 Feb 1946, Southampton

703. MARY ANN[10] RAYNOR, dau. of Hubert I.[9] and
Estelle M. (Arnold) Raynor, m. John Bilyk, Jr.,
b. 16 Apr 1913, d. 3 Dec 1983.
Issue:
  905. Deirdre Ann[11] Bilyk, b. 31 Mar 1947; m.
    _____ Raymond.

704. HUBERT I.[10] RAYNOR, JR., son of Hubert I.[9]
and Estelle M. (Arnold) Raynor, b. 1922; m. Mary
Jane Havens, b. 5 June 1933, d. 17 Jan 1982,
bur. Remsenburg Cemetery.
Issue:
  906. Scott[11] Raynor
  907. Kathleen[11] Raynor

706. LOIS HALSEY[10] RAYNOR, dau. of Halsey Jacob[9]
and Eloise M. (Rogers) Raynor, b. 1 Sept 1922,
Remsenburg; m. 28 May 1948, Lloyd Osborne Davis,
b. 2 Oct 1918, Marshallberg, NC, s/o Eugene
Ordorner and Lillian (Matney) Davis. Residence:
Remsenburg.
Issue:
*908. Chary Ann Halsey[11] Davis, b. 14 Dec 1948
  909. Stephanie Osborne[11] Davis, b. 12 Oct 1958;
    a geologist, who lives in Walnut Creek,
    CA.
  910. Louisa Matney[11] Davis, b. 28 Jan 1962; a
    college administrator, who lives in
    North Hampton, MA.

707. JEAN EDITH[10] RAYNOR, dau. of Halsey Jacob[9]
and Eloise M. (Rogers) Raynor, b. 12 Feb 1924,
Remsenburg; m. 28 July 1945, Harold Beecher
Halsey, Jr., b. 14 Apr 1922, s/o Harold Beecher
and Amy C. (Stevens) Halsey, Sr. of Westhampton
Beach. Residence: Westhampton Beach.
Issue:
*911. Sandra Eloise[11] Halsey, b. 23 Feb 1950
  912. Harold Beecher[11] Halsey III, b. 4 Dec
    1953; m. Georgeann McGuinness, b. 22
    July 1958, d/o William McGuinness.

708. HARRISON EDMUND[10] TYTE, son of Arthur Milton and Miriam Grant[9] (Corwin) Tyte, Sr., b. 9 Apr 1891, Riverhead, d. 10 May 1979; m. 23 May 1913, Edna Squires Downs, b. 26 Sept 1890, d. 22 Feb 1957; both bur. Riverhead Cemetery.
Issue:

*913. Henry Harrison ("Harry")[11] Tyte, b. 8 May 1914, Riverhead

*914. Charles Edmond[11] Tyte, b. 6 Sept 1915, Riverhead, d. 17 Oct 1969, CT, bur. Riverhead Cemetery

*915. Margaret Edna[11] Tyte, b. 14 Dec 1916, Riverhead, d. 19 Nov 1985, East Berlin, PA. bur. Union Cemetery, East Berlin, PA

*916. Lois Ethel[11] Tyte, b. 21 Dec 1922, Riverhead

*917. Miriam Ellen[11] Tyte, b. 4 Aug 1932, Riverhead

709. STEPHEN ALEXANDER[10] TYTE, son of Arthur Milton and Miriam Grant[9] (Corwin) Tyte, Sr., b. 1 Jan 1893, Riverhead, d. 6 Jan 1981; m. 19 Oct 1929, Marjorie Young, b. 31 May 1892, Baiting Hollow, d. 23 May 1979, Riverhead; both bur. Riverhead Cemetery.
Issue:

*918. Helen Bedell[11] Tyte, b. 3 July 1932, Riverhead

919. Mary Alexander[11] Tyte, b. 14 Mar 1935, d. 6 May 1935, bur. Riverhead Cemetery

710. MARY ALTHEA TERRELL[10] TYTE, dau. of Arthur Milton and Miriam Grant[9] (Corwin) Tyte, Sr., b. 29 June 1901, Riverhead, d. 28 Dec 1981; m. 24 Dec 1927 by Rev. George W. Roesch, Kenneth Gardner Regent, b. 27 Mar 1904, Patchogue, d. 9 June 1980; both bur. Riverhead Cemetery.
Issue:

*920. Joan Carolyn[11] Regent, b. 20 Oct 1928, Riverhead, d. 25 June 1990, Cutchogue, L.I., bur. Shelter Island

*921. Marcia Adelle[11] Regent, b. 28 Mar 1932,
       Riverhead
*922. Donna Althea[11] Regent, b. 7 Feb 1939,
       Greenport

711. ARTHUR MILTON[10] TYTE, JR., son of Arthur
Milton and Miriam Grant[9] (Corwin) Tyte, Sr., b.
15 May 1904, Riverhead; m. (1) 8 Oct 1923,
Marian Elizabeth Downs, b. 5 Sept 1906, d. 5
July 1976; m. (2) 10 Sept 1978, Martha Wright
Hehl, b. 9 Mar 1917.
Issue Wife (1):
 923. William Graham[11] Tyte, b. Feb 1924, d. May
       1924, bur. Riverhead Cemetery
*924. Gene Elizabeth[11] Tyte, b. 17 May 1925,
       Riverhead
*925. Norman Arthur[11] Tyte, Sr., b. 2 Dec 1927,
       Riverhead, d. 12 Apr 1990
*926. Bruce Milton[11] Tyte, b. 28 Nov 1929
*927. Elinor Marian[11] Tyte, b. 24 Nov 1934,
       Riverhead
*928. Gail Ellen[11] Tyte, b. 24 July 1950,
       Greenport

712. WICKHAM CORWIN[10] TYTE, SR., son of Arthur
Milton and Miriam Grant[9] (Corwin) Tyte, Sr., b.
6 Mar 1911, Riverhead; m. 4 Aug 1935 at the
Westhampton Presbyterian Church, Frances
Rockwell Downs, b. 2 May 1917, Manorville, d. 28
Apr 1980, East Patchogue (heart attack), d/o
Frank Edward and Marcia Rockwell (Griffin)
Downs.
Issue:
*929. Carol Frances[11] Tyte, b. 4 June 1936,
       Greenport
*930. Betsey Ann[11] Tyte, b. 8 Aug 1937,
       Riverhead
*931. Shirley Marie[11] Tyte, b. 13 Sept 1938,
       Riverhead
*932. Wickham Corwin[11] Tyte, Jr., b. 9 Oct 1939,
       Riverhead, d. 10 Oct 1969, bur. Oakwood
       Cemetery, East Quogue

*933. Stephen Edward[11] Tyte, b. 1 Mar 1948,
     Greenport
*934. Naomi Ruth[11] Tyte, b. 18 Aug 1955,
     Riverhead

714. LEONE WOODHULL[10] CORWIN, son of Hubert
Florence[9] and Minnie Cornelia (Woodhull) Corwin,
b. 2 Nov 1903, Riverhead; m. 5 May 1927,
Clarissa A. ("Sis") Fleming, b. Brooklyn, d.
1994, Riverhead, ae 91 yrs., d/o William and
Amelia Fleming. Residence: Riverhead.
Issue:
*935. Mary Louise[11] Corwin, b. 7 Sept 1930
 936. Leone Harrison[11] Corwin, b. 9 July 1934,
      d. 28 Oct 1956, bur. Riverhead Cemetery
 937. Clarissa[11] Corwin, b. 23 July 1935; m. 5
      Apr 1980, James Roesler. Residence:
      Hauppauge, L.I.

715. FLORENCE ("FLOSSIE") MILLER[10] CORWIN, dau.
of Hubert Florence[9] and Minnie Cornelia
(Woodhull) Corwin, b. 2 Sept 1909; m. (1) 13 May
1933, James Nicholson, b. 2 Nov 1904, d. 27 Sept
1975; m. (2) John Albert Litchard.
Issue Husband (1):
 938. child[11] Nicholson
 939. child[11] Nicholson
 940. child[11] Nicholson

717. MURIEL[10] CORWIN, dau. of Hubert Florence[9]
and Minnie Cornelia (Woodhull) Corwin, b. 13
June 1917; m. (1) Orville B. ("Bub") Brown; m.
(2) _____ _____. Residence: Florida and
Ephrata, PA.
Issue Husband (1):
 941. son[11] Brown
 942. son[11] Brown

718. ANTOINETTE[10] CLARK, dau. of Halsey and
Elizabeth[9] (Smith) Clark, m. _____ Ferguson
Issue:

111

943. Antoinette[11] Ferguson, m. Ira Stevens, s/o Edward H. Stevens of Westhampton Beach; residence: Westhampton.

729. DOROTHY[10] JOURNEY (?), dau. of George and Leila[9] (Baker) Journey (?), m. Merton Van Cott
Issue:
944. Alma[11] Van Cott

736. MARGARET I.[10] SATTERLY, dau. of Lewis W. and Clara L.[9] (Gildersleeve) Satterly, b. 9 Nov 1920; m. 3 May 1939, Vernon D. Hawkins of Eastport, b. 14 Nov 1916, s/o William W. and Elsie C. (Blind) Hawkins.
Issue:
*945. Leigh Davidson[11] Hawkins, b. 30 June 1940, Southampton
*946. Brian Satterly[11] Hawkins, b. 24 Mar 1942, Southampton
*947. Jon Ward[11] Hawkins, b. 6 Nov 1945, Southampton
*948. Wendy Margaret[11] Hawkins, b. 8 Feb 1955, Riverhead

742. LOUISE WANDA[10] RAYNOR, dau. of Lester White[9] and Marie Frances (Lee) Raynor, b. 20 Feb 1929; m. 6 Mar 1954, Richard Allan Pearce, b. 29 Sept 1925. Louise graduated from Russell Sage College and was a teacher.
Issue:
*949. Lynne Raynor[11] Pearce, b. 13 June 1955
*950. David Richard[11] Pearce, b. 7 Nov 1957

747. DOUGLAS C.[10] RAYNOR, son of Wilmun Halsey[9] and Dolly Eleanor (Crawford) Raynor, b. 4 May 1930; m. (1) Kaye L. Doss; m. (2) Anita J. Feltman.
Issue Wife (1):
951. child[11] Raynor
952. child[11] Raynor
953. child[11] Raynor

954. child[11] Raynor
Issue Wife (2):
955. child[11] Raynor

748. LEROY RAYNOR[10] DUNWELL, son of Percy Leroy and Edith McKay[9] (Raynor) Dunwell, b. 16 Oct 1926; m. 14 Oct 1956 in the First Presbyterian Church, Southampton, Cynthia Ann Powell, b. 30 Oct 1932, d/o Howard Earl and Helen Elizabeth (Corey) Powell.
Issue:
*956. Laurie Ann[11] Dunwell, b. 11 Aug 1957
957. LeRoy Raynor[11] Dunwell, Jr., b. 21 July 1958; m. Sandra L. Schreiber.

749. DOROTHY SEELY[10] DUNWELL, dau. of Percy Leroy and Edith McKay[9] (Raynor) Dunwell, b. 24 July 1931, Southampton; m. 11 Nov 1951 at the Bridgehampton United Methodist Church, Raymond Halsey Topping, b. 17 Nov 1927, Southampton. Residence: Bridgehampton.
Issue:
*958. Raymond Halsey[11] Topping, Jr., b. 29 Apr 1954, Southampton
*959. Diane Gail[11] Topping, b. 5 Nov 1956, Southampton
*960. Leanne Joy[11] Topping, b. 1 Dec 1960, Southampton

754. PIERSON TUTHILL[10] RAYNOR, son of Elijah Pierson[9] and Blanche Rogers (Learie) Raynor, b. 7 Mar 1912; m. 24 May 1941 in Baltimore, MD, Anne Margaret Kuhlemann, d/o G. Frederick Kuhlemann. Residence: Maryland.
Issue:
*961. Ellen[11] Raynor, b. 29 Apr 1954
962. Peggy[11] Raynor, b. 13 Jan 1957, d. 20 Apr 1965

755. CHARLES HOMER[10] RAYNOR, son of Elijah Pierson[9] and Blanche Rogers (Learie) Raynor, b.

12 July 1919; m. Marjorie Holmes, b. 27 Sept 1920, Red Bank, NJ. Residence: Fair Haven, NJ. Issue:

*963. Douglas Preston[11] Raynor, b. 24 Sept 1947, Red Bank, NJ

*964. Robert Pierson[11] Raynor, b. 17 Feb 1951, Red Bank, NJ

756. WILLIAM THEODORE ("BILL")[10] HULSE, JR., son of William Theodore and Charlotte Elizabeth[9] (Raynor) Hulse, b. 16 June 1918, Westhampton Beach; m. 17 June 1942 in Jacksonville, FL, Ella Brown Hawkins Randall, b. 31 Jan 1921, Quiogue, d. 24 Nov 1987, Southampton, bur. Westhampton Cemetery. Bill is a mechanic; Ella was a teacher. Bill still (1994) resides in the house in which he was born, on Griffing Avenue, Westhampton Beach. Issue:

*965. William Randall[11] Hulse, b. 17 Mar 1943, Southampton

757. THEODORE ORREN ("DODE")[10] HULSE, son of William Theodore and Charlotte Elizabeth[9] (Raynor) Hulse, b. 17 Jan 1923, d. 30 May 1989, Easton, PA, bur. Westhampton Cemetery; m. 8 Dec 1946, Clara Elaine Culver, of Westhampton Beach, b. 24 July 1927, d/o Harold Field and Ethel Laura (Mueller) Culver. "Dode" was Mayor of Westhampton Beach, following in his father's footsteps. Issue:

*966. Charlotte Ethel[11] Hulse, b. 23 Aug 1948, Greenburgh, NY

967. Harold William[11] Hulse, b. 31 Dec 1952, d. 1 Jan 1953, Riverhead, bur. Westhampton Cemetery

*968. Betsy Morrison[11] Hulse, b. 24 Nov 1957, Riverhead

969. Charles Louis[11] Hulse, b. 22 Feb 1960, Riverhead

970. Jamie Allyson[11] Hulse, b. 16 Sept 1965, Riverhead

758. MARION GENEVIEVE[10] RAYNOR, dau. of Clifford
Tuttle[9] and Genevieve Adele (Halsey) Raynor, b.
29 June 1921, Quiogue, Westhampton Beach; m. (1)
19 June 1941 at Westhampton Beach, Richard
Edward Ribeiro, of Riverhead; m. (2) Harry
Ellsworth Van Tassel, of Maryland. Residence:
Westhampton Beach.
Issue Husband (1):

*971. Richard Edward (Ribeiro)[11] Van Tassel, b.
10 Mar 1942, Southampton
Issue Husband (2):

*972. Kurt Raynor[11] Van Tassel, b. 6 Mar 1948
973. Gretchen Marion[11] Van Tassel, b. 7 May
1950; m. (1) Kevin Kelly; m. (2) Robert
Kirby; no issue. Residence: Fincastle,
VA.

759. DOROTHY HALSEY[10] RAYNOR, dau. of Clifford
Tuttle[9] and Genevieve Adele (Halsey) Raynor, b.
17 Mar 1924, Quiogue, Westhampton Beach; m.
William McGonigle. Residence: Haddonfield, NJ.
Issue:

*974. W. David[11] McGonigle
*975. Richard C.[11] McGonigle
*976. Kyle Raynor[11] McGonigle

761. JEAN M.[10] HULSE, dau. of Seth Wells and
Elsa E.[9] (Raynor) Hulse, m. Joseph Licopky;
residence: Chagrin Falls, OH.
Issue:

977. Robert[11] Licopky
978. Carl[11] Licopky

762. FLOYD[10] HULSE, son of Seth Wells and Elsa
E.[9] (Raynor) Hulse, m. (1) Joan Wegert; m. (2)
Barbara Wright; m. (3) Cynthia LeMinn.
Issue Wife (3):

979. John[11] Hulse, b. 12 Dec 1968
980. Marc[11] Hulse, b. 15 Nov 1970

765. HELEN LOUISE[10] RAYNOR, dau. of William Frederick[9] and Helen Page (Scribner) Raynor, b. 19 Feb 1916; m. Nov 1940, Wilbur Hampton Benjamin, Jr., of Westhampton, s/o Wilbur Hampton Benjamin, Sr.
Issue:
- 981. Wade H.[11] Benjamin, b. 23 Oct 1949, Oceanside, L.I., d. 7 July 1986, bur. Westhampton Cemetery
- 982. Sandra B.[11] Benjamin, m. (1) William Wilson; m. (2) Theodore Walser.

766. MARCIA PAGE[10] RAYNOR, dau. of William Frederick[9] and Helen Page (Scribner) Raynor, b. 21 June 1923, d. 25 Mar 1991, Portland, ME, bur. Westhampton Cemetery; m. James Edgar.
Issue:
- *983. William T.[11] Edgar, b. 19 Dec 1944, Southampton

770. STUART PAYNE[10] HOWELL, JR., son of Stuart Payne and Carrie Marguerite[9] (Raynor) Howell, b. 8 Dec 1928, Southampton; m. 20 Nov 1954 in Neubrücke, Germany, Katharina Elisabeth Herber, b. 21 Nov 1926, Oberkirchen/Saar, Germany, d/o Johann and Rosina (Dausend) Herber, of Oberkirchen. Residence: Exeter, NH.
Issue:
- *984. Mark Bryan[11] Howell, b. 28 July 1958, Riverhead
- *985. Hans-Christian[11] Howell, b. 29 Apr 1961, Riverhead

771. MARGERY DEFORREST[10] RAYNOR, dau. of Kenneth Alan[9] and Catherine Isabel (Jessup) Raynor, b. 29 June 1919; m. 29 Mar 1937, Thomas Schunk. Residence: Westhampton Beach.
Issue:
- *986. Robert Allen[11] Schunk, b. 12 Sept 1938
- 987. Alice Margaret[11] Schunk, b. 24 Sept 1941, d. Dec 1941
- 988. William[11] Schunk, b. 10 Dec 1954; m. 18

Jan 1985, Karen Holley.

772. ELIZABETH ELLISON[10] **RAYNOR**, dau. of Kenneth
Alan[9] and Catherine Isabel (Jessup) Raynor, b.
20 July 1920; m. (1) Jack Foust; m. (2) 1 Jan
1955, Andrew Barnish, b. 29 May 1920.
Residence: Westhampton Beach.
Issue Husband (1):
*989. Harold ("Buddy")[11] Foust, b. 7 Aug 1946

773. CATHERINE ISABEL[10] **RAYNOR**, dau. of Kenneth
Alan[9] and Catherine Isabel (Jessup) Raynor, b. 9
Feb 1922, d. 12 Oct 1978; m. (1) Herman L.
Bishop, s/o Herman F. and Lucy (Liedtke) Bishop;
m. (2) Gordon L. Lyons, Sr.
Issue Husband (1):
*990. Jo Ann[11] Bishop, b. ca 1946
 991. Lynn[11] Bishop, b. 3 Oct 1947
 992. Herman John[11] Bishop, twin, b. 29 July
       1948; m. 12 Aug 1979, Eileen Phieffer.
*993. Bonnie[11] Bishop, twin, b. 29 July 1948

774. WINIFRED ANN[10] **RAYNOR**, dau. of Kenneth
Alan[9] and Catherine Isabel (Jessup) Raynor, b. 4
Dec 1927; m. (1) 15 Oct 1950, Richard Lashley,
b. 26 Mar 1926, d. 21 Nov 1951, Westhampton
(killed by a train), bur. Westhampton Cemetery,
s/o Clarence J. and Elizabeth Lashley; m. (2) 1
Nov 1953, Carl Eugene Cardo, of Quogue, b. 8
July 1929. Residence: Quogue.
Issue Husband (2):
*994. Charles Kenneth[11] Cardo, b. 12 Feb 1955
*995. Randy Jay[11] Cardo, b. 8 Sept 1957

775. BARBARA JANE[10] **RAYNOR**, dau. of Kenneth
Alan[9] and Catherine Isabel (Jessup) Raynor, b.
14 Sept 1933; m. 8 Oct 1955, Raymond S. Andrews.
Residence: Water Mill, L.I.
Issue:
*996. Cathy D.[11] Andrews, b. 1 May 1957

776. JEANNETTE[10] RAYNOR, dau. of James Madison[9] and Gertrude (Blair) Raynor, b. 2 Mar 1925, d. 10 Apr 1993, Tallahassee, FL, bur. McNair-Black Cemetery, Hosford, FL; m. 10 Jan 1948, George Black, b. 10 Feb 1918.
Issue:

*997. Nancy Elizabeth[11] Black, b. 7 Mar 1951

998. James Blair[11] Black, b. 10 June 1954; m. 27 Sept 1980, Ricki Berner, b. 17 Oct 1954. Residence: Maitland, FL.

*999. Ruth Ellen[11] Black, b. 20 Aug 1956

*1000. Margaret Elecia[11] Black, b. 20 Oct 1958

*1001. Marsha Jeannette[11] Black, b. 30 Sept 1960

1002. Neil George[11] Black, b. 12 May 1965; residence: Tallahassee, FL.

777. JAMES MADISON[10] RAYNOR, JR., son of James Madison[9] and Gertrude (Blair) Raynor, b. 10 Jan 1930, Westhampton Beach, d. 28 Feb 1985, Virginia Beach, VA (primary biliary cirrhosis), ae 55 yrs., plaque at Westhampton Cemetery; m. (1) Janet Dutschman; m. (2) Rita Ann Santi, d/o Henry and Jessie Santi; m. (3) Joyce Mercurio; m. (4) Ann Thou. A graduate of Syracuse University, "Jim" was a musician and involved in the construction business.
Issue Wife (1):

1003. James Mitchell[11] Raynor, m. Debbie Thou, d/o Ann Thou.

Issue Wife (2):

1004. Amanda Jane[11] Raynor, twin, b. 2 Jan 1965, Riverhead; m. 2 June 1990, Scott McChesney.

1005. Clay Madison[11] Raynor, twin, b. 2 Jan 1965, Riverhead

1006. Chad Harrison[11] Raynor, b. 26 June 1970

778. CAROL ELIZABETH[10] RAYNOR, dau. of Emerson Mitchell[9] and Ruth Carol (Haviland) Raynor, b. 2 June 1924; m. 26 June 1948, Richard Irving Hornbeck, of New Canaan, CT. Residence: Stuart, FL.

Issue:
1007.Sahler[11] Hornbeck
1008.Stephanie[11] Hornbeck
1009.Susan[11] Hornbeck

779. PRISCILLA[10] RAYNOR, dau. of Emerson
Mitchell[9] and Ruth Carol (Haviland) Raynor, b.
27 Aug 1928; m. 13 June 1950, William Barringer.
Residence: Stuart, FL.
Issue:
1010.Robin[11] Barringer, b. 13 June 1951
1011.John[11] Barringer, b. 9 Feb 1955

781. HAROLD J.[10] RAYNOR, son of Townsend
Richard[9] and Luranna (Jimmerson) Raynor, b.
1896; m. Grace Reilly.
Issue:
1012.Harold J.[11] Raynor, Jr., b. 1928; m. E.
     Turner
1013.Ruth[11] Raynor, b. 1929
1014.Richard Locke[11] Raynor

784. JOHN ROBERT[10] WOODHULL, son of Herbert Case
and Helen Christine[9] (Moore) Woodhull, b. 27
June 1918, Patchogue, d. 23 May 1975, Baldwin,
NY; m. 1 Sept 1941, Oklahoma, Algie Nora Silsbe,
b. 18 May 1915, Jacksonville, FL, d. 24 July
1974, East Meadow, NY, bur. Patchogue, d/o
Harold and Janie (Farmer) Silsbe.
Issue:
1015.Barbara Jane[11] Woodhull, b. 11 May 1943;
     m. 27 Nov 1965, Gerald Wayne Kircher.
1016.John Robert[11] Woodhull, Jr., b. 7 July
     1951; m. Paula Foley.
1017.Thomas Alan[11] Woodhull, b. 21 Feb 1955, d.
     11 Sept 1990; m. Donna Anderson.

785. RICHARD MOORE[10] WOODHULL, son of Herbert
Case and Helen Christine[9] (Moore) Woodhull, b.
30 Aug 1922, Patchogue; m. 1 Dec 1946 in the
Gardendale Baptist Church, Gardendale, AL, Mary

Virginia Jackson, b. 1 Sept 1922, Birmingham,
AL, d/o Henry Fraley and Berlie (Russell)
Jackson.
Issue:
1018. Susan Mary[11] Woodhull, b. 28 Nov 1948; m.
12 Sept 1970, Gary Bane.
1019. Glenn Richard[11] Woodhull, b. 11 Nov 1951;
m. 27 Aug 1976, Virginia Ellen Hull.
1020. Nancy Jean[11] Woodhull, b. 21 Dec 1952; m.
7 Nov 1981, Daniel Robert Bailey.

Eleventh Generation

794. JEFFREY TERHUNE[11] SIMMONS, son of Russell
Terry[10] and Jean Annette (Terhune) Simmons, b.
28 Feb 1946, Oak Park, IL; m. 19 Dec 1970 at New
York City, Diane Beverly Curtis, b. 28 Nov 1944,
Washington, D.C.
Issue:
1021. Matthew Ryan[12] Simmons, b. 12 Aug 1974,
Chicago Heights, IL

795. STEPHEN ARTHUR[11] SIMMONS, son of Russell
Terry[10] and Jean Annette (Terhune) Simmons, b.
18 June 1950, Oak Park, IL; m. 14 Aug 1976 at
Riverside, IL, Cynthia Leslie, b. 8 Jan 19__.
Issue:
1022. Mark Leslie[12] Simmons, b. 14 Jan 1980,
Medford, OR

800. JANICE RAY[11] THOGMARTIN, dau. of Orville
Wayne and Treva May[10] (Breese) Thogmartin, b. 15
Sept 1933, Morris, IL, d. 20 Apr 1990; m. 14 Jan
1955, Frank Armour, b. 3 Mar 1931.
Issue:
1023. Thomas Wayne[12] Armour, b. 21 Dec 1955; m.
Nov 1978, Edye _____.
1024. Patrick Steven[12] Armour, b. 3 Feb 1957
1025. Laura Rae[12] Armour, b. 13 Sept 1958
1026. Jon David[12] Armour, b. 22 Feb 1961
1027. Neil Douglas[12] Armour, b. 15 Mar 1965,

d. Aug 1980 in an auto accident

801. VERN MAC[11] THOGMARTIN, son of Orville Wayne and Treva May[10] (Breese) Thogmartin, m. (1) 31 Oct 1954, Mary Catherine Jefferson, b. 11 Dec 1936; m. (2) Nov 1966, Suzie Brownfield; m. (3) 1975, Phyllis Warren Schott.
Issue Wife (1):
*1028.Lisa Ann[12] Thogmartin, b. 9 Aug 1955
1029.Kim Marie[12] Thogmartin, b. 4 Jan 1957
Issue Wife (2):
1030.Wayne James Brian[12] Thogmartin, b. Jan 1968
Issue Wife (3):
1031.Timothy Warren[12] Thogmartin, b. 9 Mar 1981

802. WAYNE KENT[11] THOGMARTIN, son of Orville Wayne and Treva May[10] (Breese) Thogmartin, m. 22 Aug 1964, Marilyn Kay Tennill, b. 11 July 1942.
Issue:
1032.David Kent[12] Thogmartin, b. 14 Jan 1971
1033.Bret Allen[12] Thogmartin, b. 1 Mar 1972
1034.Christopher[12] Thogmartin, b. 9 May 1976

803. JON BREES[11] THOGMARTIN, son of Orville Wayne and Treva May[10] (Breese) Thogmartin, m. (1) 1 Sept 1962, Marilyn Kay Winscott, b. 11 Oct 1943; m. (2) Apr 1977, Amy Lewis; m. (3) 1989, Dede Bazyk.
Issue Wife (1):
1035.Wayne Edward[12] Thogmartin, b. 9 Nov 1966
1036.Bret[12] Thogmartin, b. 1 Mar 1972

804. MARLENE ANN[11] RHINES, dau. of Merle A. and Thelma Joyce[10] (Breese) Rhines, b. 26 Dec 1935, Ottawa, IL; m. 13 Apr 1957, James E. Farrell, b. 9 Mar 1934.
Issue:
1037.Sandra Joyce[12] Farrell, b. 31 July 1965
1038.Barbara Ann[12] Farrell, twin, b. 17 Dec 1969

1039.Pamela Ann[12] Farrell, twin, b. 17 Dec
1969; m. 26 May 1990, Christopher
Whalen, b. 25 Feb 1969.

805. JAMES[11] SINGER, son of Warren and Roma
Adele[10] (Breese) Singer, b. 24 Apr 1951; m. Ruth
Ellen _____.
Issue:
1040.Jeffrey[12] Singer
1041.Jennifer[12] Singer

807. RICHARD COREY[11] BECKWITH, son of George
Corey and Anna Millicent[10] (Raynor) Beckwith, b.
23 Apr 1922, Quogue, L.I.; m. 15 Jan 1956 at the
Westhampton Presbyterian Church, Marjorie Evelyn
Helms, b. 22 Apr 1931, Hempstead, L.I.
Issue:
1042.Cheryl Ann[12] Beckwith, b. 11 July 1956,
Riverhead; m. 16 Apr 1982 at the
Presbyterian Chapel, Quogue, Gregory
Van Tuyle, b. 19 Feb 1953, Chicago, IL.
1043.Richard Corey[12] Beckwith, Jr., b. 19 Jan
1958, Riverhead

809. HERBERT CLARENCE[11] RAYNOR, son of Clarence
Elisha[10] and Lucretia Irene (Thode) Raynor, b.
19 Apr 1927, Westhampton; m. 3 Nov 1951 in NYC,
Patricia Winters, b. 25 Sept 1927, Southampton.
Issue:
1044.Denise Lee[12] Raynor, b. 22 Jan 1954,
Southampton; m. 20 Aug 1983 at
Southampton, Dennis Connors, b. 27 Nov
1927.
*1045.Dawn Marie[12] Raynor, b. 11 Feb 1956,
Southampton
1046.David Frederick[12] Raynor, b. 5 May 1960,
Southampton

810. GEORGE DAVIS[11] RAYNOR, son of Clarence
Elisha[10] and Lucretia Irene (Thode) Raynor, b. 4
Apr 1929, Westhampton, d. 9 Apr 1968,
Westhampton Beach; m. 29 June 1950 at St. Mary's

Church, Hampton Bays, Pamela Rierl, b. 25 Apr 1934, Brooklyn.
Issue:
*1047.Sharon Lee[12] Raynor, b. 26 Oct 1950, Southampton
*1048.George Thomas[12] Raynor, b. 16 Oct 1952, Riverhead
*1049.Mark Rierl[12] Raynor, b. 29 Aug 1954, Riverhead
*1050.Christopher Carl[12] Raynor, b. 6 Sept 1960, Riverhead
1051.Matthew Paul[12] Raynor, b. 3 May 1963, Riverhead, d. 16 Apr 1981, Westhampton

811. LILLIAN ANN[11] RAYNOR, dau. of Clarence Elisha[10] and Lucretia Irene (Thode) Raynor, b. 28 Dec 1931, Westhampton Beach; m. (1) 3 Sept 1949 at West Methodist Church, Westhampton, Richard Allen Bell, b. 14 Feb 1927, Speonk, d. 20 Feb 1986; m. (2) May 1955 at Westhampton Beach, Garrett Miller, b. 28 June 1931, Glenside, PA; m. (3) 23 Nov 1980, at Barton, NY, James A. Gowan, b. 14 Feb 1932.
Issue Husband (1):
1052.Robin Allen[12] Bell, b. 5 Sept 1950, Brockport, NY
*1053.Candice Ann[12] Bell, b. 27 May 1952, Brockport, NY
Issue Husband (2):
*1054.Dee Ellen[12] Miller, b. 8 Sept 1955, Allentown, PA
*1055.Garrett Emory[12] Miller III, b. 28 Aug 1956, Bellefonte, PA
*1056.Terrence Lee[12] Miller, b. 16 Feb 1959, Bellefonte, PA
*1057.Melissa Leigh[12] Miller, b. 16 Sept 1962, Bellefonte, PA

812. CORA LEE[11] RAYNOR, dau. of Clarence Elisha[10] and Lucretia Irene (Thode) Raynor, b. 9 Jan 1935, Westhampton Beach; m. (1) 12 Feb 1953, Joseph Francis Kametler, b. 13 Sept 1932,

Allentown, PA; m. (2) _____ Wegert.
Issue Husband (1):
1058.Michael Joseph[12] Kametler, b. 17 Sept
     1953, Riverhead, d. 11 Sept 1956,
     Austin, TX
*1059.James William[12] Kametler, b. 11 Sept 1956,
     Austin, TX
*1060.Robert Brian[12] Kametler, b. 19 Aug 1957,
     Riverhead
1061.Kathleen Irene[12] Kametler, b. 29 Jan 1959,
     Bethlehem, PA
1062.John Joseph[12] Kametler, b. 3 Sept 1963, Ft
     Dix, NJ
1063.Christopher Michael[12] Kametler, b. 2 Mar
     1972, Riverhead
Issue Husband (2):
1064.Terri Ann[12] Wegert, b. 7 July 1974,
     Riverhead
1065.Bradley David[12] Wegert, twin, b. 4 Dec
     1976, Southampton
1066.Daniel Paul[12] Wegert, twin, b. 4 Dec 1976,
     Southampton

813. MILTON ERNEST[11] RAYNOR, son of Clarence
Elisha[10] and Lucretia Irene (Thode) Raynor, b. 1
Oct 1940, Westhampton Beach; m. 6 Oct 1962 at
Beach Methodist Church, Westhampton Beach,
Martha C. Seitz, b. 18 July 1940, NYC.
Issue:
1067.Eric Russell[12] Raynor, twin, b. 15 June
     1971, Southampton
1068.George Alexander[12] Raynor, twin, b. 15
     June 1971, Southampton

814. CLARENCE HENRY[11] RAYNOR, son of Clarence
Elisha[10] and Lucretia Irene (Thode) Raynor, b. 1
June 1943, Southampton; m. 29 June 1963 at
Immaculate Conception Church, Westhampton Beach,
Diane Giorgi, b. 19 Dec 1944, Brooklyn.
Issue:
1069.Charles Henry[12] Raynor, b. 24 Oct 1967,
     Southampton

*1070.Leanne Barbara^{12} Raynor, b. 4 Nov 1969,
      Southampton
1071.Dyana Rose^{12} Raynor, b. 13 Mar 1972,
      Southampton

815. RICHARD ROBERT^{11} RAYNOR, son of Clarence
Elisha^{10} and Lucretia Irene (Thode) Raynor, b. 7
Oct 1946; m. 28 Aug 1971 at Setauket, Susan
Bindseil, b. 28 Sept 1950, d. 1984.
Issue:
1072.Eli William^{12} Raynor, b. 8 Sept 1975, Port
      Jefferson
1073.Jacob Richard^{12} Raynor, b. 3 Dec 1979,
      Port Jefferson

816. DAVID EUGENE^{11} RAYNOR, son of David
Lester^{10} and Marguerite Josephine (Keck) Raynor,
b. 10 Mar 1943; m. 30 May 1965, Lida Carter, of
Nova Scotia and East Quogue, b. 30 Dec 1941.
Residence: East Quogue.
Issue:
*1074.James David^{12} Raynor, b. 14 Nov 1965
1075.Jonathan Douglas^{12} Raynor, b. 15 Nov 1971;
      residence: East Quogue.

817. FAITH MILLICENT^{11} RAYNOR, dau. of David
Lester^{10} and Marguerite Josephine (Keck) Raynor,
b. 1 Apr 1946; m. 9 May 1971, Allen Robert
Stewart, Jr., b. 22 Nov 1941. Residence:
Westhampton Beach.
Issue:
1076.Stacey Ann^{12} Stewart, b. 22 Jan 1976;
      residence: Westhampton Beach.

820. JULIA EMMA^{11} RAYNOR, dau. of Everett
Clark^{10} and Marian Scudder (Hallock) Raynor, b.
19 Nov 1925, Speonk, L.I.; m. (1) Daniel J.
Galvin; m. (2) 4 July 1962, Ronald M. Loff.
Issue Husband (1):
*1077.Susan Priscilla^{12} Galvin, b. 18 Mar 1947,
       California

*1078.Daniel J.^{12} Galvin, Jr., b. 24 June 1950,
    California
*1079.Charles Everett^{12} Galvin, b. 27 Apr 1955,
    California

822. KAREN LOUISA^{11} RAYNOR, dau. of Everett
Clark^{10} and Marian Scudder (Hallock) Raynor, b.
24 Sept 1938, Southampton; m. 27 Dec 1956,
George L. Mauger.
Issue:
*1080.David L.^{12} Mauger, b. 15 Mar 1961, Arizona
*1081.Catherine G.^{12} Mauger, b. 3 May 1964,
    California

828. RUTH LOUISE^{11} RAYNOR, dau. of Charles
Marvin^{10} and Marian Louise (Payne) Raynor, b. 20
June 1945, Southampton; m. 18 Nov 1967 in the
Westhampton Presbyterian Church, Henry Schaffner
Lapp, b. 6 Sept 1944.
Issue:
  1082.Michael Alexander^{12} Lapp, b. 8 Apr 1971,
    Fairborn, OH
  1083.Katherine Louise^{12} Lapp, b. 28 July 1974,
    Dayton, OH

829. BEATRICE EILEEN^{11} RAYNOR, dau. of Charles
Marvin^{10} and Marian Louise (Payne) Raynor, b. 16
Nov 1949, Southampton; m. 18 Sept 1971 in the
Westhampton Presbyterian Church, Stephen Mason
Marcks, b. 21 Sept 1948. Beatrice was awarded
B.S. and M.S. degrees by Syracuse University.
Issue:
  1084.Peter Mason^{12} Marcks, b. 20 July 1980,
    Southampton
  1085.Melissa Raynor^{12} Marcks, b. 10 July 1984,
    Southampton

830. ARTHUR DANIEL^{11} RAYNOR, son of Daniel
Tuttle^{10} and Irene Marie (Cody) Raynor, b. 30
May 1920, Brooklyn, NY; m. 1 Jan 1944, at
Tampa, FL, Marguerite L. Day, b. 18 Feb 1923,
Jacksonville, FL, d/o Lonnie and Evelyn M.

(Seals) Day. Arthur is a musician, Mason, Life
Member of Kiwanis International, a Veteran of
World War II, and founder of the Raynor Family
Association. Arthur and Marguerite reside in
Bartow, FL.
Issue:
*1086.Pearle Marie[12] Raynor, b. 8 Apr 1945,
     Tampa, FL
*1087.Dayl Evelyn[12] Raynor, b. 25 Aug 1947,
     Tampa, FL

831. FRANCES LOUISE[11] RAYNOR, dau. of Daniel
Tuttle[10] and Irene Marie (Cody) Raynor, b. 21
June 1923, Brooklyn, N.Y.; m. (1) Robert F.
Hanley; m. (2) Salvatore Bisesi, b. 26 Aug 1926,
Baltimore, MD.
Issue Husband (1):
*1088.Kathleen[12] Hanley, b. 13 May 1944, Key
     West, FL
Issue Husband (2):
1089.Susan[12] Bisesi, b. 8 Oct 1955, Baltimore,
     MD

833. THOMAS LAMPHERE[11] GOULD, son of Frank
Datson and Florence Jerusha[10] (Grimshaw) Gould,
Sr., m. Diane Elizabeth Chillingworth.
Issue:
1090.Georgianna Grimshaw[12] Gould

835. HARRY ARNOLD[11] PUGH, JR., son of Harry
Arnold and Rose Helene[10] (Grimshaw) Pugh, m.
Madeline Stevens.
Issue:
1091.Robert Marcel[12] Pugh, m. Mary Anne McGuire
1092.Rodney[12] Pugh
1093.Michael[12] Pugh
1094.William[12] Pugh

836. RODNEY WILLIAM[11] PUGH, son of Harry Arnold
and Rose Helene[10] (Grimshaw) Pugh, m. Helen Ann
Gardner.

Issue:
1095. Randell Gardner[12] Pugh, m. Timothy Edward Landreth
1096. Gordon Grimshaw[12] Pugh

838. FRED GOULD[11] PALMER, JR., son of Fred Gould and Lilla Madelyn[10] (Grimshaw) Palmer, m. Shirley Inez Culver.
Issue:
*1097. Susan Lee[12] Palmer
*1098. Fred Gould[12] Palmer III
*1099. Cynthia Louise[12] Palmer

842. MARLEIGH ANNE[11] RAYNOR, dau. of Walter Raleigh[10] and Martha E. (Fenn) Raynor, b. 31 July 1941; m. 16 Jan 1971, Chester A. Swalina.
Issue:
1100. Chester Walter[12] Swalina, b. 6 Feb 1974

844. RACHEL LORRAINE[11] RAYNOR, dau. of George Lafayette[10] and Lorraine Irene (Lavelle) Raynor, b. 10 Sept 1961.
Issue:
1101. Leah Jeanne[12] Raynor, b. 28 June 1990

845. TERRY LYNN[11] RAYNOR, dau. of Robert A.[10] and Mildred (Skidmore) Raynor, m. 29 June 1963 in England, Rae Maw.
Issue:
1102. Michael Howard[12] Raynor, b. 6 Apr 1972

848. SANDRA VIRGINIA[11] RAYNOR, dau. of Robert A.[10] and Mildred (Skidmore) Raynor, b. 25 June 1941, Southampton; m. (1) Russell Leibig; m. (2) 16 Apr 1977, Rocco Oliveto.
Issue Husband (1):
1103. Russell Glenn[12] Leibig, b. 6 Mar 1962; m. 16 Sept 1989, Edna Jean Shefler.
1104. Denise Rae[12] Leibig, b. 27 Mar 1965; m. 15 Sept 1990, Thomas Olsen.

849. WILMUN JESSE[11] HALSEY, son of Charles Henry and Frances Jean[10] (Raynor) Halsey, b. 3 Nov 1943, Southampton; m. 21 Sept 1968 in Westhampton, Brenda James. Residence: Westhampton.
Issue:
   1105.Tonya Jean[12] Halsey, b. 29 Nov 1969, Southampton

850. CHESTER SIDNEY ("SID")[11] RAYNOR III, son of Chester Sidney[10] and Lorraine Irene (Lavelle) Raynor, Jr., b. 21 June 1939, Southampton; m. Gail Heileman. Residence: Hampton Bays.
Issue:
*1106.Chester Sidney ("Corky")[12] Raynor IV
*1107.Paul[12] Raynor, b. 13 July 1964

853. JUDITH ANN[11] CLARK, dau. of William Francis and Virginia Mae[10] (Raynor) Clark, b. 27 June 1946; m. Hugh B. Hall. Residence: Lexington, KY.
Issue:
   1108.Ashley[12] Hall
   1109.Ben[12] Hall

854. SUSAN ELIZABETH[11] CLARK, dau. of William Francis and Virginia Mae[10] (Raynor) Clark, b. 24 Feb 1949; m. (1) Steve Greenburg; m. (2) Dr. Bill Wilkes of Richmond, VA. Residence: Richmond, VA.
Issue Husband (1):
   1110.Brooke[12] Greenburg

855. JOHN RUSSELL[11] CLARK, son of William Francis and Virginia Mae[10] (Raynor) Clark, b. 11 Jan 1953; m. Karen Dillaplane. Residence: Lexington, KY.
Issue:
   1111.Brittany[12] Clark
   1112.Courtney[12] Clark
   1113.Jessica Raynor[12] Clark

857. BUFORD ALLEN[11] SHORT, JR., son of Buford
Allen and Helen Elizabeth[10] (Raynor) Short, b.
30 Mar 1955, Lexington, KY; m. (1) Jacqueline
Good; m. (2) Vickie Lee Hobbs. Buford Allen
owns and operates a scuba diving shop in
Owensboro, KY.
Issue Wife (2):
   1114.Grant[12] Short

858. VIRGINIA-EARL WILSON[11] SHORT, dau. of
Buford Allen and Helen Elizabeth[10] (Raynor)
Short, b. 17 Dec 1957, Lexington, KY; m. 5 Feb
1983, George Brain Wolfe. Virginia is a
businesswoman and George is an attorney in
Columbia, SC.
Issue:
   1115.Oliver Jordan[12] Wolfe, b. 4 July 1990

865. EDWARD ROBERT[11] CHAMIER, son of Edward
Walter[10] and Charlotte Frances (Bouma) Chamier,
b. 4 June 1947, Patterson, Passaic County, NJ;
m. 7 May 1977 in Atlanta, GA, Mary Jane
Williams, b. 15 Sept 1953, Athens, McMinn
County, TN, d/o Fredrick Lee and Linnie Black
(Martin) Williams. Edward is an architect and
Mary Jane is a speech and language pathologist.
Issue:
   1116.Russell Evan[12] Chamier, b. 12 Sept 1978,
         Jacksonville, FL, d. (in Scaklin
         Records)
   1117.Jennifer Anne[12] Chamier, b. 1 Mar 1981,
         Norcross, GA

866. KEVIN[11] CHAMIER, son of Edward Walter[10] and
Marian Elizabeth (Hulse) (Monroe) Chamier, b. 21
Apr 1954; m. Jody Belzak.
Issue:
   1118.Dana[12] Chamier
   1119.Trevor[12] Chamier

867. WILLIAM[11] CHAMIER, son of Edward Walter[10]

and Marian Elizabeth (Hulse) (Monroe) Chamier, b. 12 Dec 1957; m. Susan Allmer.
Issue:
1120.Nicole[12] Chamier
1121.Erica Lynn[12] Chamier, b. 28 Oct 1989

874. ALICE JUNE[11] RAYNOR, dau. of Joseph Fletcher[10] and Marguerite L. (White) Raynor, b. 8 Feb 1943; m. Donald K. Ruffing. Alice, a graduate of Hampton Bays High School and Suffolk Community College, is employed by N.A.F. Activities. Residence: Hampton Bays.
Issue:
1122.Donald K.[12] Ruffing, Jr., b. 16 May 1961; residence: Albuquerque, NM.
1123.Michael L.[12] Ruffing, b. 2 June 1962, d. 28 Feb 1988

876. ELLEN RAMONA[11] RAYNOR, dau. of William Thomas[10] and Margaret Elizabeth (Hudson) Raynor, b. 17 May 1937, Lewes, DE; m. 11 June 1960 in Sanford, FL, Thomas Munday of Illinois. Ellen is a school teacher.
Issue:
1124.Carol Ann[12] Munday, b. 29 Mar 1961, Sanford, FL
1125.Michael Thomas[12] Munday, b. 26 Oct 1963, Sanford, FL

877. WILLIAM THOMAS[11] RAYNOR, JR., son of William Thomas[10] and Margaret Elizabeth (Hudson) Raynor, b. 30 June 1942, Lewes, DE; m. in 1965, Ineita Thompson of Sanford, FL. William is a building contractor.
Issue:
1126.Eric Christopher[12] Raynor, b. 6 Dec 1963, Sanford, FL
1127.Elizabeth ("Beth")[12] Raynor, b. 3 Jan 1966, Sanford, FL
1128.Susan Lynn[12] Raynor, b. 22 Dec 1969, Winter Park, FL

878. ROBERT HUDSON[11] RAYNOR, son of William Thomas[10] and Margaret Elizabeth (Hudson) Raynor, b. 16 July 1946, Norfolk, VA; m. in 1971 in Aliceville, AL, Beth Owens of Aliceville, AL. Robert is an architect.
Issue:

 1129. Alan Owens[12] Raynor, b. 3 Feb 1977, Albany, GA

 1130. Laura Margaret[12] Raynor, b. 23 June 1982, Tallahassee, FL

880. WALTER LEROY[11] HILL, son of Walter Reginald and Emma Ainsley[10] (Carter) Hill, b. 10 Mar 1934, Brooklyn; m. Nancy Day Penfield. Walter "Lee" Hill is a retired Navy pilot and owns a pharmaceutical company. Residence: Oakton, VA.
Issue:

 1131. Jon[12] Hill, b. 1961

 1132. Andrew[12] Hill

 1133. Betsy[12] Hill, b. 1964

881. ROBERT REGINALD[11] HILL, son of Walter Reginald and Emma Ainsley[10] (Carter) Hill, b. 30 Sept 1938, Brooklyn; m. (1) 1963 in Roslyn, L.I., Patricia M. Lockwood, b. 15 May 1944, d/o Harold and Rita (Connolly) Lockwood; m. (2) 9 May 1987, Kathleen O'Donohoe, b. 25 Nov 1955, d/o Joseph and Margaret (Johnson) O'Donohoe. Robert is a school librarian. Residence: East Northport, L.I.
Issue Wife (1):

 1134. Robert Reginald[12] Hill, Jr., b. 25 Oct 1963, Glen Cove, L.I.

 1135. Wendy Aileen[12] Hill, b. 7 May 1967, Glen Cove, L.I.

882. ELIZABETH AINSLEY[11] HILL, dau. of Walter Reginald and Emma Ainsley[10] (Carter) Hill, b. 19 Oct 1943, Brooklyn; m. (1) at Garden City, L.I., Robert Colasimone of Canada; m. (2) 15 Sept 1979 at Silver Springs, MD, Joseph Heintz. Residence: Bowie, MD.

Issue Husband (1):
1136. Jeffrey[12] Colasimone, b. 13 Sept 1974

883. WILLIAM LAWRENCE[11] RAYNOR, son of Lawrence
Evermond and Norma Theodora[10] (Carter) Raynor,
b. 16 Sept 1949, Southampton; m. 19 Nov 1976,
Patricia Ann Zalewski, b. 31 July 1950,
Riverhead, d/o Henry and Helen Frances
(Matusaik) Zalewski. William is Head of
Maintenance at Cedar Lodge Nursing Home, Center
Moriches. Residence: Riverhead.
Issue:
1137. Jason Paul[12] Raynor, b. 3 Mar 1978, Port
Jefferson
1138. Lindsay Beth[12] Raynor, b. 20 Jan 1981,
Port Jefferson

886. ESTHER MARIE[11] FECHTMANN, dau. of Arthur
Raymond and Norma Theodora[10] (Carter) Fechtmann,
b. 12 Oct 1963, E. Patchogue; m. 18 Sept 1987 at
the Patchogue United Methodist Church, Sylvester
Francis Neville, b. 27 July 1960, Newfoundland,
Canada, s/o Michael Joseph and Celestine Mary
(Young) Neville of Sudbury, Canada. Esther
Marie was married 80 years to the day after her
grandparents, Hattie Ainsley Raynor and Harold
Leroy Carter. Esther is a professional
photographer and Sylvester is employed at the
Stony Brook, L.I. Hospital. Residence:
Eastport.
Issue:
1139. Michael Arthur[12] Neville, b. 29 July 1992,
Riverhead

887. C. KENNETH[11] MADES, son of Charles Gerald
and Emma Laverne[10] (Penny) Mades, b. 18 Apr
1938, Southampton; m. (1) in 1959, Grace A.
_____, d. 13 Apr 1980; m. (2) 24 July 1983, as
her second husband, Katherine A. Talmage, b. 8
June 1947. Residence: Hampton Bays. Katherine
has a daughter by her first husband: Wendy Diane
Talmage, b. 28 Oct 1970.
Issue Wife (1):

133

1140.William Kenneth[12] Mades, b. 16 Jan 1960,
     Southampton; resides in East Moriches.
1141.Virginia Grace[12] Mades, b. 5 Nov 1962,
     Southampton; resides in Oceanside, L.I.
1142.Robert Hans[12] Mades, twin, b. 31 Mar 1963,
     Southampton, d. Sept 1979 in an accident
1143.Barbara LaVerne[12] Mades, twin, b. 31 Mar
     1963, Southampton, d. a few days after
     birth

889. ERIC[11] ZIEMER, son of Daniel M. and Emma
Katherine[10] (Rowe) Ziemer, b. 20 Sept 1953.
Eric is a sales manager for the Los Angeles
Times.
Issue:
  1144.Craig Michael[12] Ziemer, b. 24 Sept 1989
  1145.William[12] Ziemer, b. 24 Jan 1990

890. MARK[11] ZIEMER, son of Daniel M. and Emma
Katherine[10] (Rowe) Ziemer, b. 8 Sept 1958. Mark
is an electronics engineer with Hughes Aircraft
Co. in Los Angeles, CA.
Issue:
  1146.Daniel Bruce[12] Ziemer, b. 31 Mar 1980
  1147.Matthew[12] Ziemer, b. 10 Jan 1984
  1148.Krystina[12] Ziemer, b. 13 Nov 1987

891. SYLVIA[11] BROOKER, dau. of _____ and Mamie
Aleen[10] (Rowe) Brooker, b. 20 Jan 19__; m. _____
Watson.
Issue:
*1149.Raymond[12] Watson

892. GINNIE[11] BROOKER, dau. of _____ and Mamie
Aleen[10] (Rowe) Brooker, b. 11 June 19__; m.
_____ _____.
Issue:
  1150.David[12] _____

896. REED WARREN[11] JARVIS, son of Leonard

Prescott[10] and Catherine Bennett (Reed) Jarvis,
b. 8 Nov 1932, NYC; m. (1) Anne Theresa McBride,
d. 25 June 1978; m. (2) 1 Jan 1979, Denise
Catherine Drugge, b. 18 Apr 1929, Edmonton,
Alberta, Canada. Reed was an art teacher in
Hyde Park, NY; since 1961, he has worked for the
National Park Service and is currently (1994)
Chief Ranger for the Pacific Northwest Region.
Residence: Mercer Island, WA.
Issue Wife (1):

1151. Elizabeth Anne[12] Jarvis, b. 7 Jan 1956,
        Kingston, NY; m. 2 Feb 1992, Ronald Chad
        Petrie, b. 17 Oct 1953, Aberdeen, ID.
1152. Reed Warren[12] Jarvis, Jr., b. 27 Mar 1959,
        Kingston, NY. He is Chief of
        Maintenance at a winery in Cutchogue,
        L.I. Residence: Cutchogue.
1153. Heather Patricia[12] Jarvis, b. 21 Sept
        1964, St. Louis, MO, d. 24 Oct 1982,
        Redmond, WA, in an automobile accident

904. BARBARA ANN[11] STEVENS, dau. of Thomas Henry
and Katherine Marian[10] (Parlato) Stevens, b. 14
Feb 1946, Southampton; m. 8 Sept 1969, Gerald
Joseph Robillard.
Issue:

1154. Thomas Stevens[12] Robillard, b. 22 Sept
        1972
1155. Jason Douglas[12] Robillard, b. 29 Sept 1975

908. CHARY ANN HALSEY[11] DAVIS, dau. of Lloyd
Osborne and Lois Halsey[10] (Raynor) Davis, b. 14
Dec 1948; m. (1) Gerald Lytel, d. Apr 1969; m.
(2) 12 Aug 1971, James C. Griffin, b. 30 Jan
1945, Chicago, IL. Residence: Cazenovia, NY.
Issue Husband (1):
1156. Michael[12] Griffin, b. 28 June 1968
Issue Husband (2):
1157. James C.[12] Griffin, Jr., b. 25 Sept 1975

911. SANDRA ELOISE[11] HALSEY, dau. of Harold
Beecher and Jean Edith[10] (Raynor) Halsey, Jr.,

b. 23 Feb 1950; m. (1) Richard S. Swann; m. (2) Edward S. Surgan, b. 3 July 1949.
Issue Husband (1):
  1158.Halsey S.[12] Swann, b. 12 June 1984
Issue Husband (2):
  1159.Dwight Morrison[12] Surgan, twin, b. 27 May 1988
  1160.Brooks Rogers[12] Surgan, twin, b. 27 May 1988

913. HENRY HARRISON ("HARRY")[11] TYTE, son of Harrison Edmund[10] and Edna Squires (Downs) Tyte, b. 8 May 1914, Riverhead; m. 14 Aug 1937 at the Baiting Hollow Congregational Church, Audrey Reba Seaman, b. 6 Mar 1916, d. 10 July 1984, Riverhead, bur. Riverhead Cemetery, d/o Charles Thomas and Lorreine Bernice (Lane) Seaman.
Issue:
  1161.Vivian Lorreine[12] Tyte, b. & d. 23 Sept 1938, Southampton, bur. Riverhead Cemetery
  1162.Linda Jane[12] Tyte, b. 6 Aug 1941, Southampton; m. (1) 21 Jan 1962, Thomas L. Dannenberg; m. (2) 23 Apr 1967, Louis Gatz, Jr.
  1163.Reba Lorreine[12] Tyte, b. 18 May 1945, Southampton; m. (1) James Michael McCarthy; m. (2) Thomas Leroy Downs.
  1164.Anita Beryl[12] Tyte, b. 4 Jan 1948, Southampton; m. 18 Dec 1965, Philip LaGrande Robinson.

914. CHARLES EDMOND[11] TYTE, son of Harrison Edmund[10] and Edna Squires (Downs) Tyte, b. 6 Sept 1915, Riverhead, d. 17 Oct 1969, CT, bur. Riverhead Cemetery; m. 5 Sept 1941 in the Patchogue Congregational Church, Helen Evelyn King, b. 23 Jan 1919, d/o Theodore James and Frances (Gardner) King.
Issue:
  1165.Charles Edmond[12] Tyte, Jr., b. 17 July 1944, Port Jefferson; m. (1) Aurora _____; m. (2) 29 Aug 1990 in NYC, Sumer

Aktug Agar.
1166.George Howard[12] Tyte, b. 27 Sept 1948,
Port Jefferson
1167.Richard Lawrence[12] Tyte, b. 2 Sept 1950;
m. 23 Mar 19__, Debra Jean Regan.

915. MARGARET EDNA[11] TYTE, dau. of Harrison
Edmund[10] and Edna Squires (Downs) Tyte, b. 14
Dec 1916, Riverhead, d. 19 Nov 1985, East
Berlin, PA; m. 7 July 1936 in the Aquebogue
Congregational Church, Ernest Daniel Loper, Sr.,
b. 30 Aug 1915, d. 18 Aug 1972, York, PA, s/o
Chester Ernest and Dorothy Marie (Luce) Loper.
Both Margaret and Ernest are bur. Union
Cemetery, East Berlin, PA.
Issue:
1168.Margaret Marie[12] Loper, b. 9 Mar 1937,
Greenport; m. (1) John Luther Gift; m.
(2) Emory Swartz.
1169.Arthur Chester[12] Loper, b. 9 June 1939,
Greenport, d. 3 Aug 1990, E. Harrisburg,
PA, bur. Union Cemetery, East Berlin,
PA; unmarried.
1170.Ernest Daniel[12] Loper, Jr., b. 9 Dec 1940,
Abbottstown, PA

916. LOIS ETHEL[11] TYTE, dau. of Harrison
Edmund[10] and Edna Squires (Downs) Tyte, b. 21
Dec 1922, Riverhead; m. 21 Nov 1940 in the
Riverhead Methodist Church Parsonage, Walter
DeWall, b. 4 Apr 1921, Steele, ND, s/o George
G. and Thresa Margaret (Mohan) DeWall.
Issue:
1171.William Harrison[12] DeWall, b. 10 May 1941,
Hanover, PA; m. (1) Linda Lou Richeson;
m. (2) Veda Yarrusso; m. (3) Linda K.
Myers; m. (4) Wanda Woodward Anderson.
1172.Karen Lois[12] DeWall, b. 25 May 1944,
Southampton; m. 27 June 1964, Richard
John Garritano, b. 16 Oct 1942.
1173.Peggy Ann[12] DeWall, b. 21 May 1949,
Southampton; m. 22 Aug 1970, Joseph
Louis Warnock, b. 9 May 1949.

917. MIRIAM ELLEN[11] TYTE, dau. of Harrison Edmund[10] and Edna Squires (Downs) Tyte, b. 4 Aug 1932, Riverhead; m. (1) 27 Aug 1955 in the Riverhead Methodist Church, Robert Edward Davidson, Sr., b. 21 Mar 1937, El Paso, TX, s/o Floyd Hall and Mary Florence (Fairchild) Davidson; m. (2) 11 May 1968, Lester Huntley Therrell.
Issue Husband (1):

1174. Mary Ellen[12] Davidson, b. 28 Mar 1956, Riverhead; m. 13 Apr 1982, Michael George Ryan.

1175. Robert Edward[12] Davidson, Jr., b. 24 July 1957, Riverhead; m. 24 July 1982, Nancy Lynn Sterling Conklin.

1176. Kenneth Lee[12] Davidson, twin, b. 9 July 1958, Riverhead; m. 17 Mar 1988, Karen Lorraine Dunnam.

1177. Lawrence Hall[12] Davidson, twin, b. 9 July 1958, Riverhead; m. 22 Mar 1981, Patrice Sterling.

1178. Kathleen Edna[12] Davidson, b. 11 Oct 1959, Riverhead; m. (1) Anthony White; m. (2) Richard Grodski.

1179. Nancy Elaine[12] Davidson, b. 18 Nov 1960; m. 8 Dec 1979, Robert John Frances Danowski.

Issue Husband (2):

1180. Charles Andrew[12] Therrell, b. 4 Nov 1968, Southampton

918. HELEN BEDELL[11] TYTE, dau. of Stephen Alexander[10] and Marjorie (Young) Tyte, b. 3 July 1932, Riverhead; m. 21 Oct 1950 in the Baiting Hollow Congregational Church, Reginald Walter Peterson, b. 16 June 1925, s/o Carlton V. and Ruby Roosevelt (Latham) Peterson. Residence: East Marion, L.I.
Issue:

1181. Walter Edward[12] Peterson, b. 27 Dec 1951, Greenport; m. 2 June 1973, Joann Louise Rawn, b. 17 Jan 1954.

1182.Richard David[12] Peterson, b. 30 Oct 1953,
       Greenport, d. Mar 1955, Greenport
1183.Catherine Mary[12] Peterson, b. 7 Dec 1956,
       Greenport; m. 1 Oct 1983 in the First
       Baptist Church, Greenport, Donald C.
       Wood.
1184.James Reginald[12] Peterson, b. 27 Feb 1963,
       Greenport; m. (1) 1 July 1978, Carol
       Richmond; m. (2) 1 Sept 1990 in the
       Greenport Baptist Church, Deborah Boyce.

920. JOAN CAROLYN[11] REGENT, dau. of Kenneth
Gardner and Mary Althea Terrell[10] (Tyte) Regent,
b. 20 Oct 1928, Riverhead, d. 25 June 1990,
Cutchogue, bur. Shelter Island; m. (1) 27 Aug
1949, Eugene Edwin Conover; m. (2) 28 Mar 1958
in the First Congregational Church, Riverhead,
Charles Hallett Smith, Sr., b. 23 Dec 1930,
Riverhead, d. 13 Mar 1991, Cutchogue, bur.
Shelter Island, s/o Frank J. and Helen (Hallett)
Smith.
Issue Husband (1):
  1185.Terrelle ("Terri") Allison[12] Conover, b.
       15 Oct 1952, Ann Arbor, MI; m. 14 Sept
       1975 in Mattituck, Fred Abatelli.
  1186.Dane Kenneth[12] Conover, b. 4 Nov 1954, Ann
       Arbor, MI
Issue Husband (2):
  1187.Charles Hallett[12] Smith, Jr., b. 27 Dec
       1959, Riverhead
  1188.Clara Ellen ("Nell")[12] Smith, b. 13 Jan
       1962; m. 31 Dec 1991 in Cutchogue, by
       Rev. Peter McLean, Kenneth Rorick
       of Lechworth State Park, near Rochester,
       NY.

921. MARCIA ADELLE[11] REGENT, dau. of Kenneth
Gardner and Mary Althea Terrell[10] (Tyte) Regent,
b. 28 Mar 1932, Riverhead; m. 30 Dec 1957 in the
Park Temple Methodist Church, Ft. Lauderdale,
FL, Ignace John ("Jack") Rondello, b. 21 July
1920, Trapani, Sicily, Italy, d. 29 (or 30) May
1992, WI, s/o Mario and Rosaria (Clemente)

Rondello. Residence: Eagle River, WI.
Issue:
1189.Peter Andrew[12] Rondello, b. 2 Oct 1958,
Riverhead; m. 27 Oct 1979, Cheryl Ann
Skinner.
1190.Louise Althea[12] Rondello, b. 15 Aug 1960,
Ft. Lauderdale, FL; m. Kenneth Schels;
no issue.
1191.Daniel John[12] Rondello, b. 24 Mar 1966,
Ft. Lauderdale, FL

922. DONNA ALTHEA[11] REGENT, dau. of Kenneth
Gardner and Mary Althea Terrell[10] (Tyte) Regent,
b. 7 Feb 1939, Greenport; m. (1) 19 July 1967,
John Ernest Wilbur; m. (2) 26 Sept 1981 at
Shelter Island, Timothy Sauers, b. 17 Dec 1945,
OH, s/o Jay and Dorothy (Stokes) Sauers.
Residence: Riverhead.
Issue Husband (1):
1192.Doreen Regent[12] Sauers, b. 13 Oct 1968,
Coral Gables, FL
1193.Brett Harrison[12] Sauers, b. 21 Feb 1970,
Coral Gables, FL

924. GENE ELIZABETH[11] TYTE, dau. of Arthur
Milton[10] and Marian Elizabeth (Downs) Tyte, Jr.,
b. 17 May 1925, Riverhead; m. 9 Dec 1944 in the
Riverhead Methodist Church, Harold Ellsworth
("Cappy") Goodale, b. 20 Sept 1922, Babylon, s/o
Robinson Jesse and Lavinia Olive (Ketcham)
Goodale. Residence: Riverhead.
Issue:
1194.Noel Susan[12] Goodale, b. 25 Dec 1945,
Greenport; m. 17 Aug 1968 in the Old
Steeple Church, Aquebogue, James Arthur
DeLong.
1195.Harold Ellsworth ("Bo")[12] Goodale, Jr., b.
28 May 1947, Greenport; m. 8 Mar 1969 in
Morrisville, NY, Margaret Elizabeth
("Peggy") Hildreth.
1196.Barbara Gene[12] Goodale, b. 31 May 1951,
Riverhead; m. 17 Aug 1974 in the Old
Steeple Church, Aquebogue, Marvin Lyle

Warner.

1197.June Elizabeth[12] Goodale, b. 19 Nov 1954,
    Riverhead; m. 3 Apr 1979 in Gary, IN,
    Richard Paul ("Rick") Stevenson.
1198.Holly Jo[12] Goodale, b. 7 Dec 1968,
    Riverhead

925. NORMAN ARTHUR[11] TYTE, SR., son of Arthur
Milton[10] and Marian Elizabeth (Downs) Tyte, Jr.,
b. 2 Dec 1927, Riverhead, d. 12 Apr 1990; m. 29
Mar 1952, Sophie Stephanie Moisa, b. 25 Apr
1929, Mattituck, d/o John and Apolonia
(Czykowski) Moisa. Residence: Riverhead.
Issue:
1199.Norman Arthur ("Sonny")[12] Tyte, Jr., b. 5
    May 1954, Riverhead; m. 5 May 1979,
    Alexandra Helen ("Sandy") Fedun.
1200.Evelyn Doris[12] Tyte, b. 26 Sept 1956,
    Riverhead
1201.Henry David[12] Tyte, b. 4 Sept 1957,
    Riverhead; m. 24 Aug 1985, Melissa
    Elkins.
1202.James Everett[12] Tyte, b. 1 Nov 1959,
    Riverhead
1203.Milton John[12] Tyte, b. 13 Apr 1965,
    Riverhead; m. 16 Sept 1989 at Baiting
    Hollow Congregational Church, Nicole Ann
    Shuot.

926. BRUCE MILTON[11] TYTE, son of Arthur Milton[10]
and Marian Elizabeth (Downs) Tyte, Jr., b. 28
Nov 1929; m. (1) 11 Apr 1953, Janice Yvonne
Seaman; m. (2) 1 Oct 1961 in the Cutchogue
Methodist Church, Nancy Amelia Marchais, b. 17
Aug 1930, d/o George E. and Jeanette (Johnson)
Marchais. Residence: North Carolina.
Issue Wife (2):
1204.Suzanne Elizabeth[12] Tyte, b. 2 Aug 1962,
    Greenport
1205.Jeanne Marie[12] Tyte, b. 23 July 1965,
    Greenport; m. 9 Sept 1986, Allen Lamb.

927. ELINOR MARIAN[11] TYTE, dau. of Arthur
Milton[10] and Marian Elizabeth (Downs) Tyte, Jr.,
b. 24 Nov 1934, Riverhead; m. 24 June 1955 in
the Riverhead Methodist Church, Byron Mathais
Lindsay, b. 11 Jan 1930, Wheaton, MN, s/o
Mathais Hans and Blanche Lillian (Sauby)
Lindsay. Residence: Saint Marie, MT.
Issue:

1206. Sandra Jean[12] Lindsay, b. 17 June 1956,
Wimpole Park, Arrington, England; m. 11
July 1981 in the United Methodist
Church, Riverhead, Charles John Odell,
Jr.

1207. Valerie Ann[12] Lindsay, b. & d. 2 July
1957, Wimpole Park, Arrington, England,
bur. England

1208. Loretta Gail[12] Lindsay, b. 17 May 1958,
Wimpole Park, Arrington, England; m. 18
June 1983 at Odd Fellows Hall,
Riverhead, Mark Goldberg.

1209. Deanna Marie[12] Lindsay, b. 15 Feb 1962,
Martinsburg, WV; m. 12 Feb 1989 in the
United Methodist Church, Riverhead,
Don E. Harter.

1210. David Byron[12] Lindsay, b. 15 Feb 1967,
Anchorage, AK

928. GAIL ELLEN[11] TYTE, dau. of Arthur Milton[10]
and Marian Elizabeth (Downs) Tyte, Jr., b. 24
July 1950, Greenport; m. 17 Sept 1972 in the
United Methodist Church, Riverhead, as his
second wife, Lewis Merlin ("Butch") Yeager, Jr.,
b. 15 Apr 1944, Southampton, s/o Lewis Merlin
and Leonora M. (Oppenheim) Yeager, Sr.
Residence: Riverhead.
Issue:

1211. Bonnie Gene[12] Yeager, b. 8 Apr 1977,
Southampton

1212. Bradford Jay[12] Yeager, b. 5 Nov 1979,
Southampton

1213. Drew Lewis[12] Yeager, b. 28 Feb 1986,
Southampton

1214. Blaze Harold[12] Yeager, b. 9 Feb 1990,

929. CAROL FRANCES[11] TYTE, dau. of Wickham
Corwin[10] and Frances Rockwell (Downs) Tyte, Sr.,
b. 4 June 1936, Greenport; m. 24 Aug 1958 in the
Eastport Gospel Church, Eugene Ferguson, b. 22
Jan 1934, KY, s/o Auty and Flora (Coffee)
Ferguson. Residence: Riverhead.
Issue:
1215. Beverly Hope[12] Ferguson, b. 16 Sept 1962,
Riverhead; m. 23 June 1990 in the
Westhampton United Methodist Church,
Charles John Odell, Jr.
1216. Timothy Eugene[12] Ferguson, b. 8 Feb 1964,
Riverhead
1217. Mark Andrew[12] Ferguson, b. 7 May 1965,
Riverhead; m. 15 Feb 1986 in Lake
Charles, LA, Dorena Martin.
1218. Joy Elizabeth[12] Ferguson, b. 25 June 1966,
Riverhead; m. 27 July 1985 in the
Eastport Gospel Church, Tommy Ray Davis.
1219. Dawn Marie[12] Ferguson, b. 27 Aug 1967,
Riverhead
1220. Paul David[12] Ferguson, b. 30 Nov 1968,
Riverhead
1221. Nathan Corwin[12] Ferguson, b. 23 Feb 1970,
Riverhead
1222. Jonathan Lee[12] Ferguson, b. 31 Oct 1972,
Riverhead

930. BETSEY ANN[11] TYTE, dau. of Wickham Corwin[10]
and Frances Rockwell (Downs) Tyte, Sr., b. 8 Aug
1937, Riverhead; m. (1) 24 Dec 1960, David
Jones; m. (2) _____ Porter; m. (3) 24 Aug 1968
in KY, Emmit Bruce Smith, Jr., b. 9 June 1932,
KY, s/o Emmit Bruce Smith, Sr. Residence:
Shepherdsville, KY.
Issue Husband (1):
1223. David Eugene[12] Jones, b. 14 June 1961, MO,
d. 15 June 1961, MO
1224. Melanie Anne[12] Jones, b. 15 Oct 1962,
Riverhead; m. 8 Aug 1981, David Lee

Richardson.
Issue Husband (2):
1225.Jay Allen[12] Porter, b. 22 June 1965,
       Riverhead; m. (1) Barbara Richard; m.
       (2) Sherri Patrick.
Issue Husband (3):
1226.Margaret Ann[12] Smith, b. 17 Aug 1970,
       Louisville, KY
1227.Edward Bruce[12] Smith, b. 5 Feb 1977,
       Louisville, KY

931. SHIRLEY MARIE[11] TYTE, dau. of Wickham
Corwin[10] and Frances Rockwell (Downs) Tyte, Sr.,
b. 13 Sept 1938, Riverhead; m. 15 Dec 1962, in
Riverhead, Earl David Atkinson, b. 4 Apr 1938,
WV, s/o Kenneth William and Hallie Atkinson.
Residence: Riverhead.
Issue:
1228.Deborah Lynn[12] Atkinson, b. 17 July 1961,
       Riverhead
1229.David Harvey[12] Atkinson, b. 10 Jan 1964,
       Dayton, OH; m. 22 May 1984 in Riverhead,
       Kathleen Glose.
1230.William Earl[12] Atkinson, b. 16 Oct 1972,
       E. Patchogue
1231.Daniel Wayne[12] Atkinson, b. 15 Dec 1975,
       E. Patchogue
1232.Darryl Lee[12] Atkinson, b. 7 Oct 1977, E.
       Patchogue
1233.Diane Marie[12] Atkinson, b. 7 Dec 1978,
       Southampton

932. WICKHAM CORWIN[11] TYTE, JR., son of Wickham
Corwin[10] and Frances Rockwell (Downs) Tyte, Sr.,
b. 9 Oct 1939, Riverhead, d. 10 Oct 1969, bur.
Oakwood Cemetery, East Quogue; m. 20 Nov 1960 in
Kochi-Ken, Japan, Kazue Seki, b. 13 Nov 1932,
Japan. Residence: Riverhead.
Issue:
1234.Arthur Milton[12] Tyte, b. 2 Feb 1963,
       Riverhead; m. 30 Nov 1985 in Riverhead,
       Dorothy Gretchen Rose, b. 11 Feb 1967.

1235.Wickham Corwin[12] Tyte III, b. 28 Dec 1964, Riverhead

1236.John Henry[12] Tyte, b. 4 July 1966, Riverhead; m. (1) 26 Jan 1991, Denise Kohler; m. (2) Sharon ____.

1237.William James[12] Tyte, b. 10 May 1969

933. STEPHEN EDWARD[11] TYTE, son of Wickham Corwin[10] and Frances Rockwell (Downs) Tyte, Sr., b. 1 Mar 1948, Greenport; m. 1 July 1967 in the Eastport Gospel Church, Patricia Ann Riley, b. 23 Apr 1949, d/o Richard and Mary Riley. Residence: Rosenburg, TX.
Issue:

1238.Antoinette[12] Tyte, b. 17 Jan 1969, Riverhead

1239.Stephen Edward[12] Tyte, Jr., b. 31 Mar 1971, Fairbanks, AK

1240.Richard Harrison[12] Tyte, b. 11 Mar 1973, Fairbanks, AK

934. NAOMI RUTH[11] TYTE, dau. of Wickham Corwin[10] and Frances Rockwell (Downs) Tyte, Sr., b. 18 Aug 1955, Riverhead.
Issue:

1241.Mathew Robinson[12] Tyte, b. 17 June 1976, E. Patchogue

935. MARY LOUISE[11] CORWIN, dau. of Leone Woodhull[10] and Clarissa A. (Fleming) Corwin, b. 7 Sept 1930; m. Frank J. Conti, Jr. Residence: Scottsdale, AZ.
Issue:

1242.Regina[12] Conti, m. ____ Harrison

1243.Frank Corwin[12] Conti

945. LEIGH DAVIDSON[11] HAWKINS, son of Vernon D. and Margaret I.[10] (Satterly) Hawkins, b. 30 June 1940, Southampton; m. 22 June 1963, Priscilla F. Huddleston, b. 13 Jan 1943, d/o Frederick George and Winifred Elizabeth (Mack) Huddleston of England.

Issue:

1244.Catherine Ann[12] Hawkins, b. 27 Apr 1964
1245.Alan Lewis[12] Hawkins, b. 14 Jan 1966

946. BRIAN SATTERLY[11] HAWKINS, son of Vernon D.
and Margaret I.[10] (Satterly) Hawkins, b. 24 Mar
1942, Southampton; m. 7 Sept 1969, Annette
Mezzapelle, b. 22 July 1944, d/o Peter and Rose
Mezzapelle.
Issue:

1246.Rebecca Ann[12] Hawkins, b. 11 Apr 1972
1247.Mark John[12] Hawkins, b. 26 Mar 1974

947. JON WARD[11] HAWKINS, son of Vernon D. and
Margaret I.[10] (Satterly) Hawkins, b. 6 Nov 1945,
Southampton; m. (1) Margaret Reska, b. 20 Mar
1946, d/o Paul and Helen Reska; m. (2) Rose
Mannino Melesh, b. 10 July 1950, d/o Anthony and
Gilda Mannino.
Issue Wife (1):

1248.Elizabeth Ann[12] Hawkins, b. 22 Nov 1968

948. WENDY MARGARET[11] HAWKINS, dau. of Vernon D.
and Margaret I.[10] (Satterly) Hawkins, b. 8 Feb
1955, Riverhead; m. 17 Feb 1973, Robert P. Rice,
s/o Robert P. and Frances (Day) Rice.
Issue:

1249.Kenneth Hawkins[12] Rice, b. 30 Sept 1977,
        Clinton, CT
1250.Charles Robert[12] Rice, b. 11 July 1979,
        Clinton, CT
1251.Eric Vernon[12] Rice, b. 15 Nov 1980, New
        Haven, CT

949. LYNNE RAYNOR[11] PEARCE, dau. of Richard
Allan and Louise Wanda[10] (Raynor) Pearce, b. 13
June 1955; m. 1 Aug 1981, Michael John
Kelleher, b. 17 Apr 1952.
Issue:

1252.Matthew Pearce[12] Kelleher, b. 11 Nov 1985
1253.Amy Raynor[12] Kelleher, b. 22 July 1988

950. DAVID RICHARD[11] PEARCE, son of Richard Allan and Louise Wanda[10] (Raynor) Pearce, b. 7 Nov 1957; m. 14 Mar 1987, Susan Marie Zampi, b. 17 Mar 1958.
Issue:
1254. Cassandra Zampi[12] Pearce, b. 5 Dec 1989
1255. Austin Lester[12] Pearce, b. 13 July 1991

956. LAURIE ANN[11] DUNWELL, dau. of LeRoy Raynor[10] and Cynthia Ann (Powell) Dunwell, b. 11 Aug 1957; m. 15 Oct 1977, James Joseph Collins, Jr., b. 16 Nov 1953.
Issue:
1256. James Joseph[12] Collins III, b. 1 Dec 1978
1257. Patrick Joseph[12] Collins, b. 4 Oct 1980
1258. Tara Ann Dunwell[12] Collins, b. 31 May 1988

958. RAYMOND HALSEY[11] TOPPING, JR., son of Raymond Halsey and Dorothy Seely[10] (Dunwell) Topping, b. 29 Apr 1954, Southampton; m. 8 Mar 1975 in the Bridgehampton United Methodist Church, Lyllis Ann Granger, b. 17 Dec 1958, Huntington. Residence: Bridgehampton.
Issue:
1259. Raymond James[12] Topping, b. 22 Mar 1975, Southampton
1260. Kimberly Anne[12] Topping, b. 10 June 1979, Southampton

959. DIANE GAIL[11] TOPPING, dau. of Raymond Halsey and Dorothy Seely[10] (Dunwell) Topping, b. 5 Nov 1956, Southampton; m. 17 Oct 1981 in the Bridgehampton United Methodist Church, Donald James Howe, b. 15 Feb 1952, Riverhead. Residence: Water Mill, L.I.
Issue:
1261. Devan Alysa[12] Howe, b. 15 Apr 1986, Riverhead
1262. Danielle Lynn[12] Howe, b. 14 Feb 1989, Riverhead

960. LEANNE JOY[11] TOPPING, dau. of Raymond
Halsey and Dorothy Seely[10] (Dunwell) Topping, b.
1 Dec 1960, Southampton; m. 30 Nov 1991 at the
First Presbyterian Church of East Hampton, Amos
Benjamin Hostetter, Jr., b. 7 Sept 1947,
Harrisonburg, VA. Residence: Bridgehampton.
Issue:
1263. Jacob Topping[12] Hostetter, twin, b. 20 May
1994, Southampton
1264. Joshua Samuel[12] Hostetter, twin, b. 20 May
1994, Southampton

961. ELLEN[11] RAYNOR, dau. of Pierson Tuthill[10]
and Anne Margaret (Kuhlemann) Raynor, b. 29 Apr
1954; m. Gary Wingate. Residence: Reisterstown,
MD.
Issue:
1265. Kara[12] Wingate
1266. Gregory[12] Wingate

963. DOUGLAS PRESTON[11] RAYNOR, son of Charles
Homer[10] and Marjorie (Holmes) Raynor, b. 24 Sept
1947, Red Bank, NJ; m. 1 Nov 1969, Patricia
Coleman, b. 7 Feb 1950.
Issue:
1267. Douglas Coleman[12] Raynor, b. 9 June 1971
1268. Scott Charles[12] Raynor, b. 3 Apr 1975

964. ROBERT PIERSON[11] RAYNOR, son of Charles
Homer[10] and Marjorie (Holmes) Raynor, b. 17 Feb
1951, Red Bank, NJ; m. 4 Oct 1980, Susan
Coleman, b. 15 Oct 1953.
Issue:
1269. Sara Frances[12] Raynor, b. 18 May 1983,
Charleston, SC
1270. Eliot Pierson[12] Raynor, b. 28 Feb 1985,
Charleston, SC

965. WILLIAM RANDALL[11] HULSE, son of William
Theodore[10] and Ella Brown Hawkins (Randall)

Hulse, Jr., b. 17 Mar 1943, Southampton; m. 17 Sept 1977 at Southampton, Janet Lorraine De Castro, b. 14 June 1955, NYC. William is Westhampton Beach Village Historian; Janet is a teacher.
Issue:

1271.Meredith Sayre[12] Hulse, b. 16 Apr 1979, NYC

966. CHARLOTTE ETHEL[11] HULSE, dau. of Theodore Orren[10] and Clara Elaine (Culver) Hulse, b. 23 Aug 1948, Greenburgh, NY; m. 15 Oct 1969 at Greenburgh, NY, Clarence Arthur Lander, Jr., b. 7 Sept 1948, White Plains, NY.
Issue:

1272.Arthur Edward[12] Lander, b. 21 Apr 1970, Loring, ME, d. 24 Apr 1970
1273.Stephanie Anne[12] Lander, b. 12 Oct 1971, White Plains, NY
1274.Clarence Arthur[12] Lander, 3rd, b. 18 Apr 1974, White Plains, NY

968. BETSY MORRISON[11] HULSE, dau. of Theodore Orren[10] and Clara Elaine (Culver) Hulse, b. 24 Nov 1957, Riverhead; m. 29 July 1979 at Westhampton Beach, David William Doyle, b. 23 July 1956, Southampton.
Issue:

1275.Sean Patrick[12] Doyle, b. 18 Feb 1982, Southampton
1276.Corydon James[12] Doyle, b. 29 Oct 1985, Southampton
1277.Robert Ryan[12] Doyle, b. 25 Apr 1988, Riverhead

971. RICHARD EDWARD (RIBEIRO)[11] VAN TASSEL, son of Richard Edward and Marion Genevieve[10] (Raynor) Ribeiro, b. 10 Mar 1942, Southampton; m. Nancy Lee Binns. Residence: Westhampton Beach.
Issue:

1278.Richard Edward[12] Van Tassel, Jr., b. 21

July 1964, Southampton; m. 17 Oct 1992,
Helen Drew of Vero Beach, FL.
Residence: Vero Beach, FL.
1279.Dean Warrick[12] Van Tassel, b. 13 Sept
1968, Southampton

972. KURT RAYNOR[11] VAN TASSEL, son of Harry
Ellsworth and Marion Genevieve[10] (Raynor) Van
Tassel, b. 6 Mar 1948; m. (1) Anita Romano; m.
(2) Nancy Rodgers of Columbia, SC. Residence:
York, SC.
Issue Wife (1):
1280.Amy Jean[12] Van Tassel, b. 20 Mar 1970,
Southampton; m. 17 July 1991 in Kennett,
MO, Eric Tyler. Amy Jean is a member of
the U.S. Air Force.
1281.Andrew Clifford[12] Van Tassel, b. 4 Feb
1974, Southampton
Issue Wife (2):
1282.Jeffrey Rodgers[12] Van Tassel, b. 16 Aug
1987, Charlotte, NC
1283.Marion Emily Rodgers[12] Van Tassel, b. 29
Aug 1988, Charlotte, NC

974. W. DAVID[11] MCGONIGLE, son of William and
Dorothy Halsey[10] (Raynor) McGonigle, m. (1)
Nancy Johnson; m. (2) Nancy McDonald.
Issue Wife (2):
1284.David B.[12] McGonigle, b. 28 Jan 1974
1285.Kerry A.[12] McGonigle, b. 5 Feb 1977

975. RICHARD C.[11] MCGONIGLE, son of William and
Dorothy Halsey[10] (Raynor) McGonigle, m. (1)
Nancy Evans; m. (2) Rebecca Adams.
Issue Wife (1):
1286.Brian Andrew[12] McGonigle, b. 28 May 1979
1287.Bradford Evans[12] McGonigle, b. 18 Apr 1982
Issue Wife (2):
1288.Bret Adams[12] McGonigle, b. 24 Apr 1990

976. KYLE RAYNOR[11] MCGONIGLE, son of William and

Dorothy Halsey[10] (Raynor) McGonigle, m. Karen Schetter.
Issue:
1289.Kara Mia[12] McGonigle, b. 11 Jan 1990
1290.Leah Suzanne[12] McGonigle, b. 18 May 1993

983. WILLIAM T.[11] EDGAR, son of James and Marcia Page[10] (Raynor) Edgar, b. 19 Dec 1944, Southampton; m. 10 July 1971, Karen Honsberger, of Skaneateles, NY.
Issue:
1291.Amy[12] Edgar, b. 9 Oct 1973
1292.William[12] Edgar, b. 7 Feb 1977
1293.Caroline[12] Edgar, b. 20 Mar 1979

984. MARK BRYAN[11] HOWELL, son of Stuart Payne[10] and Katharina Elisabeth (Herber) Howell, Jr., b. 28 July 1958, Riverhead; m. 16 May 1987 at Sudbury, MA, Helen Pollari, d/o Theodore and Rachel (Marak) Pollari, of Fort Mill, SC. Residence: Acton, MA.
Issue:
1294.Benjamin Marak[12] Howell, b. 15 Mar 1990
1295.Devin Christian[12] Howell, b. 26 Jan 1993

985. HANS-CHRISTIAN[11] HOWELL, son of Stuart Payne and Katharina Elisabeth (Herber) Howell, Jr., b. 29 Apr 1961, Riverhead; m. 13 Oct 1990 at Andover, MA, Barbara Barletta. Residence: Maynard, MA.
Issue:
1296.Samantha Linn[12] Howell, b. 15 Feb 1992, Boston, MA
1297.Nicole Grace[12] Howell, b. 20 Feb 1994, Framingham, MA

986. ROBERT ALLEN[11] SCHUNK, son of Thomas and Margery DeForrest[10] (Raynor) Schunk, b. 12 Sept 1938; m. 30 June 1968, Cynthia McAvoy. Residence: Westhampton Beach.
Issue:

1298.Darryl[12] Schunk, b. 29 Nov 1969
1299.Allan[12] Schunk, b. 28 Aug 1972

989. HAROLD ("BUDDY")[11] FOUST, son of Jack and
Elizabeth Ellison[10] (Raynor) Foust, b. 7 Aug
1946; m. (1) Elizabeth Caroline McGarvey; m. (2)
18 Sept 1988, Mary Jane Bennett.
Issue Wife (1):
1300.Jennifer Ruth[12] Foust, b. 23 Apr 1973
1301.Michael Andrew[12] Foust, b. 23 Sept 1974
1302.Sarah Lillian[12] Foust, b. 23 Feb 1977
1303.John Joseph[12] Foust, b. 24 Mar 1980

990. JO ANN[11] BISHOP, dau. of Herman L. and
Catherine Isabel[10] (Raynor) Bishop, b. ca 1946;
m. _____ Freid.
Issue:
1304.Phillip Forrest[12] Freid
1305.Christopher[12] Freid

993. BONNIE[11] BISHOP, dau. of Herman L. and
Catherine Isabel[10] (Raynor) Bishop, twin, b. 29
July 1948; m. Peter Sereduke.
Issue:
1306.Brian[12] Sereduke

994. CHARLES KENNETH[11] CARDO, son of Carl Eugene
and Winifred Ann[10] (Raynor) Cardo, b. 12 Feb
1955; m. Aug 1990, Sarah Degre.
Issue:
1307.Ayla[12] Cardo, b. 11 Jan 1991

995. RANDY JAY[11] CARDO, son of Carl Eugene and
Winifred Ann[10] (Raynor) Cardo, b. 8 Sept 1957;
m. 8 Sept 1984, Beverley Bittner.
Issue:
1308.Kristen B.[12] Cardo, b. 17 Aug 1986

996. CATHY D.[11] ANDREWS, dau. of Raymond S. and
Barbara Jane[10] (Raynor) Andrews, b. 1 May 1957;

m. 5 Oct 1989, John S. Distefano, s/o Salvatore
and Evelyn (Honnett) Distefano.
Issue:
1309.Andrew John[12] Distefano, b. 28 Dec 1991

997. NANCY ELIZABETH[11] BLACK, dau. of George and
Jeannette[10] (Raynor) Black, b. 7 Mar 1951; m. 1
July 1978, Edward Wilson Stewart, b. 28 May
1950. Residence: Tallahassee, Florida.
Issue:
1310.Christopher Edward[12] Stewart, b. 9 Nov
     1985

999. RUTH ELLEN[11] BLACK, dau. of George and
Jeannette[10] (Raynor) Black, b. 20 Aug 1956; m. 3
July 1982, Scott Gryzich, b. 27 Nov 1955.
Residence: Orlando, Florida.
Issue:
1311.Laura Ruth[12] Gryzich, b. 21 Feb 1986

1000. MARGARET ELECIA[11] BLACK, dau. of George
and Jeannette[10] (Raynor) Black, b. 20 Oct 1958;
m. 2 Mar 1981, William Gilbert Sparks, b. 23 Feb
1958. Residence: Gainesville, Florida.
Issue:
1312.Mary Elizabeth[12] Sparks, b. 23 Aug 1981

1001. MARSHA JEANNETTE[11] BLACK, dau. of George
and Jeannette[10] (Raynor) Black, b. 30 Sept 1960;
m. 28 Dec 1986, Stephen Craig Mayers, b. 24 Sept
1950. Residence: Brandon, Florida.
Issue:
1313.Elizabeth Blair[12] Mayers, b. 24 June 1988
1314.Stephen Craig[12] Mayers, II, b. 13 Sept
     1991

Twelfth Generation

1028. LISA ANN[12] THOGMARTIN, dau. of Vern Mac[11]
and Mary Catherine (Jefferson) Thogmartin, b. 9
Aug 1955; m. _____ Purifoy.

Issue:
1315.Keith Ray[13] Purifoy, b. 5 July 1971

1045. DAWN MARIE[12] RAYNOR, dau. of Herbert
Clarence[11] and Patricia (Winters) Raynor, b. 11
Feb 1956, Southampton; m. 22 May 1982 at
Loveland, CO, Jonathan Mielke, b. 10 Mar 1950.
Issue:
1316.Mackenzie Patricia[13] Mielke, b. 14 Dec
1982
1317.Amanda Marie[13] Mielke, b. 31 Jan 1984

1047. SHARON LEE[12] RAYNOR, dau. of George
Davis[11] and Pamela (Rierl) Raynor, b. 26 Oct
1950, Southampton; m. (1) 3 Mar 1968 at St.
Mark's Episcopal Church, Westhampton Beach,
Robert Molloy, b. 4 Sept 1948, Binghamton, NY;
m. (2) 1 Dec 1984 at St. Ann's Church,
Bridgehampton, Charles Johnson, b. 12 Oct 1941,
Brooklyn.
Issue Husband (1):
1318.Kristen Lee[13] Molloy, b. 22 Mar 1968,
Southampton
*1319.Stacey Jean[13] Molloy, b. 6 Mar 1970,
Southampton
1320.Jennifer Reeves[13] Molloy, b. 1 Dec 1974,
Riverdale, GA

1048. GEORGE THOMAS[12] RAYNOR, son of George
Davis[11] and Pamela (Rierl) Raynor, b. 16 Oct
1952, Riverhead; m. 22 Apr 1978 at St. Mark's
Episcopal Church, Westhampton Beach, Paula
Bossung, b. 27 Feb 1956, Sumter, SC.
Issue:
1321.Melissa Jane[13] Raynor, b. 17 Sept 1981,
Southampton
1322.Megan Pamela[13] Raynor, b. 9 Dec 1983,
Southampton
1323.Kevin Thomas[13] Raynor, b. 30 July 1986,
Southampton

1049. MARK RIERL[12] RAYNOR, son of George Davis[11]

and Pamela (Rierl) Raynor, b. 29 Aug 1954,
Riverhead; m. 23 Sept 1979 (or 1980) at
Immaculate Conception Church, Westhampton Beach,
Mary Teresa Smith, b. 15 July 1957, Brooklyn.
Issue:
1324.James Matthew[13] Raynor, b. 15 Apr 1983,
     Southampton
1325.Justin Mark[13] Raynor, b. 1 Sept 1985,
     Southampton

1050. CHRISTOPHER CARL[12] RAYNOR, son of George
Davis[11] and Pamela (Rierl) Raynor, b. 6 Sept
1960, Riverhead; m. 28 Apr 1991 at St. John's
Church, Center Moriches, Janine Oldham, b. 22
May 1963, Patchogue.
Issue:
1326.Nikki Marie[13] Raynor, b. 18 June 1993,
     Southampton

1053. CANDICE ANN[12] BELL, dau. of Richard Allen
and Lillian Ann[11] (Raynor) Bell, b. 27 May 1952,
Brockport, NY; m. 1 May 1983 at Port Jefferson,
L.I., Edward Collins, b. 6 Aug 1940, Queens
Village, NY.
Issue:
1327.Brendon Patrick[13] Collins, b. 15 Feb 1986,
     Port Jefferson
1328.Timothy Andrew[13] Collins, b. 15 Sept 1988,
     Port Jefferson

1054. DEE ELLEN[12] MILLER, dau. of Garrett and
Lillian Ann[11] (Raynor) Miller, b. 8 Sept 1955,
Allentown, PA; m. 29 May 1982 at Nichols United
Methodist Church, Nichols, NY, Randy Wayne
Bennett, b. 28 Apr 1953, Waverly, NY.
Issue:
1329.Ashley Anne[13] Bennett, b. 28 Oct 1987,
     Sayre, PA
1330.Kristin Nichole[13] Bennett, b. 8 Apr 1989,
     Sayre, PA

1055. GARRETT EMORY[12] MILLER III, son of Garrett

and Lillian Ann[11] (Raynor) Miller, b. 28 Aug 1956, Bellefonte, PA; m. 5 Nov 1988 in Richmond, VA, Pam Frank, b. 12 Feb 1958, Ebinsburg, PA. Issue:

  1331.Gina Leigh[13] Miller, b. 18 Sept 1975, Sayre, PA

1056. TERRENCE LEE[12] MILLER, son of Garrett and Lillian Ann[11] (Raynor) Miller, b. 16 Feb 1959, Bellefonte, PA; m. 2 Nov 1985 at Tioga, NY, Melanie Miller, b. 9 Sept 1963, Oradell, NJ. Issue:

  1332.Nathan Robert[13] Miller, b. 28 May 1986, Sayre, PA

  1333.Stefanie Irene[13] Miller, b. 24 Nov 1988, Sayre, PA

  1334.Daniel Matthew[13] Miller, b. 8 Dec 1990, Sayre, PA

1057. MELISSA LEIGH[12] MILLER, dau. of Garrett and Lillian Ann[11] (Raynor) Miller, b. 16 Sept 1962, Bellefonte, PA; m. 17 Feb 1989 at Nichols, NY, Kevin James Brown, b. 3 Feb 1958, Endicott, NY. Issue:

  1335.Alexis Jae[13] Brown, b. 25 Apr 1986, Sayre, PA

  1336.Lukas Garrett[13] Brown, b. 11 Oct 1989, Sayre, PA

1059. JAMES WILLIAM[12] KAMETLER, son of Joseph Francis and Cora Lee[11] (Raynor) Kametler, b. 11 Sept 1956, Austin, TX; m. 20 Apr 1986 at Quogue, Pamela Rae Brin, b. 26 Jan 1947, Bloomington, IL. Issue:

  1337.Krissy Elizabeth[13] Kametler, b. 6 Oct 1986, Brookhaven, L.I.

1060. ROBERT BRIAN[12] KAMETLER, son of Joseph Francis and Cora Lee[11] (Raynor) Kametler, b. 19 Aug 1957, Riverhead; m. 20 May 1989 at

Immaculate Conception Church, Westhampton Beach,
Kim Marie Klein, b. 6 May 1964, Brookhaven.
Issue:

    1338.Heather Rae[13] Kametler, b. 16 Dec 1990,
        Riverhead

1070. LEANNE BARBARA[12] RAYNOR, dau. of Clarence
Henry[11] and Diane (Giorgi) Raynor, b. 4 Nov
1969, Southampton; m. 23 June 1990 at Immaculate
Conception Church, Westhampton Beach, Rodger A.
Hubbard, b. 18 Nov 1966, Oyster Bay, L.I.
Issue:

    1339.Hillary Anne[13] Hubbard, b. 14 Nov 1991,
        West Islip

1074. JAMES DAVID[12] RAYNOR, son of David
Eugene[11] and Lida (Carter) Raynor, b. 14 Nov
1965; m. 10 Nov 1985, (Alba) Iris Perez, of East
Moriches, b. 9 Feb 1966.
Issue:

    1340.Ileana Natalia[13] Raynor, b. 31 Dec 1990

1077. SUSAN PRISCILLA[12] GALVIN, dau. of Daniel
J. and Julia Emma[11] (Raynor) Galvin, b. 18 Mar
1947, CA; m. (1) in 1966, Theodore Gudmondsen;
m. (2) in 1973, Jeff Perkins.
Issue Husband (1):

    1341.Scott D.[13] Gudmondsen, b. 14 Oct 1966
Issue Husband (2):

    1342.Debra D.[13] Perkins, b. 16 July 1975

1078. DANIEL J.[12] GALVIN, JR., son of Daniel J.
and Julia Emma[11] (Raynor) Galvin, b. 24 June
1950, CA; m. (1) 18 June 1969, Linda Melton; m.
(2) 22 June 1985, Cheryl Lucia. Daniel is a
general manager for G.T.E. in Dallas, TX.
Issue Wife (1):

    1343.Jason J.[13] Galvin, b. 8 Apr 1970

    1344.Shannon L.[13] Galvin, b. 24 Feb 1974
Issue Wife (2):

    1345.Garon[13] Galvin, b. 12 Sept 1979

1346.Shea[13] Galvin, b. 27 May 1981

1079. CHARLES EVERETT[12] GALVIN, son of Daniel J.
and Julia Emma[11] (Raynor) Galvin, b. 27 Apr
1955, CA; m. (1) 28 Sept 1980, Michelle Herrera;
m. (2) 24 Aug 1991, Sally Anne Epling. Charles
is a service and sales representative for AT&T,
Thousand Oaks, CA.
Issue Wife (1):
  1347.Sean Everett[13] Galvin, b. 2 July 1981
  1348.Ryan Patrick[13] Galvin, b. 12 June 1983
Issue Wife (2):
  1349.Marilyn Raynor[13] Galvin, b. 9 Jan 1993

1080. DAVID L.[12] MAUGER, son of George L. and
Karen Louisa[11] (Raynor) Mauger, b. 15 Mar 1961,
AZ; m. 14 July 1984, Jo Anne Ramirez.
Issue:
  1350.Courtenay N.[13] Mauger, b. 31 Dec 1985

1081. CATHERINE G.[12] MAUGER, dau. of George L.
and Karen Louisa[11] (Raynor) Mauger, b. 3 May
1964, CA; m. 14 June 1986, Troy Meikel.
Issue:
  1351.Lindsay G.[13] Meikel, b. 23 Apr 1989
  1352.Rex B.[13] Meikel, b. 7 Mar 1991

1086. PEARLE MARIE[12] RAYNOR, dau. of Arthur
Daniel[11] and Marguerite L. (Day) Raynor, b. 8
Apr 1945, Tampa, FL; m. 15 June 1969 at Bartow,
FL, Thomas Maxwell Wood, s/o Dennis and Elaine
Wood, of Vero Beach, FL.
Issue:
  1353.Daniel Thomas[13] Wood, b. 28 Feb 1978,
        Winter Springs, FL
  1354.Margaret Evelyn[13] Wood, b. 7 Dec 1980,
        Winter Springs, FL

1087. DAYL EVELYN[12] RAYNOR, dau. of Arthur
Daniel[11] and Marguerite L. (Day) Raynor, b. 25
Aug 1947, Tampa, FL; m. (1) 22 Mar 1969 at

Bartow, FL, Don Wayne Davis; m. (2) 20 Dec 1980 at Lake Wales, FL, Michael Gerlosky.
Issue Husband (1):
1355.Donna Marie[13] Davis, b. 20 Oct 1973, Madison, FL
Issue Husband (2):
1356.Michelle Denise[13] Gerlosky, b. 20 Mar 1983, Lake Wales, FL
1357.Gregory Michael[13] Gerlosky, b. 25 May 1984, Lake Wales, FL

1088. KATHLEEN[12] HANLEY, dau. of Robert F. and Frances Louise[11] (Raynor) Hanley, b. 13 May 1944, Key West, FL; m. Edward Metzger.
Issue:
1358.Drew[13] Metzger, b. 7 May 1974, Baltimore, MD

1097. SUSAN LEE[12] PALMER, dau. of Fred Gould[11] and Shirley Inez (Culver) Palmer, Jr., m. William Claude Everly.
Issue:
1359.Briget Mary[13] Everly

1098. FRED GOULD[12] PALMER III, son of Fred Gould[11] and Shirley Inez (Culver) Palmer, Jr., m. Irene Shea O'Brien Baker.
Issue:
1360.Patrick Thomas Baker[13] Palmer
1361.Fred Gould[13] Palmer IV

1099. CYNTHIA LOUISE[12] PALMER, dau. of Fred Gould[11] and Shirley Inez (Culver) Palmer, Jr., m. Charles Davis II.
Issue:
1362. Charles[13] Davis III
1363. Wesley Phillips[13] Davis

1106. CHESTER SIDNEY ("CORKY")[12] RAYNOR IV, son of Chester Sidney[11] and Gail (Heileman) Raynor III, resides in Sugarland, TX.

Issue:
1364.Chester Sidney[13] Raynor V, b. July 1983
1365.Cristina[13] Raynor
1366.Dustin[13] Raynor, b. 21 May 1986
1367.Aaron[13] Raynor, b. 16 Apr 1988

1107. PAUL[12] RAYNOR, son of Chester Sidney[11] and
Gail (Heileman) Raynor III, b. 13 July 1964; m.
Dawn Lovell, b. 11 May 1967. Residence: Hampton
Bays.
Issue:
1368.Mallory[13] Raynor, b. 10 Jan 1990

1149. RAYMOND[12] WATSON, son of _____ and
Sylvia[11] (Brooker) Watson.
Issue:
1369.Gabriel (or Gabēriel)[13] Watson

Thirteenth Generation

1317. STACEY JEAN[13] MOLLOY, dau. of Robert and
Sharon Lee[12] (Raynor) Molloy, b. 6 Mar 1970,
Southampton; m. 18 May 1991 at Barrington, NJ,
David Taylor, b. 8 Nov 1962, Camden, NJ.
Issue:
1370.Kaitlynn Marie[14] Taylor, b. 16 Apr 1992,
     Voorhees, NJ

Name | Page
ABATELLI, Fred, 139
ADAMS, Rebecca, 150
AFFRON, Carol, 89
AGAR, Aktug, 137
ALBERTSON, Elizabeth, 10
ALDRIDGE, Daniel, 20
  Mercy W., 10
ALLEN, William, 101
ALLMER, Susan, 131
ANDERSON, Donna, 119
  Wanda Woodward, 137
ANDREWS, Bertha M., 65
  Cathy D., 117, 152
  Raymond S., 117
ARMOUR, Edye, 120
  Frank, 120
  Jon David, 120
  Laura Rae, 120
  Neil Douglas, 120
  Patrick Steven, 120
  Thomas Wayne, 120
ARNOLD, Estelle M., 82
ARNTZEN, Mary E., 45
ARTHUR, William T., 29
ATKINSON, Daniel, 144
  Darryl Lee, 144
  David Harvey, 144
  Deborah Lynn, 144
  Diane Marie, 144
  Earl David, 144
  William Earl, 144
BAILEY, Daniel, 120
BAISDEN, Shermanton, 83
BAKER, Bess, 59
  George, 59
  Irene Shea, 159
  Leila, 59, 85
BANE, Gary, 120
BANNON, Susan, 105
BARLETTA, Barbara, 151
BARNES, Rose C., 67

Name | Page
BARNISH, Andrew, 117
BARRINGER, John, 119
  Robin, 119
  William, 119
BARTEAU, Henrietta, 66
BAZYK, Dede, 121
BECKWITH, Cheryl, 122
  George Corey, 95
  Herman Douglas, 95
  Richard C., 95, 122
  Richard C., Jr., 122
BEECHER, James F., 43
BELL, Candice, 123,155
  Richard Allen, 123
  Robin Allen, 123
BELLOWS, Sarah M., 52
BELZAK, Jody, 130
BENJAMIN, Almine, 18
  Alta, 79
  Amelia H., 33
  Clarence F., 79
  Harriet H., 33
  Henrietta, 33
  James Harvey, 33
  Leonard, 79
  Louisa Raynor, 73
  Mary Amelia, 33
  Mary Frances, 51
  Nancy W., 33
  Sandra B., 116
  Wade H., 116
  Wilbur H., Jr., 116
  William H., 33
BENNETT, Ashley, 155
  Kristin Nichole, 155
  Mary Jane, 152
  Norstrand, 20
  Randy Wayne, 155
BERNER, Ricki, 118
BILYK, Deirdre, 108
  John, Jr., 108
BINDSEIL, Susan, 125
BINNS, Nancy Lee, 149

BISESI, Salvatorre,127
  Susan, 127
BISHOP, Bonnie,117,152
  Caroline, 84
  Earldine, 84
  Earle, 84
  Florence, 26, 39, 47
  Frank, 64
  George P., 26
  Harriet, 14
  Harriet M., 26
  Herman D., 21
  Herman John, 117
  Herman L., 117
  Ida May, 37, 55
  Jo Ann, 117, 152
  Joseph L., 64
  Lynn, 117
  Patricia, 84
  Rogers, 37
  Stanton Rogers, 37
  William, 26, 64
BITTNER, Beverley, 152
BLACK, Allen J., 56
  George, 118
  James Blair, 118
  Mabel Eliza, 56
  Margaret E., 118,153
  Marsha J., 118, 153
  Nancy E., 118, 153
  Neil George, 118
  Ruth Ellen, 118, 153
BLACKBURN, Mabel, 51
BLACKWOOD, Bertha, 54
BLAIR, Gertrude, 91
BOSSUNG, Paula, 154
BOUMA, Charlotte, 102
BOUVIER, Estelle, 107
BOWERS, Jerusha, 5
BOYCE, Deborah, 139
BREESE, Agnes, 25, 47
  Alma Lucina, 46
  Ambrose, 24
  Amelia, 25
  Augustin, 25, 46
  Augustus, 15, 25

BREESE, Cecil, 24
  Cora May,43,67
  David, 24
  David Raynor, 15, 24
  Edwin A., 24, 45
  Eliza Lindsley, 15
  Ella F., 24, 45
  Ellis E., 43
  Ellsworth C., 46, 70
  Elmer E., 43
  Emma, 25, 47
  Ernest A., 46
  Eugenia A., 24, 45
  Finley, 24
  Flora I., 71, 94
  Frances, 25
  Hannah, 15, 24, 25
  Harriet Maria, 24,45
  Henrietta R., 24, 44
  Howard L., 68
  John H., 24, 43
  John R., 15
  Karl, 46
  Kathryn E., 68
  LaRue F., 46
  Larwill W., 46
  Laura, 25
  Lizzie, 25, 47
  Lloyd E., 71
  Lucilla L., 24, 43
  Marian, 46
  Marion L., 68
  Mary Ann, 15, 25
  Mary E., 24, 43
  Mathew L., 68
  Minnie Bell, 45, 70
  Minnie E., 46
  Nellie V., 43
  Nora Bell, 43, 67
  Peter R., 94
  Phebe, 15
  Ralph G.; 71, 94
  Robert, 24
  Robert F., 15, 24
  Robert V., 71
  Roma Adele, 71, 95

BREESE, Sarah, 15, 25
  Silas G., 15, 23
  Silas H., 24, 45
  Susan, 25
  Susan Day, 15
  Thelma J., 71, 95
  Thurlow E., 24, 46
  Treva May, 71, 94
  Verne G., 46, 71
  Walter D., 43, 68
  Will L., 43, 68
BREWSTER, Eliza, 21
  John Sills, 21
  Milicent, 21
  Millicent, 6
  William, 21
BRIN, Pamela Rae, 156
BROOKER, _____, 106
  Ginnie, 106, 134
  Sylvia, 106, 134
BROUWER, Theophilus,
          84
BROWN, Alexis J., 156
  Elizabeth, 66
  Kevin J., 156
  Laura, 46
  Lukas G., 156
  Orville B., 111
BROWNFIELD, Suzie, 121
BROWNING, Jennie, 37
BURNETT, Benjamin, 9
BURNS, Adeline, 65
BURTSELL, Symes, 59
CARDO, Ayla, 152
  Carl Eugene, 117
  Charles K., 117, 152
  Kristen B., 152
  Randy Jay, 117, 152
CARDWELL, Margaret, 94
CARMAN, Elizabeth, 85
CARPENTER, Harriet, 37
CARTER, Emma A., 79, 104
  Genevieve E., 79
  Guy Lancelot, 52
  Harold Leroy, 79
  Harriet E., 54

CARTER, Lida, 125
  Norma T., 79, 104
  Sarah Jane, 29
CHAMIER, Aimee M., 103
  Claire L., 78, 103
  Colin, 103
  Courtney, 103
  Craig, 103
  Dana, 130
  Edward, 78
  Edward R., 103, 130
  Edward W., 78, 102
  Erica Lynn, 131
  Jennifer A., 130
  Kevin, 103, 130
  Nicole, 131
  Russell E., 130
  Scott L., 78, 103
  Trevor, 130
  William, 103, 130
CHAPMAN, John, 81
  LeGrant, 81
CHILLINGWORTH, Diane,
          127
CINQUEMANI, Joan, 103
CLARK, Anna, 25, 47
  Antoinette, 84, 111
  Brittany, 129
  Courtney, 129
  Emily, 25
  Frank, 25
  Halsey, 84
  Jessica Raynor, 129
  John R., 101, 129
  Judith Ann, 101, 129
  Lizzie, 25
  Susan E., 101, 129
  Thomas, 25
  William F., 101
CLIFTON, Margaret, 81
COADY, Edwin F., 99
  James F., 99
  Leah Mae, 99
  Michael J., 99
CODY, Irene M., 98
COLASIMONE, Jeffrey, 133

COLASIMONE, Robert,132
COLEMAN, Patricia, 148
  Susan, 148
COLLINS, Brendon, 155
  Edward, 155
  James J., Jr., 147
  James J. III, 147
  Patrick J., 147
  Tara Ann D., 147
  Timothy A., 155
COMPTON, Grace, 65
CONARD, Bessie O., 44
  Burton L., 44
  Byron, 69
  Clara R., 43
  Edna L., 44
  Frank R., 69
  George T., 44, 68
  Hattie E., 44
  Ida May, 68, 93
  Irene, 69
  James W., 43
  Lorenzo D., 68
  Lucian C., 69
  Mabel I., 44, 68
  Nettie F., 44, 69
  Ruby, 69
  Sarah L., 68
  Viola E., 44, 69
  Waldo L., 44, 69
CONKLIN, Alena, 43
  David F., 42
  Hattie M., 43
  Howard S., 42
  Nancy Lynn S., 138
CONNORS, Dennis, 122
CONOVER, Dane K., 139
  Eugene E., 139
  Terrelle A., 139
CONTI, Frank C., 145
  Frank J., Jr., 145
  Regina, 145
COOK, Sarah Jane, 32
COOLS, Fred A., 96
CORBET, _____, 25
CORCORAN, Dianah, 9

CORWIN, Clarissa, 111
  Cornelia, 84
  Dwight T., 58, 83
  Edith E., 83
  Florence M., 84, 111
  Frank H., 40
  Harriet E., 34
  Helen F., 35
  Henry H., 34, 57
  Henry W., 34
  Hubert F., 58, 83
  Hulda A., 18
  Leone H., 111
  Leone W., 84, 111
  Mary L., 111, 145
  Mary M., 35
  Miriam G., 58, 83
  Muriel, 84, 111
  Percy, 58
  William W., 34
CRAWFORD, Dolly E., 87
CREEF, Russel H., 80
CROSS, Samuel, 82
CULVER, Benson R., 107
  Clara E., 114
  Deborah A., 107
  Lynn Rogers, 107
  Richard D., 82
  Richard D., Jr., 107
  Richard F., 81
  Sarah, 58
  Shirley I., 128
CURTIS, Diane B., 120
DANNENBERG, Thomas,
              136
DANOWSKI, Robert, 138
DAVIDSON, Kathleen,138
  Kenneth Lee, 138
  Lawrence H., 138
  Mary Ellen, 138
  Nancy Elaine, 138
  Robert E., 138
  Robert E., Jr., 138
DAVIS, Charles II, 159
  Charles III, 159
  Chary Ann, 108, 135

DAVIS, Don Wayne, 159
  Donna Marie, 159
  J. Frank, 35
  Joanna, 14
  Lloyd Osborne, 108
  Louisa M., 108
  Stephanie O., 108
  Tommy Ray, 143
  Wesley P., 159
DAY, Bethuel, 9
  Marguerite L., 126
DEAL, Sandra, 102
DEALY, Mannie L., 72
DEAN, Glentis F., 81
DECASTRO, Janet, 149
DEEMER, Helen, 55
DEGRASS, Dean, 47
  Ellen Dean, 47
DEGRE, Sarah, 152
DELONG, James A., 140
DEWALL, Karen L., 137
  Peggy Ann, 137
  Walter, 137
  William H., 137
DILLAPLANE, Karen, 129
DISTEFANO, Andrew, 153
  John S., 153
DODERER, Bernice, 70
  Doris M., 70
  Fred, 70
DOLBEY, Betty Ann, 51
DOMINY, Emma A., 68
DOSS, Kaye L., 112
DOWER, Lena, 71
DOWNS, Edna S., 109
  Florence M., 34
  Frances R., 110
  Marian E., 110
  Thomas L., 136
DOYLE, Corydon J., 149
  David W., 149
  Robert R., 149
  Sean P., 149
DREW, Helen, 150
DRUGGE, Denise, 135
DUNGAN, Anna M., 31.

DUNNAM, Karen L., 138
DUNWELL, Dorothy S.,
    87, 113
  Laurie Ann, 113, 147
  LeRoy Raynor, 87,113
  Percy Leroy, 87
DUTSCHMAN, Janet, 118
EDGAR, Amy, 151
  Caroline, 151
  James, 116
  William, 151
  William T., 116, 151
EDWARDS, Elanora, 36
  Lulu, 86
EHLERS, Helen E., 76
ELKINS, Melissa, 141
EMMONS, _____, 10
EPLING, Sally Ann, 158
ESSEX, William, 44
EVANS, Nancy, 150
EVERLY, Briget M., 159
  William Claude, 159
FAHY, _____, 64
FARRELL, Barbara, 121
  James E., 121
  Louis E., 94
  Pamela A., 122
  Sandra J., 121
FARROW, Richard, 78
FECHTMANN, Arthur, 105
  Esther M., 105, 133
  Paul R., 105
FEDUN, Alexandra, 141
FELTMAN, Anita J., 112
FENN, Martha E., 99
FERGUSON, _____, 111
  Antoinette, 112
  Beverly H., 143
  Dawn M., 143
  Eugene, 143
  Jonathan L., 143
  Joy E., 143
  Mark A., 143
  Nathan C., 143
  Paul D., 143
  Timothy E., 143

165

FILER, Charlotte, 71
  Emmett S., 47, 71
  Emmett V. W., 47
FLEET, Annie A., 50
FLEMING, Clarissa, 111
FOLEY, Paula, 119
FORDHAM, Tryphenia, 8
FOSTER, _____, 12
  C. Irving, 76
  Daniel, 14
  Jerusha, 13
  Mary, 30
  Sarah, 14
  Sophia, 23
FOURNIER, Helen L., 74
FOUST, Harold, 117,152
  Jack, 117
  Jennifer R., 152
  John J., 152
  Michael A., 152
  Sarah Lillian, 152
FOWLER, Submit, 9
FRANK, Pam, 156
FREID, _____, 152
  Christopher, 152
  Phillip F., 152
FREY, George C., 90
GALVIN, Charles E., 125, 158
  Daniel J., 126
  Daniel J., Jr., 126, 157
  Garon, 157
  Jason J., 157
  Marilyn Raynor, 158
  Ryan Patrick, 158
  Sean Everett, 158
  Shannon L., 157
  Shea, 158
  Susan P., 125, 157
GARDINER, Henry, 21
GARDNER, Helen A., 127
GARRITANO, Richard,137
GATZ, Louis, Jr., 136
GERLOSKY, Gregory, 159
  Michael, 159

GERLOSKY, Michelle,159
GIFT, John Luther, 137
GILBERT, Anna, 54
  Anthony M., 54
  Emily, 54
  Mary, 54
GILDERSLEEVE, Bertha, 59
  Betsy, 86
  Clara L., 59, 85
  Dewitt, 59
  Effie, 59, 85
  Gladys M., 59
  Hettie R., 59, 85
  Isaac D., 59
  Raymond S., 59, 86
  Richard, 86
  Shirley, 86
  Wilbur, 86
GIORGI, Diane, 124
GIRARD, Lulu M., 53
GLOSE, Kathleen, 144
GOLDBERG, Mark, 142
GOLDER (GOULDER), Harriett N., 37
GOLDSMITH, Isabella,41
GOOD, Jacqueline, 130
GOODALE, Barbara, 140
  Harold E., 140
  Harold E., Jr., 140
  Holly Jo, 141
  June E., 141
  Noel Susan, 140
GOODRICH, Carrie, 44
GORDON, George H., 50
  Josephine H., 50
  Minnie J., 50, 76
  Nathan H., 50
  Philip, 59
GOULD, Florence H., 98
  Frank D., Sr., 98
  Frank D., Jr., 98
  Georgianna G., 127
  Thomas L., 98, 127
GOWAN, James A., 123
GRAHAM, C. R., 8

GRAHAM, Christine, 70
GRANGER, Lyllis, 147
GRAVES, Grace, 45
  Irving, 45
  Worth, 45
GREENBURG, Brooke, 129
  Steve, 129
GREMMO, John J. III,
    103
GRIFFIN, James C., 135
  James C., Jr., 135
  Michael, 135
GRIFFING, Stephen, 81
  Stephen, Jr., 81
GRIMSHAW, Florence J.,
    75, 98
  Geraldine, 75
  Leah F., 75, 99
  Lilla Madelyn, 75,99
  Roger W., 75
  Rose Helene, 75, 98
  Wesley S., 75
  William S., 75
GRODSKI, Richard, 138
GRONNER, Ruth S., 94
GRYZICH, Laura R., 153
  Scott, 153
GUDMONDSEN, Scott, 157
  Theodore, 157
GUTMAN, Brian, 103
  Charles J., 103
  Keith, 103
HALL, Ashley, 129
  Ben, 129
  Hugh B., 129
HALLOCK, Marian S., 97
HALSEY, Charles H.,100
  Genevieve Adele, 88
  Harold B., Jr., 108
  Harold B. III, 108
  Harriet, 18
  Jesse, 39
  Mary A., 34
  Sandra E., 108, 135
  Sarah, 7
  Tonya Jean, 129

HALSEY, Wilmun,100,129
HAMOR, Grace F., 99
HANLEY, Kathleen, 127,
    159
  Robert F., 127
HARRIS, Henry, 80
HARRISON, _____, 145
HARTER, Don E., 142
HARWOOD, Arthur, 46
HAVENS, Mary J., 108
HAVILAND, Ruth C., 92
HAWKINS, Alan L., 146
  Albert E., 65
  Amanda Gould, 52
  Brian S., 112, 146
  Catherine Ann, 146
  Chauncey L., 41, 66
  Edward Eugene, 42
  Eleanor T., 65
  Elizabeth, 41, 64
  Elizabeth Ann, 146
  Elizabeth C., 66
  Ella C., 42
  Ella Rose, 66
  Elmira, 23, 41
  Elsie A., 65
  Evelyn B., 65
  Fannie C., 66
  Forest F., 65
  Frederick L., 65
  George Frank, 42
  George Lewis, 66
  Gilbert Rose, 42
  Grace H., 75
  Henry E., 41, 66
  Herbert M., 42, 67
  James H., 41, 65
  Joel, 22
  John Shirley, 65
  Jon Ward, 112, 146
  Laura Blackburn, 48
  Leah E., 65
  Leigh D., 112, 145
  Leonard Vernon, 65
  Lewis, 41
  Mark John, 146

HAWKINS, Mary, 42
  Mary Jane, 35
  Merten Jarvis, 30
  Mildred Lydia, 67
  Nancy, 23, 41
  Nettie, 66
  Phebe G., 75
  Phebe Rose, 41, 64
  Ralph Stout, 67
  Rebecca Ann, 146
  Robert W., 65
  Samuel A., 41, 65
  Selah, 41, 66
  Susan R., 65
  Sylvester, 23, 41
  Theodore Judson, 42
  Vernon D., 112
  Walter, 41
  Wendy M., 112, 146
  William Henry, 23,42
  William P., 41, 65
  William S., 66
HEATH, Anna, 24
  Nellis E., 68
HEDGES, Jeremiah, 21
HEHL, Martha W., 110
HEILEMAN, Gail, 129
HEINTZ, Joseph, 132
HELM, Eunice, 72
HELMS, Marjorie, 122
HEMBURY, Howard E., 76
HENDERS, Dwight P., 70
  Norman Arthur, 70
HERBER, Katharina, 116
HERRERA, Michelle, 158
HERRICK, Irene, 3
HILDRETH, Margaret,140
HILL, Aileen J., 104
  Andrew, 132
  Betsy, 132
  Elizabeth A.,104,132
  Jon, 132
  Robert R., 104, 132
  Robert R., Jr., 132
  Walter L., 104, 132
  Walter R., 104

HILL, Wendy Aileen,132
HOBBS, Vickie Lee, 130
HOFFMAN, Mary, 17
HOLLEY, Georgia A., 64
  Karen, 117
HOLLIS, Ida, 67
HOLMES, Marjorie, 114
HOMAN, Ellen, 42
  Huldah, 39
HONSBERGER, Karen, 151
HORNBECK, Richard, 118
  Sahler, 119
  Stephanie, 119
  Susan, 119
HOSTETTER, Amos B.,148
  Jacob Topping, 148
  Joshua Samuel, 148
HOWE, Danielle L., 147
  Devan Alysa, 147
  Donald James, 147
HOWELL, Benjamin, 151
  Devin Christian, 151
  Ella Marguerite, 90
  George, 9
  Hans-Christian, 116,
           151
  Harmony, 20
  Hiram, 10
  Lucile Elizabeth, 90
  Mark Bryan, 116, 151
  Nicole Grace, 151
  Ruth Marguerite, 90
  Samantha Linn, 151
  Stuart Payne, 90
  Stuart Payne, Jr.,
           90, 116
  Warren, 10
HOXIE, Charles W., 67
  Lowell H., 67
HUBBARD, Charles, 53
  Elijah, 31, 53
  Erastus, 31
  Hillary Anne, 157
  Robert, 53
  Rodger A., 157
  William, 31, 53

HUDDLESTON, Priscilla,
   145
HUDSON, Margaret, 104
HULL, Virgina E., 120
HULSE, Betsy, 114, 149
  Charles Louis, 114
  Charlotte E.,114,149
  Esther, 36
  Everett, 40
  Floyd, 89, 115
  Harold W., 114
  Jamie Allyson, 114
  Jean M., 89, 115
  John, 115
  Marc, 115
  Meredith Sayre, 149
  Seth Wells, 89
  Theodore O., 88, 114
  William R., 114, 148
  William Theodore, 88
  William T., Jr., 88,
   114
HUTCH, William, 52
INMAN, Sarah J., 45
JACKSON, Mary V., 120
JAGGER, Harriett, 19
  Mehitable, 18
JAMES, Brenda, 129
JARVIS, Elizabeth, 135
  Gertrude E., 81
  Heather P., 135
  Helen L., 80, 106
  Ida M., 80
  Leonard P., 81, 107
  Nan Mary, 107
  Reed W., 107, 134
  Reed W., Jr., 135
  Roscoe W., 80
  William J., 80
JEFFERSON, Mary, 121
JERSTAD, Luther, 107
JESSUP, Apollos, 12
  Catherine I., 91
  Daniel R., 28
  Ebenezer, 12
  Egbert, 20, 39

JESSUP, Eliza H., 50
  Fannie J., 39
  Florence B., 47, 71
  Florence Bishop, 72
  George H., 40, 58
  George P., 48, 72
  Henry, 12
  Isabel, 58, 84
  Laura P., 28
  Lester R., 58
  Lewis, 12
  Mary Jane, 20
  Mary S., 72
  Mehetabel, 12
  Nancy W., 48, 72
  Richard, 11, 28
  Ruth, 12
  Sarah, 12
  Silas, 12, 20, 21
  Silas B., 39
  Silas Egbert, 39, 47
  Stephen, 28
  Susan M., 39, 64
  William, 28
  William C., 28
  William H., 40, 58
  William Henry, 20,39
JIMMERSON, Luranna, 92
JOHNSON, Charles, 154
  Lee, 78
  Nancy, 150
JONES, David, 143
  David Eugene, 143
  Melanie Anne, 143
JOURNEY, Dorothy, 85,
   112
  George, 85
KAMETLER, Christopher,
   124
  Heather Rae, 157
  James W., 124, 156
  John Joseph, 124
  Joseph Francis, 123
  Kathleen Irene, 124
  Krissy E., 156
  Michael Joseph, 124

KAMETLER, Robert B.,
    124, 156
KECK, Marguerite, 96
KELLEHER, Amy R., 146
    Matthew P., 146
    Michael J., 146
KELLY, Kevin, 115
KERR, Carlyle A., 93
    John Charles, 93
    Ruth E., 93
KETCHAM, Aleta, 51, 77
    John, 51
KING, Helen E., 136
    Tealie L., 77
KINNAN, I. R., 8
KIRBY, Robert, 115
KIRCHER, Gerald, 119
KLAUS, Walter, 82
KLEIN, Kim Marie, 157
KOHLER, Denise, 145
KRUPSKI, Helen, 95
KUHLEMANN, Anne, 113
LAMB, Allen, 141
LANDER, Arthur E., 149
    Clarence A., Jr.,149
    Clarence A. 3rd, 149
    Stephanie Anne, 149
LANDRETH, Timothy, 128
LAPP, Henry S., 126
    Katherine L., 126
    Michael A., 126
LARWILL, Henrietta, 24
LASHLEY, Richard, 117
LAUBE, Elizabeth, 73
LAVELLE, Lorraine, 100
LAWRENCE, Edith F., 68
    George, 25
LAWS, Ann, 8
LEACH, Benjamin, 9
LEARIE, Blanche, 88
LEE, Barbara Joy, 87
    Harriet Virginia, 87
    Marie Frances, 86
    Philo Stephen, 87
    Philo William, 87
LEIBIG, Denise R., 128

LEIBIG, Russell, 128
    Russell Glenn, 128
LEMINN, Cynthia, 115
LENZ, Louise, 57
LEONARD, Edith, 47
    Henry, 47
LESLIE, Cynthia, 120
LEVELLEY, Sarah, 20
LEWIS, Amy, 121
    Elizabeth, 43
LICOPKY, Carl, 115
    Joseph, 115
    Robert, 115
LINDGREN, Carl, 96
    Wilhelmina E., 96
LINDSAY, Byron M., 142
    David Byron, 142
    Deanna Marie, 142
    Loretta Gail, 142
    Sandra Jean, 142
    Valerie Ann, 142
LINDSLEY, Elizabeth, 8
LITCHARD, John A., 111
LITTLEJOHN, Lorraine,
        106
    Lyance G., Sr., 106
    Lyance G., Jr., 106
    William L., 106
LOCKWOOD, Patricia,132
LOFF, Ronald M., 125
LOPER, Arthur C., 137
    Ernest Daniel, 137
    Ernest D., Jr., 137
    Margaret Marie, 137
LORD, Eddie, 25
LOVE, Jay, 94
    Joy, 94
    John J., 94
    Peter Michael, 94
LOVELL, Dawn, 160
    Luther S., 93
    Mary E., 93
LOVSEY, Fannie, 66
LUCE, Harold D., 73
LUCIA, Cheryl, 157
LYDAMORE, Leslie, 69

LYDAMORE, Milton C.,69
  William H., 69
LYONS, Gordon L., 117
LYTEL, Gerald, 135
MADES, Barbara L., 134
  C. Kenneth, 106, 133
  Charles Gerald, 105
  Donald John, 106
  Grace A., 133
  Robert H., 134
  Virginia Grace, 134
  William K., 134
MARCHAIS, Nancy, 141
MARCKS, Melissa, 126
  Peter Mason, 126
  Stephen Mason, 126
MARSCHALK, Lottie, 5
MARTIN, Dorena, 143
MATTAX, Rebecca, 15,26
MATTOX, John, Jr., 15
MAUGER, Catherine G.,
         126, 158
  Courtenay N., 158
  David L., 126, 158
  George L., 126
MAW, Rae, 128
MAYERS, Elizabeth, 153
  Stephen Craig, 153
  Stephen Craig II,153
MCATEE, Clinton, 45
  Hettie Essie, 45
  Rollo Dale, 45
  Thomas, 45
  Thomas Cecil, 45
MCAVOY, Cynthia, 151
MCBRIDE, Anne T., 135
MCCARTHY, James, 136
MCCAWLEY, Thomas, 72
MCCHESNEY, Scott, 118
MCCOY, Maude, 74
MCDONALD, Nancy, 150
MCGARVEY, Elizabeth,
         152
MCGONIGLE, Bradford,
         150
  Bret Adams, 150

MCGONIGLE, Brian, 150
  David B., 150
  Kara Mia, 151
  Kerry A., 150
  Kyle Raynor, 115,150
  Leah Suzanne, 151
  Richard C., 115, 150
  W. David, 115, 150
  William, 115
MCGUINNESS, Georgeann,
         108
MCGUIRE, Mary Anne,127
MCKENSEY, M. R., 8
MCLAIN, Ramona, 79
MCLOUGHLIN, Ann, 56
MCMAHON, Mary E., 44
MEIKEL, Lindsay, 158
  Rex B., 158
  Troy, 158
MELESH, Rose M., 146
MELTON, Linda, 157
MERCER, ____, 93
  Clarence A., 68, 93
  Eunice Lucilla, 93
  Hazel Elizabeth, 93
  Marica, 68
  Rhetta, 69
  William Allen, 68
  William E., 68, 93
MERCURIO, Joyce, 118
METZGER, Drew, 159
  Edward, 159
MEYER, Henry, 22
MEZZAPELLE, Annette,
         146
MIELKE, Amanda M., 154
  Jonathan, 154
  Mackenzie P., 154
MILLER, Daniel M., 156
  Dee Ellen, 123, 155
  Edward G. B., 62
  Garrett, 123
  Garrett E., 123, 155
  Gina Leigh, 156
  Melanie, 156
  Melissa L., 123, 156

MILLER, Nathan R., 156
  Stefanie Irene, 156
  Terrence L., 123,156
MITCHELL, Ella, 47
  Ernest, 47
  Garfield Arthur, 47
  Will, 47
MOISA, Sophie S., 141
MOLD, Doris, 92
MOLLOY, Jennifer, 154
  Kristen Lee, 154
  Robert, 154
  Stacey Jean, 154,160
MONROE, Marian E., 102
MOORE, Egbert J., 64
  Fannie Mae, 64
  Helen C., 64, 92
  Howard Raymond, 64
  Isaac Terry, 64
MORGAN, ____, 86
MORRIS, Lila Grace, 63
MOSSLANDER, Almira, 66
MUNDAY, Carol Ann, 131
  Michael Thomas, 131
  Thomas, 131
MYERS, Linda K., 137
NADTERHOFF, Olive, 93
NEUFER, Richard, 56
NEVILLE, Michael, 133
  Sylvester F., 133
NEVINS, Paul, 99
NEWEY, Ethel, 66
NEWINS, Elizabeth, 42
NICHOLS, Adolph, 51,77
  Christopher W., 51
  David, 102
  Elizabeth, 77, 102
  Eugene, 77
  Lillian R., 51
  Louis W., 51
  Wilson, 77, 102
NICHOLSON, James, 111
NIGHTSER, Jeptha, Jr.,
    26
  William Morgan, 26
O'BRYAN, Eliza, 48

ODELL, Charles J., 142
  Charles J., Jr., 143
O'DONOHOE, Kathleen,
    132
OLDHAM, Janine, 155
OLIVETO, Rocco, 128
OLSEN, Ellen, 54
  Thomas, 128
OVERTON, Florence, 52
  Frank, 43
  Henry Warren, 52
OWENS, Beth, 132
PALMER, Cynthia L.,
    128,159
  Fred Gould, 99
  Fred G., Jr., 99,128
  Fred G. III, 128,159
  Fred G. IV, 159
  Patrick T., 159
  Susan Lee, 128, 159
PARKS, Alma, 66
PARLATO, Elizabeth, 82
  John, 107
  Katherine, 82, 107
  Louis Oliver, 82,107
  Michael J., 82
  Robert, 107
PATRICK, Sherri, 144
PAYNE, Maria H., 30
  Maria Woodhull, 32
  Marian Louise, 98
PEARCE, Austin L., 147
  Cassandra Zampi, 147
  David R., 112, 147
  Lynne R., 112, 146
  Richard Allan, 112
PECK, ____, 73
PELLETREAU, Jesse, 28
PENFIELD, Nancy, 132
PENNY, Abigail, 16
  Catherine R., 16
  Donald Remson, 80
  Emma L., 80, 105
  Frances Matilda, 16
  George Sylvanus, 16
  Harriet Amanda, 16

PENNY, Harvey, 16
    Isabelle, 80
    John, 13
    Mary Jane, 16, 26
    Phebe R., 16
    William, 16
    William A., 80
PEREZ, (Alba) Iris,157
PERKINS, Debra D., 157
    Jeff, 157
PERSALL, Ann, 39
PETERMAN, Connie, 102
PETERSON, Catherine,
            139
    James Reginald, 139
    Reginald Walter, 138
    Richard David, 139
    Walter Edward, 138
PETRIE, Ronald C., 135
PHIEFFER, Eileen, 117
PHILLIPS, Fred M., 85
    Jeannette M., 85
    Murray G., 85
PIERSON, Bertram, 71
    C. Floyd, 59, 85
    Enoch H., 59
    Katherine J., 72
    Lee, 59
    Lena B., 85
    Marian, 85
    Mary, 11, 59
    Ruth, 14
    Sarah, 3, 26
    _____, 14
POLLARI, Helen, 151
PORTER, Jay Allen, 144
    _____, 143
POTTER, Annie, 31
POWELL, Cynthia, 113
PUGH, Gordon G., 128
    Harry Arnold, 99
    Harry A., Jr.,99,127
    Michael, 127
    Randell Gardner, 128
    Robert Marcel, 127
    Rodney, 127

PUGH, Rodney W., 99,
            127
    Rose Marie, 99
    William, 127
PUGSLEY, Lavinia, 90
PURIFOY, _____, 153
    Keith Ray, 154
RAMIREZ, Jo Anne, 158
RANDALL, Ella B.H.,114
RAWN, Joann Louise,138
RAYMOND, _____, 108
RAYNOR, Aaron, 160
    Abbie Louise, 74
    Abigail, 3, 7, 9,
            10, 14, 16
    Addison O., 33
    Adonijah, 4, 5
    Adonijah, Jr., 5, 9
    Alan Owens, 132
    Alice C., 64
    Alice June, 103, 131
    Amy B., 62
    Amanda Jane, 118
    Angelina, 27
    Anna, 32
    Anna M., 72, 95
    Antoinette H., 35,58
    Archie W., 50, 75
    Arthur, 30
    Arthur Daniel,98,126
    Arthur Halsey, 49,73
    Augustus H., 38, 61
    Azur (Asa), 8
    Barbara Jane, 91,117
    Beatrice, 98
    Beatrice A., 73
    Beatrice E., 98, 126
    Blanche A., 73, 96
    Caleb S., 11, 18
    Carol E., 92, 118
    Carol Susan, 105
    Carrie M., 63, 90
    Catherine, 9, 15, 17
    Catherine I., 91,117
    Chad Harrison, 118
    Charity, 10

173

RAYNOR, Charles, 9,
   17, 31, 39, 63
Charles A., 22
Charles B., 52, 78
Charles D., 64
Charles E., 38, 61
Charles F., 40
Charles Henry, 124
Charles Homer,88,113
Charles L., 20
Charles Luther, 33,
         37, 55
Charles Luther, Jr.,
         55
Charles M., 73, 98
Charles Russell, 27
Charles W., 29, 50
Charlotte E., 29,
   50, 61, 88
Chester S., 50, 76
Chester S., Jr., 76,
         100
Chester S. III, 100,
         129
Chester S. IV, 129,
         159
Chester S. V, 160
Christine M., 78
Christopher, 123,155
Clara Gertrude, 74
Clarence E., 72, 95
Clarence H., 96, 124
Clarence R., 48, 72
Clarissa, 8
Clark Sidney, 51, 77
Clay Madison, 118
Clifford T., 62, 88
Cora Lee, 96, 123
Cornelius, 22
Cristina, 160
Cyrenus, 9
Cyrus Timothy, 22,40
Cyrus T., Jr., 40
Daniel, 17, 30
Daniel Lindsley, 8
Daniel Tuttle, 74,98

RAYNOR, David, 4, 5
David, Jr., 5, 7
David Eugene, 96,125
David Frederick, 122
David Lester, 72, 96
Dawn Marie, 122, 154
Dayl Evelyn, 127,158
Deborah, 3, 52
Denise Lee, 122
Dorothy H., 89, 115
Douglas C., 87, 112
Douglas Coleman, 148
Douglas P., 114, 148
Dustin, 160
Dwight Elijah, 38
Dyana Rose, 125
Ebba, 97
Edith McKay, 60, 87
Eli William, 125
Elihu, 4, 6, 10, 11,
         17, 31
Elihu Jotham, 31, 54
Elijah, 12, 21
Elijah Pierson, 20,
         37, 61, 87
Eliot Pierson, 148
Eliott Joshua, 62
Eliza Kate, 35
Elizabeth, 1, 2, 6,
   10,17,19,57,82
Elizabeth "Beth",131
Elizabeth "Betty",56
Elizabeth "Betsey",
         13, 22
Elizabeth E., 91,117
Elizabeth "Eliza",
         17, 30
Elizabeth H., 49, 72
Elizabeth L., 8, 15
Ella Grace, 31
Ella Mae, 49
Ellen, 113, 148
Ellen R., 104, 131
Elsa E., 62, 89
Elsie Faye, 73
Emerson M., 63, 91

RAYNOR, Emma Lenora,53
   Erastus W., 31,35,53
   Eric Christopher,131
   Eric Russell, 124
   Ernest Preston, 52
   Ethel Emma, 53, 79
   Eunice, 9
   Everett Clark, 73,96
   Everett C., Jr.,97
   Faith M., 96, 125
   Fannie, 20
   Fletcher, 97
   Frances Ellen, 99
   Frances H., 49, 74
   Frances J., 76, 100
   Frances L., 98, 127
   Frank Lawrence, 60
   Franklin C., 38, 60
   Fred, 30
   Frederic C., 49, 74
   Frederick, 63
   Frederick C., 34, 57
   Frederick M., 64
   Frederick W., 38, 62
   George, 9, 17, 32,39
   George Alexander,124
   George Clinton,29,49
   George Davis, 96,122
   George L., 75,99,100
   George T., 123, 154
   George W., 27, 28,
         48, 64
   Gideon Henry, 31
   Grace, 30
   Grace Alice, 30
   Halsey Gilbert, 74
   Halsey J., 57, 82
   Hannah, 2,3,8,9,13,
       17,23,27,34
   Harold Hastings, 63
   Harold J., 92, 119
   Harold J., Jr., 119
   Harold Wilson, 76
   Harriet, 12,14,18,
       21, 33
   Harriet Halsey, 33

RAYNOR, Harriet H., 88
   Harriet J., 35,60,87
   Harrison Strong, 57
   Hattie Ainsley,53,79
   Helen E., 77, 101
   Helen Louise, 90,116
   Henry, 4, 6, 7, 13
   Henry Proud, 60, 86
   Henry T., 21
   Henry William, 40
   Herbert C., 96, 122
   Herbert L.,100
   Herrick, 10, 18, 32
   Herrick J., 18, 32
   Hettie Jane, 29, 51
   Hetty, 32
   Holmes, 77, 102
   Hubert I., 57, 82
   Hubert I., Jr.,82,
        108
  Hugh, 4, 7
  Ichabod, 6
  Ileana Natalia, 157
  Irene, 8
  Isaac, 3
  Isabel M., 53, 80
  Isabelle, 92
  Jacob A., 11,19,34
  Jacob Richard, 125
  James, 7, 12, 22
  James A., 22
  James David, 125,157
  James Hewitt, 12, 22
  James Huit, 22
  James Madison, 63,91
  James M., Jr.,91,118
  James Matthew, 155
  James Mitchell, 118
  Jane, 7, 12
  Jane Alice, 22
  Jason Paul, 133
  Jean Edith, 82, 108
  Jeanne Grace, 101
  Jeannette, 91, 118
  Jerusha, 6, 13
  Joanna, 13

RAYNOR, Joffy, 12
    John, 3, 20, 32
    John Cook, 10, 17
    John Everett, 33, 56
    John F., 104
    John Fletcher, 30,52
    John Gilbert, 29, 49
    John G., Jr., 49, 75
    John Lawrence, 22
    John M. B., 38, 63
    John Morrison, 18,32
    John Roscoe, 32, 55
    John W., 57
    Jonathan, 3,4,5,8,9
    Jonathan Douglas,125
    Jonathan "Jotham",
            10, 16
    Joseph, 1,2,3,19,34
    Joseph Clark, 27
    Joseph F., 78, 103
    Joshua, 27
    Josiah, 3
    Josiah Woodhull, 6,
            10, 11
    Julia C., 60
    Julia Emma, 97, 125
    Juliana, 5
    Justin Mark, 155
    Karen Louisa, 97,126
    Kate, 31, 54
    Kathleen, 108
    Kathryn E., 57, 82
    Kathy, 89
    Kenneth Alan, 63, 91
    Kenneth D., 92
    Kevin, 63
    Kevin Thomas, 154
    Kingsley, 63
    Laura Margaret, 132
    Laura P., 30
    Laura Vincent, 55,81
    Laurens Tyler, 90
    Lawrence E., 105
    Leah Jeanne, 128
    Leanne B., 125, 157
    Lester James Huit,40

RAYNOR, Lester, 60, 86
    Lewis, 12, 22
    Lillian, 52, 57
    Lillian Ann, 96, 123
    Lindsay Beth, 133
    Lois Halsey, 82, 108
    Louis B., 73, 97
    Louise Preston, 73
    Louise Rushmore, 76
    Louise Wanda, 86,112
    Lusie, 54
    Luther, 13
    Lydia, 1, 2
    Lydia Young, 61
    Mallory, 160
    Marcia Page, 90, 116
    Margery D., 91, 116
    Maria, 17
    Marian S., 73
    Marion G., 89, 115
    Mark Rierl, 123, 154
    Marleigh Anne,99,128
    Marriette, 20
    Martha, 4, 8, 19, 30
    Martha "Patty", 6
    Mary, 2, 11, 22, 32,
            72, 74
    Mary Alice, 30
    Mary Alida, 53, 79
    Mary Ann, 82, 108
    Mary C., 33, 55
    Mary Elizabeth, 49
    Mary Ellen, 54, 80
    Mary Frances, 21, 40
    Mary J. "Polly", 20
    Mary Jagger, 32, 54
    Mary T., 17
    Matthew, 5
    Matthew Paul, 123
    Megan Pamela, 154
    Mehitable "Hetty", 6
    Melissa Jane, 154
    Melodie Ann, 102
    Melvinna, 22
    Merritt, 13
    Michael Howard, 128

RAYNOR, Michael, 102
  Mildred E., 73
  Mildred F., 55, 81
  Milicent, 20
  Millicent, 17, 27,
    28, 29, 50
  Milton Ernest, 96, 124
  Minnie M., 53
  Miriam, 13
  Miriam Wickes, 19, 34
  Mulford T., 20, 39
  Nancy, 10, 13, 30
  Nancy P., 20, 37
  Naomi, 8
  Nathan, 4, 5, 10, 17, 29
  Nathan H., 31
  Nathan Sidney, 29, 50
  Nathaniel, 6
  Nathaniel W., 11, 20
  Nels, 98
  Nicholas, 22
  Nikki Marie, 155
  Norman Hiram, 62, 89
  Olin Shepherd, 74
  Oliver, 9
  Oliver J., 34, 56, 57
  Oscar Bingley, 18, 32
  Oscar Bishop, 55
  Pamella, 8
  Paul, 129, 160
  Pearl, 52, 78
  Pearle M., 127, 158
  Peggy, 113
  Phebe, 6, 8, 9
  Phebe Ann, 22
  Philip Russell, 72
  Phoebe, 7, 13, 17
  Pierson T., 88, 113
  Priscilla, 92, 119
  Priscilla C., 97
  Prudence, 7, 9, 14, 15
  Rachel, 39
  Rachel L., 100, 128
  Ralph L., 54
  Ralph Morrison, 55
  Raymond Louis, 97

RAYNOR, Rebecca, 9
  Rena, 6
  Rexford Lee, 86
  Richard Locke, 119
  Richard R., 96, 125
  Robert A., 76, 100
  Robert H., 104, 132
  Robert P., 114, 148
  Robert W., 40
  Roger, 63
  Roscoe, 76
  Rose Belle, 29
  Royal W., 92
  Ruby LeMay, 52, 78
  Russell W., 51, 76
  Ruth, 10, 119
  Ruth Louise, 98, 126
  Sandra V., 100, 128
  Sara Frances, 148
  Sarah, 1, 2, 4, 6
  Sarah Louise, 35, 54
  Sarah R. "Sally", 17
  Sarah Rupell, 29, 51
  Sarah Tuthill, 30, 52
  Sarah V. "Sally", 56
  Scott, 108
  Scott Charles, 148
  Selah, 13, 23
  Sharon Lee, 123, 154
  Sharon Leigh, 102
  Sherry, 97
  Shuah, 8
  Sidney Eliot, 89
  Sidney F., 73, 97
  Sophia, 12
  Stephen, 7, 9
  Susan, 20, 36
  Susan E., 26
  Susan Lynn, 131
  Susannah, 12, 20, 21
  Sylvanus, 9
  Terry Lynn, 100, 128
  Thurston, 1, 2
  Thurston Herrick, 32
  Timothy, 11
  Townsend R., 63, 92

RAYNOR, Triphena, 9
Uriah, 17, 30
Virginia, 76
Virginia Mae, 77,101
Wallace Alfred, 72
Walter, 49
Walter Austin, 52
Walter Benjamin, 52
Walter Raleigh,75,99
Walter Scott, 29, 51
William,4,6,9,10,11,
17,27,30,32,52,89
William A., 30, 53
William Clark, 29,48
William Clifford, 73
William Corwin, 54
William Fletcher,
49, 73
William Foster, 23
William Frederick,
62, 90
William Jagger,19,35
William L., 105, 133
William R., 11, 19
William S., 38
William T., 79, 104
William T., Jr.,
104, 131
William Uriah, 53,78
Wilmun Halsey, 60,87
Winifred Ann, 91,117
Woodhull, 55
REARDON, Lottie T., 74
REED, Catherine B.,107
REEVE, Baylis, 82
Ida, 86
Rodney, 82
REGAN, Debra J., 137
REGENT, Donna, 110,140
Joan Carolyn,109,139
Kenneth Gardner, 109
Marcia A., 110, 139
REILLY, Grace, 119
RESKA, Margaret, 146
RHINES, Marlene,95,121
Merle A., 95

RIBEIRO, Richard, 115
RICE, Charles R., 146
Eric Vernon, 146
Kenneth Hawkins, 146
Robert P., 146
RICHARD, Barbara, 144
RICHARDSON, David, 144
RICHESON, Linda L.,137
RICHMOND, Carol, 139
RIERL, Pamela, 123
RIGBY, Alfred, 33
RIGGS, P. R., 8
S. R., 8
RILEY, Patricia A.,145
RIPLEY, Thomas P., 16
ROBERTS, Patricia, 81
ROBERTSON, _____, 10
ROBILLARD, Gerald, 135
Jason Douglas, 135
Thomas Stevens, 135
ROBINSON, Beulah, 36
Charles Henry, 42
Davis, 36
Ellen Grace, 49
Frances J., 32
Georgiana, 42
Huldah J., 65
James T., 50
Jessie, 50
Norton F., 16
Philip L., 136
Phineas, 42
Sally A., 42
Sarah Ann, 27
Wesley, 50
RODGERS, Nancy, 150
ROESLER, James, 111
ROGERS, Alanson N., 85
Alanson Pierson, 84
Angeline C., 23, 42
Charles, 84
Constance, 84
Daisy, 58, 84
David Roswell, 36,58
Edith, 57
Elinor, 84

ROGERS, Eloise M., 82
  Frances H., 36,40,58
  Gilbert D., 56
  Helen Cook, 56, 81
  Henry Merritt, 23
  J. Dwight, 56
  Jennie B., 36, 58
  Jeremiah, 23
  John N., 36
  Larsan, 36
  Lester G., 35
  Lillie F., 56
  Mary G., 36
  May, 84
  Millicent B., 36, 59
  Oscar B., 56
  Sophia, 58, 84
  Susan Halsey, 36, 59
  Thomas, 58, 84
ROMANO, Anita, 150
RONDELLO, Daniel, 140
  Ignace John, 139
  Louise Althea, 140
  Peter Andrew, 140
RORICK, Kenneth, 139
ROSE, Albert E., 48
  Dorothy G., 144
  Israel M., 29, 48
  James Monroe, 48
  John Mitchell, 48
  Millicent, 48
ROSS, Michael, 99
ROWE, Alonzo Dial, 80
  Emma K. "Kay",80,106
  Isabelle V., 80
  Mamie Aleen, 80, 106
  William D., 80
  William L., 80
RUFFING, Donald K.,131
  Donald K., Jr., 131
  Michael L., 131
RYAN, Michael G., 138
SAGE, Charity E., 67
  Ellis Douglas, 43,67
  Seth Solomon, 43
SANTI, Rita Ann, 118

SATTERLY, Geraldine,86
  Lewis W., 85
  Margaret I., 86, 112
SAUERS, Brett H., 140
  Doreen Regent, 140
  Timothy, 140
SAXON, Nancy, 13
SAXTON, Georgianna, 23
SCHELS, Kenneth, 140
SCHETTER, Karen, 151
SCHOTT, Phyllis, 121
SCHREIBER, Sandra, 113
SCHULTZ, _____, 106
SCHUNK, Alice M., 116
  Allan, 152
  Darryl, 152
  Robert A., 116, 151
  Thomas, 116
  William, 116
SCRIBNER, Helen P., 90
SEAMAN, Audrey R., 136
  Janice Yvonne, 141
SECOR, John, 9
SEITZ, Martha C., 124
SEKI, Kazue, 144
SEREDUKE, Brian, 152
  Peter, 152
SHALER, Olivia, 13
SHAY, Elizabeth, 22
SHEFLER, Edna J., 128
SHEPARD, Nellie M., 69
SHORT, Buford A., 101
  Buford A., Jr., 102,
              130
  Elizabeth R., 102
  Grant, 130
  Virginia-Earl W.,
              102, 130
SHUOT, Nicole Ann, 141
SILSBE, Algie N., 119
SIMMONS, Arthur H., 70
  Jeffrey T., 94, 120
  Mark Leslie, 120
  Matthew Ryan, 120
  Russell Terry, 70,94
  Stephen A., 94, 120

SIMMONS, Virginia ,70,
        93
SINCLAIR, Bessie, 71
SINGER, James, 95, 122
    Jeffrey, 122
    Jennifer, 122
    Ruth Ellen, 122
    Thomas, 95
    Warren, 95
SKIDMORE, Mildred, 100
SKINNER, Cheryl A.,140
SLOCUM, William B., 22
SMITH, Charles H., 139
    Charles H., Jr., 139
    Clara Ellen, 139
    Cyril Glenn, 44
    Dill Ellsworth, 44
    Edward Bruce, 144
    Edward Charles, 58
    Elizabeth, 58, 84
    Elton Lee, 44
    Emmit Bruce, Jr.,143
    Gertrude Brooks, 44
    Ida May, 65
    Leon Ruber, 44
    Margaret Ann, 144
    Mary Teresa, 155
    Nettie, 74
    Rosina Jane, 44, 69
    Wilson Lee, 44
SOMMERS, Albert, 77
    Audrey, 77
    Douglas, 77
    Frank, 77
    Marjorie, 77
SOYARS, Alexander, 85
    George, 85
    Vinton, 85
SPARKS, David, 97
    Mary Elizabeth, 153
    William Gilbert, 153
STERLING, Patrice, 138
STEVENS, Abraham, 27
    Abraham Howell, 29
    Abram Howell, 48
    Barbara Ann, 107,135

STEVENS, Charles, 72
    Charles B., 28
    Hannah R., 28, 48
    Hubert F., 28
    Ira, 112
    John Mitchell, 28,48
    Lina, 28
    Mabel Blackburn, 48
    Madeline, 127
    Nancy, 28
    Sarah, 28
    Silas Abram, 50
    Thomas H., Jr., 107
    William, 25
STEVENSON, Richard,141
STEWART, Allen R.,Jr.,
        125
    Christopher E., 153
    Edward Wilson, 153
    Stacy Ann, 125
STONE, Ada A., 65
STOUT, Harriette, 67
STOWE, Clarence, 92
STRONG, Elizabeth, 63
SURGAN, Brooks R., 136
    Dwight Morrison, 136
    Edward S., 136
SWALINA, Chester, 128
    Chester Walter, 128
SWANN, Halsey S., 136
    Richard S., 136
SWARTZ, Emory, 137
TALMAGE, Anna M., 40
    Caroline Bishop, 40
    Henry Raynor, 40
    Katherine, 133
    Nathaniel M., 40
    Wendy Diane, 134
TAYLOR, David, 160
    Kaitlynn Marie, 160
TEEPLE, Libbie, 25
    Susan, 25
    Thomas, 25
TENNILL, Marilyn, 121
TERHUNE, Jean A., 94
TERRELL, Sarah E., 57

TERRY, Eliza E., 27
 Hannah, 21
THERRELL, Charles, 138
 Lester Huntley, 138
THODE, Lucretia I., 96
THOGMARTIN, Bret, 121
 Bret Allen, 121
 Christopher, 121
 David Kent, 121
 Janice Ray, 95, 120
 Jon Brees, 95, 121
 Kim Marie, 121
 Lisa Ann, 121, 153
 Orville Wayne, 95
 Timothy Warren, 121
 Vern Mac, 95, 121
 Wayne Edward, 121
 Wayne James B., 121
 Wayne Kent, 95, 121
THOMPSON, Ineita, 131
THOU, Ann, 118
 Debbie, 118
THURSTON, Galen, 70
 Ruth Henrietta, 70
 Vivian Elizabeth, 70
 William Harrison, 69
TILLOTSON, Anna, 22
TISCHLER, Lawrence, 94
TOMPKINS, Rose, 46
TOPPING, Diane Gail,
             113, 147
 Kimberly Anne, 147
 Leanne Joy, 113, 148
 Raymond Halsey, 113
 Raymond Halsey, Jr.,
             113, 147
 Raymond James, 147
TOWNSEN, Carrie, 84
TRANBERG, Ruth, 70
TRASK, A. Frank, 16
TRIPLETT, _____, 102
TURNER, E., 119
TUTHILL, Beulah, 52
 Charles, 13
 Charlotte M., 78
 Daniel, 14

TUTHILL, Isaac, 14
 Josiah, 14
 Oliver, 13
 Orville B., 52
 Richard, 14
 Seth, 13
 Susan Margaret, 28
 Zophar, 14
TUTTLE, Grace A., 61
 Hannah Maria, 31
 Perry, 37
 Sarah A., 16
 William, 13
TYLER, Eric, 150
 Harriet L., 36
 John Lester, 36
 Lindley Benton, 36
 Marguerite D., 62
 Roscoe Conklin, 36
 Susan Frances, 36
 William Lindley, 36
TYTE, Anita Beryl, 136
 Antoinette, 145
 Arthur Milton, 144
 Arthur Milton, Sr.,
             83
 Arthur Miton, Jr.,
             83, 110
 Aurora, 136
 Betsey Ann, 110, 143
 Bruce M., 110, 141
 Carol F., 110, 143
 Charles E., 109, 136
 Charles E., Jr., 136
 Elinor M., 110, 142
 Evelyn Doris, 141
 Gail Ellen, 110, 142
 Gene E., 110, 140
 George Howard, 137
 Harrison E., 83, 109
 Helen B., 109, 138
 Henry David, 141
 Henry H., 109, 136
 James Everett, 141
 Jeanne Marie, 141
 John Henry, 145

TYTE, Linda Jane, 136
   Lois Ethel, 109, 137
   Margaret E., 109,137
   Mary Alexander, 109
   Mary Althea, 83, 109
   Mathew Robinson, 145
   Milton John, 141
   Miriam E., 109, 138
   Naomi R., 111, 145
   Norman A., 110, 141
   Norman A., Jr., 141
   Reba Lorreine, 136
   Richard Harrison,145
   Richard Lawrence,137
   Sharon, 145
   Shirley M., 110, 144
   Stephen A., 83, 109
   Stephen E., 111, 145
   Suzanne E., 141
   Vivian Lorreine, 136
   Wickham C., 83, 110
   Wickham C., Jr.,
         110, 144
   Wickham C. III, 145
   William Graham, 110
   William James, 145
VAIL, Clifford R., 55
   Daniel Morrison, 55
   Hannah, 24
   Herbert Germond, 54
   Kenneth A., 55
   Roscoe Philip, 55
VAN COTT, Alma, 112
   Clifford, 76, 101
   Elbert, 76
   Leona, 101
   Merton, 112
VAN FLEET, Victor, 25
   Will, 25
VAN POPERING, Bernard,
         85
VAN TASSEL, Amy J.,150
   Andrew Clifford, 150
   Dean Warrick, 150
   Gretchen Marion, 115
   Harry Ellsworth, 115

VAN TASSEL, Jeffrey,
         150
   Kurt Raynor, 115,150
   Marion Emily R., 150
   Richard E., 115, 149
   Richard E., Jr., 149
VAN TUYLE, Gregory,122
VERITY, Azalia, 42
WADE, Benjamin, 16, 26
   Edgar, 26
   Jared (Jeremiah), 16
   Jared, Jr., 16
   Lillie, 26, 47
   Oliver, 26
   Oliver R., 16, 26
WALSER, Theodore, 116
WARNER, Elmer, 72
   Marvin Lyle, 141
WARNOCK, Joseph L.,137
WARREN, _____, 102
WATSON, Gabriel, 160
   Grace Edna, 93
   Raymond, 134, 160
   _____, 134
WEBBER, Pauline, 72
WEGERT, Bradley, 124
   Daniel Paul, 124
   Joan, 115
   Terri Ann, 124
   _____, 123
WELLS, Ellen E., 40
   Julia (Foster), 30
   Mary L., 65
   Nancy, 39
WHALEN, Christopher,
         122
WHAYLAND, Irene, 102
WHITE, Amy Louise, 60
   Anthony, 138
   Jerusha, 9
   Marguerite L., 103
   Nellie L., 38
WHITED, Charles B., 74
WHITMORE, Alphin H.,45
   Bernice Breese,46,70
   Helen Herberta, 46

182

WHITMORE, Maude D.,
    46, 70
  Ora Rosina, 45
WHITTEMORE, Robert, 22
WILBUR, John E., 140
WILKES, Bill, 129
WILKINSON, Frederick,
    64
  William, 64
WILLIAMS, Durward, 45
  Edwin Forrest, 48
  Joseph A., 16
  Laura Eldridge, 86
  Mary Jane, 130
WILLIAMSON, Sarah, 77
WILSON, Blanche E., 67
  Edith May, 67
  Hollace Margretta, 67
  Lola Edgerton, 77
  Robert Gerald, 67
  Robert W., 67
  Violet Jeanette, 67
  William, 116
  William H., 48
WILTSHIRE, Eva, 60
WINGATE, Gary, 148
  Gregory, 148
  Kara, 148
WINNE, Rachel, 25
  _____, 25
WINSCOTT, Marilyn, 121
WINTERS, Patricia, 122
WISE, Arrene, 83
WOLFE, George B., 130
  Oliver Jordan, 130
WOOD, Alexander, 69
  Clara Hazel, 69, 93
  Daniel Thomas, 158
  Donald C., 139
  Emma Goldsmith, 67
  Fred Alexander, 69

WOOD,Jennie Mabel, 69
  Margaret Evelyn, 158
  Martha, 2
  Thomas Maxwell, 158
WOODHULL, Barbara, 119
  Esther, 6
  Glenn Richard, 120
  Herbert Case, 92
  John Robert, 92, 119
  Minnie Cornelia, 83
  Nancy Jean, 120
  Richard M., 92, 119
  Susan Mary, 120
  Thomas Alan, 119
WRIGHT, Barbara, 115
  Carol Jean, 94
  Janet Evelyn, 94
  Wesley Hastings, 93
YARRUSSO, Veda, 137
YEAGER, Blaze H., 142
  Bonnie Jean, 142
  Bradford Jay, 142
  Drew Lewis, 142
  Lewis M., Jr., 142
YOUNG, Ida Johnson, 54
  Marjorie, 109
YOUNGS, Helen E., 61
  Henrietta M., 49
ZAHARIS, Hannah, 74
ZALEWSKI, Patricia A.,
    133
ZIEMER, Craig M., 134
  Daniel Bruce, 134
  Daniel M., 106
  Eric, 106, 134
  Krystina, 134
  Mark, 106, 134
  Matthew, 134
  William, 134
ZUDE, Mary Emily, 97

1. Contributors

The author gratefully acknowledges the enormous contributions of the following individuals and organizations to *THE RAYNORS OF KETCHAPONACK:*

Elizabeth (Raynor) Barnish, Priscilla (Raynor) Barringer, Richard Beckwith, Louise (Raynor) Benjamin, Herman John "Bo" Bishop, Jeannette (Raynor) Black, Winifred (Raynor) Cardo, Elbert N. "Nate" Carter, Marion Carter, Edward Chamier, Laurie Collins, Wilhelmina Cools, Samuel Cross, Lois (Raynor) Davis, Lois DeWall, James Edgar, Marlene Farrell, Norma Fechtmann, Charlotte Filer, Lucile Frey, Frank D. Gould, Jr., Lillian (Raynor) Gowan, Frances (Raynor) Halsey, Jean (Raynor) Halsey, Margaret Hawkins, Floyd Hulse, William R. Hulse, William T. Hulse, Jr., J. Larry Jacobson, Reed Jarvis, Sharon (Raynor) Johnson, Sarah (Raynor) Lind, Julia (Raynor) Loff, Emma Mades, Mary McCawley, Kristen Molloy, Shirley Perry, Art Raynor, C. Marvin Raynor, Charles Homer Raynor, Gerald V.S. Raynor, Grace (Mrs. Harold) Raynor, Helen E. (Mrs. Harold) Raynor, Joseph F. Raynor, Marian Hallock Raynor, Martha C. (Mrs. Milton) Raynor, Rachel Lorraine Raynor, Rita Raynor, Ruth Raynor, William T. and Margaret E. Raynor, Alice (Raynor) Ruffing, Emma Schultz, Margery (Raynor) Schunk, Helen (Raynor) Short, Faith (Raynor) Stewart, Dorothy Topping, Phebe Tuttle, Marion (Raynor) Van Tassel, Richard Woodhull, East Hampton Free Library, Suffolk County Historical Society, and Westhampton Beach Free Library.

2. Bibliography

1. "Additions to the Genealogy of Raynor of Southampton, L.I., N.Y.", from the Mss. of Herrick J. Raynor, Elijah Raynor and other sources, by Lucy D. Ackerly
2. AMERICAN BIOGRAPHICAL DIRECTORIES
3. AMERICAN FAMILIES OF HISTORIC LINEAGE,

Long Island Edition, William S.
Pelletreau and John Howard Brown, Vol. I
4. "Bible Records," compiled by members of
the Southampton Colony Chapter, D.A.R.
5. THE BOROUGHS OF BROOKLYN AND QUEENS, AND
THE COUNTIES OF NASSAU AND SUFFOLK, LONG
ISLAND, N.Y., 1609-1924, Vols. IV and V,
Henry I. Hazelton, 1925
6. BURKE'S GENERAL ARMORY
7. COLLECTIONS OF THE N.Y. STATE HISTORICAL
SOCIETY FOR THE YEAR 1892, Vol. I, 1665-
1707, "Abstracts of Wills on File in the
Surrogate's Office, City of N.Y."; Vol.
III, "Abstracts of Wills"
8. COMPLETE HISTORY OF CONNECTICUT, Benjamin
Trumbull
9. D.A.R. Birth, Marriage and Death Records,
Southampton Colony Chapter
10. Death Certificates (Southampton Town) of
#330. Frank C.[8] Raynor, #334. Frederick
Woodhull[8] Raynor, and Harriett N.
(Golder) Raynor
11. DOCUMENTARY HISTORY OF THE STATE OF NEW
YORK, E. B. O'Callaghan
12. THE EARLY HISTORY OF SOUTHAMPTON, L.I.,
N.Y., George Rogers Howell, 2nd Edition,
1887
13. EARLY LONG ISLAND WILLS OF SUFFOLK COUNTY,
William S. Pelletreau, 1897
14. EDWARD JESSUP AND HIS DESCENDANTS, H. G.
Jessup
15. FOUNDERS OF NEW ENGLAND, Drake, Oct. 1860
16. A GENEALOGICAL DICTIONARY OF THE FIRST
SETTLERS OF NEW ENGLAND, James Savage
17. "Genealogical Research in England," 1912
18. GENEALOGY - JOHN WILLIAMS AND THANKFUL
BARLOW, compiled by Charles Tomlin and
Clarence R. Brooks, 1931
19. GENEALOGIES OF LONG ISLAND FAMILIES,
Charles J. Werner
20. HAMPTON CHRONICLE, Westhampton Beach, N.Y.
21. "Historical and Biographical Sketch of the
Rayner, Raynor Family," James Madison
Raynor, Sr.
22. HISTORICAL SKETCH OF WESTHAMPTON BEACH,

Beatrice Rogers, 1953
23. HISTORY OF LONG ISLAND, Thompson
24. A HISTORY OF MATTITUCK, L.I., N.Y., Rev. Charles E. Craven, 1906
25. HISTORY OF STAMFORD, CONNECTICUT, Huntington
26. HISTORY OF SUFFOLK COUNTY, H. W. Munsell, 1884
27. HOTTEN'S ORIGINAL LISTS
28. Index to Births and Baptisms, Marriages, and Deaths, East Hampton (N.Y.) Free Library
29. THE INDIAN PLACE NAMES ON LONG ISLAND, William Wallace Tooker, 1911
30. "Inscriptions in Westhampton," Lucy D. Ackerly, 1910-11
31. LONG ISLAND TRAVELER, 24 Feb 1882
32. Manuscript of Elbert N. Carter, "Descendants of David and Mary Pauline (Garrigues) Carter"
33. Manuscript of Henry Raynor, "Genealogical History of the Raynor and Tuttle Families Commenced 1878," with Footnotes and Additions by Lillian Raynor, 1911
34. Marriage Certificate of #165. Elijah Pierson[7] Raynor and Harriet N. Carpenter
35. Mattituck Church Records
36. NEW ENGLAND HISTORICAL AND GENEALOGICAL REGISTER, 66: 164-167
37. NEW YORK GENEALOGICAL AND BIOGRAPHICAL RECORD, Vol. 37, 1906
38. "Parish Registers of Mattituck and Aquebogue"
39. "The Pierson Kinship Historical Newsletter," complied and published by Elmer E. Meyer, Atlantic Highlands, NJ
40. PLANTERS OF THE COMMONWEALTH, Dr. Charles E. Banks, 1930
41. PORTRAIT OF BIOGRAPHICAL RECORD OF SUFFOLK COUNTY, Chapman Publishing Co., 1896
42. THE RAYNOR (RAYNER)-BURNHAM FAMILIES, compiled by Emma Machacek, Route 2, Schuyler, NE 68661, 1965
43. RAYNOR FAMILY HISTORY, Clinton E. Metz, Freeport (L.I.) Village Historian

44. "Raynor Notes: Long Island," Donald Lines Jacobus
45. Records of the First Church of Morristown, New Jersey
46. RECORDS OF THE TOWN OF SOUTHAMPTON, N.Y.: 1639-1925, Vols. 1, 2, 3, 4 and 6
47. REFUGEES OF 1776 FROM LONG ISLAND TO CONNECTICUT, Frederick Gregory Mather
48. "Remsenburg Cemetery Inscriptions," Mrs. Elijah P. Raynor
49. SAG HARBOR EXPRESS, Jan. 4, 1883; Dec. 20, 1888
50. THE SALMON RECORDS, William Salmon; ed. by William A. Robbins, 1918
51. Southampton Town Censuses: 1698; 1776; 1790; 1865; 1870
52. Southold Town Census of 1850
53. Suffolk County, N.Y. Clerk's Office, Riverhead, N.Y.: Deeds
54. Suffolk County Historical Society's Card File
55. Suffolk County Surrogate's Office, Riverhead, N.Y.: Wills and Probate Files
56. Suffolk County Wills, N.Y. Historical Society's Collection
57. SUFFOLK GAZETTE, Sag Harbor, N.Y., 1804-1809
58. "Tombstone Inscriptions in Southampton and East Hampton Towns," compiled by members of the Southampton Colony Chapter, D.A.R., June 1939
59. "Tombstone Inscriptions," L. B. Ackerly
60. TOPPING GENEALOGY
61. U.S. Census Records, 1790-1890, National Archives, Washington, D.C.
62. VAIL GENEALGOY
63. VITAL RECORDS OF THE PRESBYTERIAN CHURCH, Sag Harbor, N.Y.
64. WADE'S SYMBOLISMS OF HERALDRY
65. Wedding Announcement of #334. Frederick Woodhull[8] Raynor and Marguerite DeForrest Tyler
66. Westhampton Beach Village Historian's Card Files
67. ZACHARIAH HAWKINS AND HIS DESCENDANTS

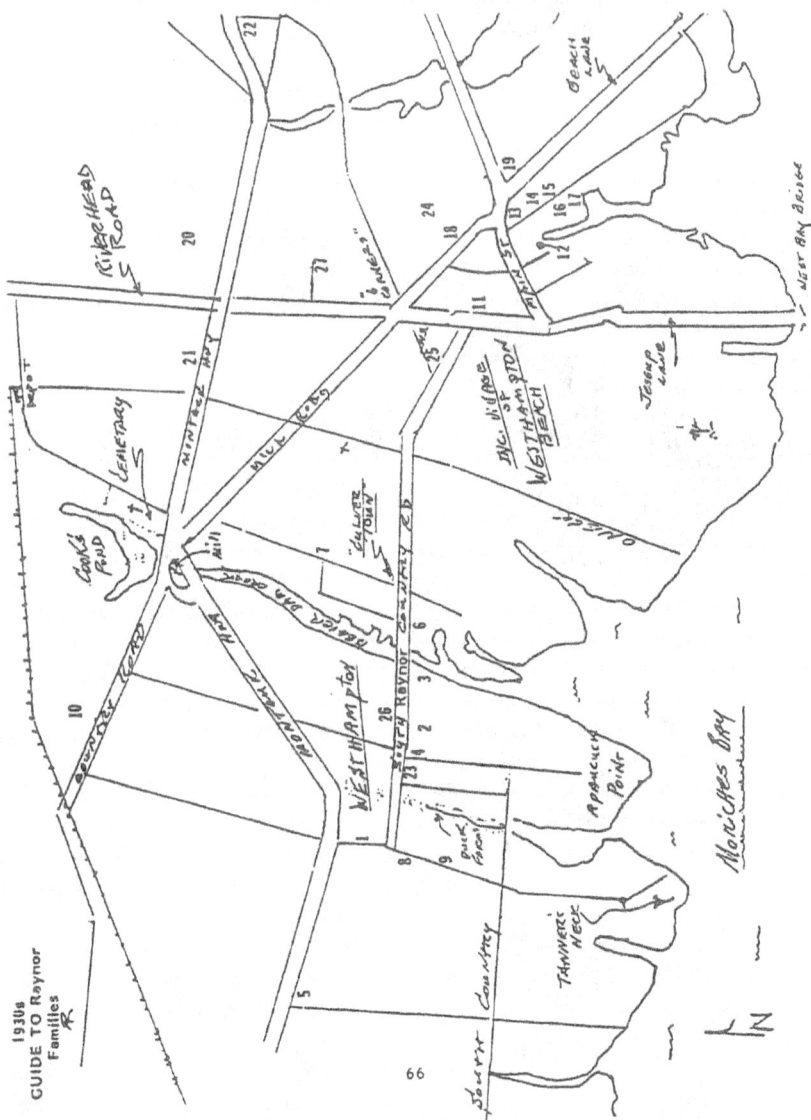

1930s
GUIDE TO Raynor
Families

N

APPENDIX

1930s Guide to Raynor Families
Westhampton and Westhampton Beach, L.I.

1. Daniel T., wife Irene, children Frances
   and Arthur D.   4
2. Arthur H., wife Helen   2
3. John G., Jr., wife Phoebe, sons
   G. Lafayette and Walter Raleigh   4
4. Thurston H.   1
5. Ansel V., wife Florence Mae, children
   Gwendolyn, Alberta, Vernon, Clifton,
   Edward   7
6. W. Fletcher, wife Louisa, children Beatrice,
   Sidney, Louis, Louise, C. Marvin   7
7. Fred, wife Lottie, children Olin & Gertrude   4
8. Archie, wife Grace, children Robert,
   Virginia, Harold   5
9. Chester S., wife Louise, children Frances
   and Chester, Jr.   4
10. Ralph, wife Bertha   2
11. Elijah P., wife Blanche, children Charles
    Homer, Pierson T. and Harriet   5
12. Kenneth A., wife Catherine, daughters
    Margery, Elizabeth, Catherine, Winifred,
    and Barbara   7
13. Elijah P. (see 11. above) summer home
14. James Madison, wife Gertrude, children
    Jeannette and James, Jr.   4
15. J. Mitchell, wife Elizabeth (Libby)   2
16. Clifford, wife Genevieve, daughters Marion
    and Dorothy   4
17. August, wife Grace, son Norman & wife,
    Carol   4
18. William, wife Helen, children Laurens,
    Louise and Marcia   5
19. Helen (Mrs. Charles), daughter Lydia   2
20. Dwight ("Doc")   1
21. Clarence Russell ("Russ"), wife Pauline   2
22. Jesse, wife Edna   2
23. Mabel (Mrs. "Big John"), daughters Sarah &
    Elizabeth*   3
24. Emerson M., wife Ruth, daughters Carol &
    Priscilla   4

25. Frederick W. (lived with daughter, Carrie
     Howell, & grandchildren Lucile & Stuart) 1
26. Everett Clark, wife Marian, children
     Everett, Jr., Julia, Priscilla & Karen   6
27. Clarence E., wife Irene, children Herbert,
     George, Lillian, Cora (children Milton,
     Clarence & Richard were born in the 40's) 6
                                              ̅ ̅
                                               98

     98 RAYNORS in 27 homes in 3/4 mile radius!
Not including Raynor women such as Carrie Raynor
Howell, Frances Raynor Grimshaw, Dolly Raynor
Stevens, Hettie Raynor Nichols, Elsie Raynor
Hulse, Charlotte Raynor Hulse, and many more.

     * Site of Raynor Lane. Map used with
permission of Westhampton Beach Chamber of
Commerce. (modified to include "South RAYNOR
Country Road" - a first...may it ever be.)

                                   - Art Raynor

www.ingramcontent.com/pod-product-compliance
Lightning Source LLC
Chambersburg PA
CBHW070912270326
41927CB00011B/2544